Milton Friedman's Monetary Framework

Milton Friedman's Monetary Framework

A Debate with His Critics

Edited by
Robert J. Gordon

Milton Friedman
Karl Brunner and
Allan H. Meltzer
James Tobin
Paul Davidson
Don Patinkin

The
University
of Chicago
Press
*Chicago
and London*

The University of Chicago Press, Chicago 60637
The University of Chicago Press, Ltd., London

© 1970, 1971, 1972, 1974 by The University of Chicago
All rights reserved. Published 1974. Second Impression 1977
Printed in the United States of America

Library of Congress Catalog Card Number:73-92599
International Standard Book Number:0-226-26407-6 clothbound

Contents

To Miguel Sidrauski*

We are all of us teachers, and we all know that the greatest reward of our career is the rare student who has the touch of genius, who absorbs what we have to teach, and repays by teaching us—the intellectual child in whose reflected glory we bask. Miguel was such a one. Of Polish descent but reared and schooled in Argentina, Miguel came to the University of Chicago as a graduate student only a few years ago. He happened to take one of my courses in one of his first quarters at Chicago. It was a large class and he did not speak up much, so I did not single him out until the first examination. That opened my eyes, and thenceforth he was a marked man. The same experience was repeated in course after course, and all of us quickly came to know that here was a student who was destined not only to use economics but to be of that small band who make economics.

Miguel's intellectual drive, his urge to get things straight, to get to the heart of the matter, shone through in every paper he wrote, in every conversation with him. So did his character: straightforward, confident but not arrogant, warm, generous, and sympathetic. He was a truly fine human being, who quickly became a leader among his fellow students.

Miguel became interested in monetary theory. He then also came under the influence of my colleague, Hirofumi Uzawa, who has had such a far-reaching influence on so many young men. Miguel had not only a fine mathematical mind, dissatisfied with any analysis that lacked complete rigor, but like Hiro he had that clarity of mind that picks out the key elements of a problem, strips away all irrelevant complications, and produces the kind of simplicity that is the height of sophistication. Like Hiro also, he had the real instincts of an economist, so that he was dissatisfied with any purely mathematical analysis unless the results had a meaningful economic interpretation. His dissertation reveals these qualities. It is a sophisticated yet simple analysis of a complex economic problem, mathematically rigorous yet always economically motivated and interpreted. It has already had considerable influence and will have more.

Two years ago, just as he was finishing his degree, Miguel's lovely fiancée came to the United States. After their marriage, they moved to Cambridge, where Miguel started his career as an assistant professor of

*This statement was made in honor of Miguel Sidrauski at the American Bankers Association–University Professors' Conference, Ditchley House, England, which was held September 10-13, 1968. It is reprinted with permission of the *Journal of Money, Credit, and Banking* 1 (May 1969): 129-30.

economics at Massachusetts Institute of Technology. We wanted, in our own interests, to keep him at Chicago, and offered him the opportunity to stay. But we also advised him that our interests were not necessarily his and that it would very likely be better for him and more stimulating to move into a new and different intellectual environment. I was pleased when he visited us a year later to find that our advice to him had been good—that he had found stimulus and challenge, difference of opinion without intolerance, that he felt that both he and his colleagues had benefited from the intellectual diversity. And I was equally pleased to hear from his MIT colleagues how high an opinion they had come to form of him, both of his intellect and his character.

The death of any young man is a personal tragedy for his family and his friends. The death of this young man is a grievous loss to our profession and to the world. Here was a man who would have pushed out the frontiers of our subject, would have changed and added to economic analysis, would have enlightened and informed generations of students—struck down at the very beginning of his career, full of promise but as yet almost bereft of fulfillment.

MILTON FRIEDMAN
University of Chicago

Introduction

The publication in 1963 of *A Monetary History of the United States,* by Milton Friedman and Anna Schwartz (1963*b*), represents a landmark in the development of monetary economics. Through its demonstration of a consistent relationship between fluctuations in the money supply and national income over the period 1867–1960, and through its proposition that a one-third decline in the money supply between 1929 and 1933 was primarily responsible for the severity and duration of the Great Depression, it was probably the most important single contribution to the revival of interest in monetary economics which has occurred during the past fifteen years. Several reviewers of the book, however, criticized the absence of an explicitly stated theory of the role of money in income determination capable of generating the propositions supported by the extensive empirical investigation.[1] While Friedman had previously presented his general theoretical approach in "The Quantity Theory of Money—a Restatement," there was widespread interest in a more formal and complete statement in which Friedman would analyze the channels by which money influences income and spending, explore the dynamics of the money-income relationship, and compare his quantity theory approach with the neo-Keynesian doctrines which at that time dominated the teaching of macroeconomic theory in American universities.[2]

Friedman responded with his "Theoretical Framework for Monetary Analysis," which was first published in the *Journal of Political Economy* in early 1970 (Friedman 1970*a*). One year later he added another, shorter supplementary paper, "A Monetary Theory of Nominal Income," which provided an additional model of income determination (Friedman 1971). Both papers were then combined and republished in one volume by the National Bureau of Economic Research.[3] The NBER version of the two Friedman papers is the first item reprinted in this book.[4]

[1] See Culbertson (1964), Meltzer (1965), and Tobin (1965*a*). It should be noted that several reviewers also made substantive critical comments on the basic empirical propositions summarized in the previous sentence.

[2] See Friedman (1956).

[3] Milton Friedman, *A Theoretical Framework for Monetary Analysis,* Occasional Paper 112 (New York: National Bureau of Economic Research, 1971).

[4] Most of pp. 31–48 in the NBER version is taken from "A Monetary Theory of Nominal Income" (Friedman 1971), whereas the remainder of that version is taken from the 1970 version of "A Theoretical Framework" (Friedman 1970*a*), with the exception of four new paragraphs added to the NBER version (from the paragraph beginning "Another, more subtle, difference . . ." on p. 27 to the end of sec. 5 at the top of p. 29). The NBER version

The present version of "A Theoretical Framework" begins (pp. 1-15) with a comparison of four versions of the quantity theory, the Irving Fisher transactions version, the income version, the Cambridge cash-balances approach, and the Friedman restatement. Next (pp. 15-31) the basic elements in Keynes's *General Theory* are summarized, and the analytical approach of Keynes's followers (the "Keynesians") is contrasted with that of Friedman and his associates, with major emphasis placed on the tendency of the Keynesians to regard the price level as fixed and to concentrate on a narrower range of assets in their analysis of the channels by which money influences income.[5] The major elements in Keynesian analysis and the quantity theory are summarized in a "simple common model," involving seven unknown variables but only six equations, with the two theoretical approaches characterized by the different seventh or "missing" equation which must be added to make the "simple common model" determinate. The simple Keynesian theory fixes the price level, the simple quantity theory fixes the level of real output, and a third approach suggested by Friedman, "the simple monetary theory of nominal income" (pp. 34-48), fixes the difference between the anticipated real interest rate and the real secular rate of growth of output. A final section on dynamic adjustment analyzes the effects of a change in the rate of growth of the money supply on the rate of growth of nominal income, and on the division of the latter between changes in the rate of growth of real output and in the rate of growth of the price level.

Because Friedman's statement was important and controversial, both as a commentary on the history of economic thought and as a theoretical contribution to be considered in its own right, I began in late 1970 to solicit critical reviews from a number of noted monetary theorists. Fortunately, almost all of my invitations were accepted, and four papers, by Karl Brunner and Allan Meltzer, James Tobin, Paul Davidson, and Don Patinkin, were finished in summer 1971 and submitted to Friedman, whose reply was written in late 1971. One round of revisions followed during the winter of 1971-72 in which all authors revised their papers to minimize misunderstandings and maximize attention to substantive issues. The symposium appeared in print in the September/October 1972 issue of the *Journal of Political Economy*.[6]

---

will also appear in adapted form as chap. 2 of a National Bureau of Economic Research monograph by Milton Friedman and Anna J. Schwartz, *Monetary Trends in the U.S. and the U.K.*, which is near completion.

[5]It should be noted that the emphasis on the narrower range of assets was added in the NBER version and was not present in the initial *JPE* paper.

[6]The comments of the critics appeared in the *JPE* symposium in the order in which

My original invitation placed no restriction on the aspects of Friedman's papers to be considered by each reviewer, and so the critics' papers overlap to some degree and cover a variety of topics. Brunner and Meltzer concentrate on elements which they feel are important but which Friedman omits from his "simple common model," particularly the effects of fiscal policy, interest-bearing government debt, the distinction between money and bank credit, and the distinction between nominal and real interest rates.[7] In contrast to Friedman's charcterization of a Keynesian model with fixed prices and a quantity theory model with fixed output, Tobin argues that the crucial issue is not the fixity or flexibility of prices but, rather, the assumed insensitivity of monetary velocity to interest rates. Tobin also criticizes Friedman's third approach to the problem of the missing equation, the "monetary theory of nominal income." Davidson emphasizes several factors, particularly the role of uncertainty, that he believes are basic elements of Keynes's approach but that he claims are missing from Friedman's characterization of Keynesian economics. Patinkin devotes most of his attention to issues in doctrinal history and provides textual evidence to show that Friedman incorrectly interpreted the nature of both the quantity theory and Keynesian economics, thus continuing his theme in an earlier article that Friedman's theoretical framework is more in the tradition of Keynes than in the tradition of the quantity theory.

All of the major points raised by the critics are discussed in Friedman's reply, which clarifies and expands on his original themes. Some interesting new material is included, particularly his contrast (in his reply to Patinkin) of the different views held in the early 1930s by Chicago and "London-Austrian" economists regarding the causes of the Great Depression. Also of interest is his analysis of the elements in Keynes's *General Theory* that are not uniquely "Keynesian," that is, introduced first in the *General Theory*, but, rather, that were developed by Keynes and others in earlier "classical" writings.

The purpose of the present volume is simply to combine in one location Friedman's NBER monograph, the comments of the critics, and Friedman's reply, for the convenience of scholars and students. Although several of the critics requested the right to present rebuttals to Friedman's reply for this volume, these requests were denied on the twin grounds that

---

Friedman chose to respond to them. The listing of authors' names on the title page of this volume reflects this order.

[7]They recently published a paper presenting an alternative model in which these items are incorporated (Brunner and Meltzer 1972).

(1) the etiquette of academic journals reserves the final word to the original author and (2) Friedman had already devoted a great deal of time to revising the first draft of his reply to minimize misunderstandings and problems of communication with the critics. Thus, the critics have not been given the chance to evaluate the sections of Friedman's reply that in the previous paragraph I refer to as "interesting new material," and at least one critic has indicated to me his doubts as to whether the material is either new, valid, or relevant.

Since the critics were originally asked to respond to the two separate *JPE* articles before the NBER version was completed, in the present volume all of the critics have made minor changes in their comments to take account of the additional passages on pages 27–29 (see n. 4 above) that were added by Friedman in the process of combining the two separate articles into the NBER volume. The changes are in the form of additional footnotes in the comments by Davidson and Patinkin and short postscripts by Tobin and Davidson. Other than these minor changes, the debate remains as originally published, and readers are invited to reach their own conclusions on the many fascinating issues discussed between these covers.[8]

ROBERT J. GORDON, Coeditor
Journal of Political Economy, 1970–73

Evanston, Illinois
February 1974

[8] Other minor changes are the combined set of references at the end of the volume, the combined index, and page number references to reflect the NBER version instead of, as originally, the two *JPE* papers.

A Theoretical Framework for Monetary Analysis

Milton Friedman

Every empirical study rests on a theoretical framework, on a set of tentative hypotheses that the evidence is designed to test or to adumbrate. It may help the reader of the series of monographs on money that Anna J. Schwartz and I have been writing to set out explicitly the general theoretical framework that underlies them.[1]

That framework is the quantity theory of money—a theory that has taken many different forms and traces back to the very beginning of systematic thinking about economic matters. It has probably been "tested" with quantitative data more extensively than any other set of propositions in formal economics—unless it be the negatively sloping demand curve. Nonetheless, the quantity theory has been a continual bone of contention. Until the past three decades, it was generally supported by serious students of economics, those whom we would today term professional economists, and rejected by laymen. However, the success of the Keynesian revolution led to its rejection by perhaps most professional economists. Only recently has it experienced a revival so that it once again commands the adherence of many professional economists. Both its acceptance and its rejection have been grounded basically on judgments about empirical regularities.

1. The Quantity Theory: Nominal versus Real Quantity of Money

In all its versions, the quantity theory rests on a distinction between the *nominal* quantity of money and the *real* quantity of money. The nominal quantity of money is the quantity expressed in whatever units are used

[1]I am, as always, heavily indebted to Anna Schwartz. I have also benefited from discussion of some parts of this article in a number of classes in monetary theory at the University of Chicago and a number of meetings of the Workshop in Money and Banking of the University of Chicago. H. G. Johnson read the semifinal draft and made many useful suggestions for revision. I am grateful to the staff reading committee of the National Bureau: Irving B. Kravis, Chairman, Gary S. Becker, and Richard T. Selden, and to the reading committee of the National Bureau's Board of Directors: Otto Eckstein, Walter E. Hoadley, and James J. O'Leary.

1

to designate money—talents, shekels, pounds, francs, lire, drachmas, dollars, and so on. The real quantity of money is the quantity expressed in terms of the volume of goods and services that the money will purchase.

There is no unique way to express the real quantity of money. One way to express it is in terms of a specified standard basket of goods and services. That is what is implicitly done when the real quantity of money is calculated by dividing the nominal quantity of money by a price index. The standard basket is then the basket the components of which are used as weights in computing the price index—generally, the basket purchased by some representative group in a base year.

A different way to express the real quantity of money is in terms of the time durations of the flows of goods and services the money could purchase. For a household, for example, the quantity of money can be expressed in terms of the number of weeks of the household's average level of consumption that it could finance with its money balances, or, alternatively, in terms of the number of weeks of its average income to which its money balances are equal. For a business enterprise, the real quantity of money it holds can be expressed in terms of the number of weeks of its average purchases, or of its average sales, or of its average expenditures on final productive services (net value added) to which its money balances are equal. For the community as a whole, the real quantity of money can be expressed in terms of the number of weeks of aggregate transactions of the community, or aggregate net output of the community, to which it is equal.

The reciprocal of any of this latter class of measures of the real quantity of money is a velocity of circulation for the corresponding unit or group of units. In every case, the calculation of the real quantity of money or of velocity is made at the set of prices prevailing at the date to which the calculation refers. These prices are the bridge between the nominal and the real quantity of money.

The quantity theory of money takes for granted that what ultimately matters to holders of money is the real quantity rather than the nominal quantity they hold and that there is a fairly definite real quantity of money that people wish to hold under any given circumstances. Suppose that the nominal quantity that people hold at a particular moment of time happens to correspond at current prices to a real quantity larger than the quantity that they wish to hold. Individuals will then seek to dispose of what they regard as their excess money balances; they will try to pay out a larger sum for the purchase of securities, goods and services, for the repayment of debts, and as gifts than they are receiving from the corresponding sources. However, they cannot as a group succeed. One man's expenditures are another's receipts. One man can reduce his nominal money balances only by persuading someone else to increase his. The community as a whole cannot in general spend more than it receives.

The attempt to do so will nonetheless have important effects. If prices and income are free to change, the attempt to spend more will raise the volume of expenditures and receipts, expressed in nominal units, which will lead to a bidding up of prices and perhaps also to an increase in output. If prices are fixed by custom or by government edict, the attempt to spend more will either be matched by an increase in goods and services or produce "shortages" and "queues." These, in turn, will raise the effective price and are likely sooner or later to force changes in official prices.

The initial excess of nominal balances will therefore tend to be eliminated, even though there is no change in the nominal quantity of money, by either a reduction in the real quantity available to hold through price rises or an increase in the real quantity desired through output increases. And conversely for an initial deficiency of nominal balances.

It is clear from this discussion that changes in prices and nominal income can be produced either by changes in the real balances that people wish to hold or by changes in the nominal balances available for them to hold. Indeed, it is a tautology, summarized in the famous quantity equation, that all changes in nominal income can be attributed to one or the other—just as a change in the price of any good can always be attributed to a change in either demand or supply. The quantity theory is not, however, this tautology. On an analytical level, it is an analysis of the factors determining the quantity of money the community wishes to hold; on an empirical level, it is the generalization that changes in desired real balances (in the demand for money) tend to proceed slowly and gradually or to be the result of events set in train by prior changes in supply, whereas, in contrast, substantial changes in the supply of nominal balances can and frequently do occur independently of any changes in demand. The conclusion is that substantial changes in prices or nominal income are almost invariably the result of changes in the nominal supply of money.

2. Quantity Equations

The tautology embodied in the quantity equation is a useful device for clarifying the variables stressed in the quantity theory. The quantity equation has taken different forms, according as quantity theorists have stressed different variables.

a) Transactions Equation

The most famous version of the quantity equation is doubtless the transactions version popularized by Irving Fisher (Fisher 1911, pp. 24–54):

$$MV = PT, \tag{1}$$

or

$$MV + M'V' = PT. \tag{2}$$

In this version, the elementary event is a transaction: an exchange in which one economic actor transfers to another economic actor goods or services or securities and receives a transfer of money in return. The right-hand side of the equations corresponds to the transfer of goods, services, and securities; the left-hand side, to the matching transfer of money.

Each transfer of goods, services, or securities is regarded as the product of a price and a quantity: wage per week times number of weeks, price of a good times number of units of the good, dividend per share times number of shares, price per share times number of shares, and so on. The right-hand side of equations (1) and (2) is the aggregate of such payments during some interval, with P a suitably chosen *average* of the prices, and T a suitably chosen *aggregate* of the quantities during that interval, so that PT is the total nominal value of the payments during the interval in question. The units of P are dollars per unit of quantity; the units of T are number of unit quantities per period of time. We can convert the equation from an expression applying to an *interval* of time to one applying as of a *point* in time by the usual limiting process of letting the interval of time for which we aggregate payments approach zero, and expressing T not as an aggregate but as a rate of flow (that is, the limit of the ratio of aggregate quantities to the length of the interval as the length of the interval approaches zero). The magnitude T then has the dimension of quantity per unit time. The product of P and T then has the dimension of dollars per unit time.

Because the right-hand side is intended to summarize a continuing process, a flow of physical goods and services, the physical item transferred (good, service, or security) is treated as if it disappeared from economic circulation once transferred. If, for example, a single item, say, a house, were transferred three times in the course of the time interval for which *PT* is measured, it would enter into *T* as three houses for that time interval. Further, only those physical items that enter into transactions are explicitly included in *T*. The houses that exist but are not bought or sold during the time interval are omitted, though, if they are rented, the rental values of their services will be included in *PT* and the number of dwelling-unit years per year will be included in *T*. Clearly, *T* is a rather special kind of index of quantities: it includes service flows (man-hours, dwelling-unit years, kilowatt hours) but also capital items yielding flows (houses, electric generating plants), weighting each of these capital items in accordance with the number of times it enters into exchanges (its "velocity of circulation" in strict analogy with the "velocity of circulation" of money). Similarly, *P* is a rather special kind of price index.

The monetary transfer analyzed on the left-hand side of equations (1) and (2) is treated very differently. The money that changes hands is treated as retaining its identity, and all money, whether used in transactions during the time interval in question or not, is explicitly accounted for. Money is treated as a stock, not a flow or a mixture of a flow and a stock. For a single transaction, the breakdown into *M* and *V* is trivial: the cash that is transferred is turned over once, or $V = 1$. For all transactions during an interval, we can, in principle, classify the existing stock of dollars of money according as each dollar entered into 0, 1, 2, . . . transactions, that is, according as each dollar "turned over" 0, 1, 2, . . . times. The weighted average of these numbers of turnover, weighted by the number of dollars that turned over that number of times, is the conceptual equivalent of *V*. The dimensions of *M* are dollars; of *V*, number of turnovers per unit time; so, of the product, dollars per unit time.[2]

Equation (2) differs from equation (1) by dividing payments into two categories: those effected by the transfer of hand-to-hand currency (including coin) and those effected by the transfer of deposits. In equation (2) *M* stands solely for the volume of currency and *V* for

[2] A common criticism of the quantity equation is that, while it takes account of the velocity of circulation of money, it does not take account of the velocity of circulation of goods. As the preceding two paragraphs make clear, while this criticism is not literally valid, it has a real point. The velocity of circulation of money is explicit; the velocity of circulation of goods is implicit. It might well make the right-hand side of equations (1) and (2) more meaningful to make it the sum of two components—one, the total value of transactions involving continuing flows, the other, the value of transfers of existing items of wealth—and to express the second component as a price times a velocity times a stock. In effect, the shift to the income version of the equation resolves the issue by completely neglecting transfers of existing items of wealth.

the velocity of currency, M' for the volume of deposits and V' for the velocity of deposits.

One reason for the emphasis on this particular division was the persistent dispute about whether the term "money" should include only currency or deposits as well (Friedman and Schwartz 1970, chap. 2). Another reason was the direct availability of figures on $M'V'$ from bank records of clearings or of debits to deposit accounts. These make it possible to calculate V' in a way that it is not possible to calculate V.[3]

Equations (1) and (2), like the other quantity equations I shall discuss, are intended to be identities—a special application of double-entry bookkeeping, with each transaction simultaneously recorded on both sides of the equation. However, as with the national income identities with which we are all familiar, when the two sides, or the separate elements on the two sides, are estimated from independent sources of data, many differences between the two sides emerge (Mitchell 1927, pp. 128–39). This has been less obvious for the quantity equations than for the national income identities—with their standard entry "statistical discrepancy"—because of the difficulty of calculating V directly. As a result, V in equation (1) or V and V' in equation (2) have generally been calculated as the numbers having the property that they render the equations correct. These calculated numbers therefore embody the whole of the counterpart to the "statistical discrepancy."

Just as the left-hand side of equation (1) can be divided into several components, as in equation (2), so also can the right-hand side. The emphasis on transactions reflected in this version of the quantity equation suggests dividing total transactions into categories of payments for which payment periods or practices differ: for example, into capital transactions, purchases of final goods and services, purchases of intermediate goods, payments for the use of resources, perhaps separated into wage and salary payments and other payments. The observed value of V might well be a function of the distribution of total payments among categories. Alternatively, if the quantity equation is interpreted not as an identity but as a functional relation expressing desired velocity as a function of other variables, the distribution of payments may well be an important set of variables.

b) The Income Form of the Quantity Equation

Despite the large amount of empirical work done on the transactions equations, notably by Irving Fisher and Carl Snyder (Fisher 1911, pp.

[3] For an extremely ingenious indirect calculation of V, not only for currency as a whole but for particular denominations of currency, see Laurent (1969).

280–318; Fisher 1919; Snyder 1934), the ambiguities of the concepts of "transactions" and the "general price level"—particularly those arising from the mixture of current and capital transactions—were never satisfactorily resolved. The more recent development of national or social accounting has stressed income transactions rather than gross transactions and has explicitly and satisfactorily dealt with the conceptual and statistical problems of distinguishing between changes in prices and changes in quantities. As a result, the quantity equation has more recently tended to be expressed in terms of income rather than of transactions. Let $Y =$ nominal national income, $P =$ the price index implicit in estimating national income at constant prices, and $y =$ national income in constant prices, so that

$$Y = Py. \tag{3}$$

Let M represent, as before, the stock of money; but define V as the average number of times per unit time that the money stock is used in making *income* transactions (that is, payments for final productive services or, alternatively, for final goods and services) rather than all transactions. We can then write the quantity equation in income form as

$$MV = Py, \tag{4}$$

or, if it is desired to distinguish currency from deposit transactions, as

$$MV + M'V' = Py. \tag{5}$$

Although the symbols P, V, and V' are used both in equations (4) and (5) and in equations (1) and (2), they stand for different concepts in each pair of equations.

Equations (4) and (5) are both conceptually and empirically more satisfactory than equations (1) and (2). However, they have the disadvantage that they completely neglect both the ratio of intermediate to final transactions and transactions in existing capital assets.

In the transactions version of the quantity equation, each intermediate transaction—that is, purchase by one enterprise from another—is included at the total value of the transaction, so that the value of wheat, for example, is included once when it is sold by the farmer to the mill, a second time when the mill sells flour to the baker, a third time when the baker sells bread to the grocer, a fourth time when the grocer sells bread to the consumer. In the income version, only the net value added by each of these transactions is included. To put it differently, in the transactions version, the elementary event is an isolated exchange of a physical item for money—an actual, clearly observable event. In the income version, the elementary event is a hypothetical event that can be inferred from observation but is not directly observable. It is a complete series of transactions involving the exchange of productive services for final goods, via a sequence of money payments, with all the intermediate transactions in this income circuit netted out. The total value of all transactions is therefore a multiple of the value of income transactions only.

For a given flow of productive services or, alternatively, of final products (two of the multiple faces of income), the volume of transactions will clearly be affected by vertical integration or disintegration of enterprises, which reduces or increases the number of transactions involved in a single income circuit, or by technological changes that lengthen or shorten the process of transforming productive services into final products. The volume of income will not be thus affected.

Similarly, the transactions version includes the purchase of an existing asset—a house or a piece of land or a share of equity stock—precisely on a par with an intermediate or final transaction. The income version excludes such transactions completely.

Are these differences an advantage or disadvantage of the income version? That clearly depends on what it is that determines the amount of money people want to hold. Do changes of the kind considered in the preceding paragraphs, changes that alter the ratio of intermediate and capital transactions to income, also alter in the same direction and by the same proportion the amount of money people want to hold? Or do they tend to leave this amount unaltered? Or do they have a more complex effect?

Clearly, the transactions and income versions of the quantity theory involve very different conceptions of the role of money. For the transactions version, the most important thing about money is that it is transferred. For the income version, the most important thing is that it is held. This difference is even more obvious from the Cambridge cash-balances version of the quantity equation. Indeed, the income version can perhaps best be regarded as a way station between the Fisher and the Cambridge versions.

c) Cambridge Cash-Balances Approach

The essential feature of a money economy is that it enables the act of purchase to be separated from the act of sale. An individual who has something to exchange need not seek out the double coincidence—someone who both wants what he has and offers in exchange what he wants. He need only find someone who wants what he has, sell it to him for general purchasing power, and then find someone who has what he wants and buy it with general purchasing power.

In order for the act of purchase to be separated from the act of sale, there must be something which everybody will accept in exchange as "general purchasing power"—this is the aspect of money emphasized in the transactions approach. But also there must be something which can serve as a temporary abode of purchasing power in the interim between sale and purchase. This is the aspect of money emphasized in the cash-balances approach.

How much money will people or enterprises want to hold for this purpose? As a first approximation, it has generally been supposed that the amount bears some relation to income, on the assumption that this affects the volume of potential purchases for which the individual or enterprise wishes to hold a temporary abode of purchasing power. We can therefore write

$$M = kPy, \tag{6}$$

where M, P, and y are defined as in equation (4), and k is the ratio of money stock to income—either the observed ratio so calculated as to make equation (6) an identity, or the "desired" ratio so that M is the "desired" amount of money, which need not be equal to the actual amount. In either case, k is numerically equal to the reciprocal of the V in equation (4), the V in one case being interpreted as measured velocity and in the other as desired velocity.

Although equation (6) is simply a mathematical transformation of equation (4), it brings out much more sharply the difference between the aspects of money stressed by the transactions approach and those stressed by the cash-balances approach. This difference makes different definitions of money seem natural and leads to emphasis being placed on different variables and analytical techniques.

The transactions approach makes it natural to define money in terms of whatever serves as the medium of exchange in discharging obligations. By stressing the function of money as a temporary abode of purchasing power, the cash-balances approach makes it seem entirely appropriate to include also such stores of value as demand and time deposits not transferable by check, although this approach clearly does not require their inclusion (Friedman and Schwartz 1970, chap. 3).

Similarly, the transactions approach leads to stress being placed on such variables as payments practices, the financial and economic arrangements for effecting transactions, and the speed of communication and transportation as it affects the time required to make a payment—essentially, that is, to emphasis on the mechanical aspects of the payments process. The cash-balances approach, on the other hand, leads to stress being placed on variables affecting the usefulness of money as an asset: the costs and returns from holding money instead of other assets, the uncertainty of the future, and so on—essentially, that is, to emphasis on the role of cash in a portfolio.

Of course, neither approach enforces the exclusion of the variables stressed by the other—and the more sophisticated economists who have used them have had broader conceptions than the particular approach they adopted. The portfolio aspects enter into the costs of effecting transactions and hence affect the most efficient payment arrangements; the mechanical aspects enter into the returns from holding cash and hence affect the usefulness of cash in a portfolio.

Finally, with regard to analytical techniques, the cash-balances approach fits in much more readily with the general Marshallian demand-supply apparatus than does the transactions approach. Equation (6) can be regarded as a demand function for money, with P and y on the right-hand side being two of the variables on which demand for money depends, and with k symbolizing all the other variables, so that k is to be regarded not as a numerical constant but as itself a function of still other variables. For completion, the analysis requires another equation showing the supply of money as a function of other variables. The price level or the level of nominal income is then the resultant of the interaction of the demand and supply functions.

The quantity theory in its cash-balances version thus suggests organizing an analysis of monetary phenomena in terms of (1) the factors determining the nominal quantity of money to be held—the conditions determining supply—and (2) the factors determining the real quantity of money the community wishes to hold—the conditions determining demand.

3. Supply of Money in Nominal Units

The factors determining the nominal quantity of money available to be held depend critically on the monetary system. For systems like those which have prevailed in the United States and in the United Kingdom during the past century, they can usefully be analyzed under the three main headings that we have termed the proximate determinants of the money stock: (1) the amount of high-powered money—for any one country this is determined through the balance of payments under an international commodity standard, by the monetary authorities, under a fiduciary standard; (2) the ratio of bank deposits to bank holdings of high-powered money—this is determined by the banking system subject to whatever requirements are imposed on them by law or the monetary authorities; and (3) the ratio of the public's deposits to its currency holdings—this is determined by the public (Friedman and Schwartz 1963*b*, pp. 776–98; Cagan 1965).

4. The Demand for Money

J. M. Keynes's liquidity preference analysis (discussed further in section 5, below) reinforced the shift of emphasis from the transactions version of the quantity equation to the cash-balances version—a shift of emphasis from mechanical aspects of the payments process to the qualities of money as an asset. Keynes's analysis, though strictly in the Cambridge cash-balances tradition, was much more explicit in stressing the role of money as one among many assets, and of interest rates as the relevant cost of holding money.

More recent work has gone still further in this direction, treating the demand for money as part of capital or wealth theory, concerned with the composition of the balance sheet or portfolio of assets.

From this point of view, it is important to distinguish between ultimate wealth holders, to whom money is one form in which they choose to hold their wealth, and enterprises, to whom money is a producer's good like machinery or inventories (Friedman 1956).

a) Demand by Ultimate Wealth Holders

For ultimate wealth holders, the demand for money, in real terms, may be expected to be a function primarily of the following variables:

i) *Total wealth.*—This is the analogue of the budget constraint in the usual theory of consumer choice. It is the total that must be divided among various forms of assets. In practice, estimates of total wealth are seldom available. Instead, income may serve as an index of wealth. However, it should be recognized that income as measured by statisticians may be a defective index of wealth because it is subject to erratic year-to-year fluctuations, and a longer-term concept, like the concept of permanent income developed in connection with the theory of consumption, may be more useful (Friedman 1957, 1959; Brunner and Meltzer 1963; Meltzer 1963).

The emphasis on income as a surrogate for wealth, rather than as a measure of the "work" to be done by money, is conceptually perhaps the basic difference between more recent work and the earlier versions of the quantity theory.

ii) *The division of wealth between human and nonhuman forms.*— The major asset of most wealth holders is their personal earning capacity, but the conversion of human into nonhuman wealth or the reverse is subject to narrow limits because of institutional constraints. It can be done by using current earnings to purchase nonhuman wealth or by using nonhuman wealth to finance the acquisition of skills but not by purchase or sale and to only a limited extent by borrowing on the collateral of earning power. Hence, the fraction of total wealth that is in the form of nonhuman wealth may be an additional important variable.

iii) *The expected rates of return on money and other assets.*—This is the analogue of the prices of a commodity and its substitutes and complements in the usual theory of consumer demand. The nominal rate of return on money may be zero, as it generally is on currency, or negative, as it sometimes is on demand deposits subject to net service charges, or positive, as it sometimes is on demand deposits on which interest is paid and generally is on time deposits. The nominal rate of return on other assets consists of two parts: first, any currently paid yield or cost, such as interest on bonds, dividends on equities, and storage costs on physical assets, and, second, changes in their nominal prices. The second part will, of course, be especially important under conditions of inflation or deflation.

iv) *Other variables determining the utility attached to the services rendered by money relative to those rendered by other assets—in Keynesian terminology, determining the value attached to liquidity proper.*—One such variable may be one already considered—namely, real wealth or income, since the services rendered by money may, in principle, be regarded by wealth holders as a "necessity," like bread, the consumption of which increases less than in proportion to any increase in income, or as a "luxury," like recreation, the consumption of which increases more than in proportion.

Another variable that is likely to be important empirically is the degree of economic stability expected to prevail in the future. Wealth holders are likely to attach considerably more value to liquidity when they expect economic conditions to be unstable than when they expect them to be highly stable. This variable is likely to be difficult to express quantitatively even though the direction of change may be clear from qualitative information. For example, the outbreak of war clearly produces expectations of instability, which is one reason why war is often accompanied by a notable increase in real balances—that is, a notable decline in velocity.

Still another variable may be the volume of capital transfers relative to income—of trading in existing capital goods by ultimate wealth holders. The higher the turnover of capital assets, the higher the fraction of total assets people may find it useful to hold as cash. This variable corresponds to the class of transactions neglected in going from the transactions version of the quantity equation to the income version.

We can symbolize this analysis in terms of the following demand function for money for an individual wealth holder:

$$\frac{M}{P} = f\left(y, w; r_m, r_b, r_e, \frac{1}{P}\frac{dP}{dt}; u\right), \tag{7}$$

where $M, P,$ and y have the same meaning as in equation (6) except that they relate to a single wealth holder; w is the fraction of wealth in nonhuman form (or, alternatively, the fraction of income derived from property); r_m is the expected nominal rate of return on money; r_b is the expected nominal rate of return on fixed-value securities, including expected changes in their prices; r_e is the expected nominal rate of return on equities, including expected changes in their prices; $(1/P)(dP/dt)$ is the expected rate of change of prices of goods and hence the expected nominal rate of return on real assets; and u is a portmanteau symbol standing for whatever variables other than income may affect the utility attached to the services of money. Each of the four rates of return stands, of course, for a set of rates of return, and for some purposes it may be important to classify assets still more finely —for example, to distinguish currency from deposits, long-term from short-term fixed-value securities, risky from relatively safe equities, and one kind of physical assets from another.[4]

The usual problems of aggregation arise in passing from equation (7) to a corresponding equation for the economy as a whole—in particular, they arise from the possibility that the amount of money demanded may depend on the distribution among individuals of such variables as y and w and not merely on their aggregate or average value. If we neglect these distributional effects, equation (7) can be

[4] Under some assumed conditions, the four rates of return may not be independent. For example, in a special case considered in Friedman (1956, pp. 9–10),

$$r_b = r_e + (1/P)(dP/dt).$$

regarded as applying to the community as a whole, with M and y referring to per capita money holdings and per capita real income, respectively, and w to the fraction of aggregate wealth in nonhuman form.

The major problems that arise in practice in applying equation (7) are the precise definitions of y and w, the estimation of *expected* rates of return as contrasted with actual rates of return, and the quantitative specification of the variables designated by u.

b) *Demand by Business Enterprises*

Business enterprises are not subject to a constraint comparable with that imposed by the total wealth of the ultimate wealth holder. The total amount of capital embodied in productive assets, including money, is a variable that can be determined by an enterprise to maximize returns, since it can acquire additional capital through the capital market. Hence, there is no reason on this ground to include total wealth, or y as a surrogate for total wealth, as a variable in the business demand function for money.

It may, however, be desirable to include a somewhat similar variable defining the "scale" of the enterprise on different grounds—namely, as an index of the productive value of different quantities of money to the enterprise. This is more nearly in line with the earlier transactions approach emphasizing the "work" to be done by money. It is by no means clear what the appropriate variable is: total transactions, net value added, net income, total capital in nonmoney form, or net worth. The lack of availability of data has meant that much less empirical work has been done on the business demand for money than on an aggregate demand curve encompassing both ultimate wealth holders and business enterprises. As a result there are as yet only faint indications about the best variable to use.

The division of wealth between human and nonhuman form has no special relevance to business enterprises, since they are likely to buy the services of both forms on the market.

Rates of return on money and on alternative assets are, of course, highly relevant to business enterprises. These rates determine the net cost to them of holding the money balances. However, the particular rates that are relevant may be quite different from those that are relevant for ultimate wealth holders. For example, rates charged by banks on loans are of minor importance for wealth holders yet may be extremely important for businesses, since bank loans may be a way in which they can acquire the capital embodied in money balances.

The counterpart for business enterprises of the variable u in equation

(7) is the set of variables other than scale affecting the productivity of money balances. At least one of these—namely, expectations about economic stability—is likely to be common to business enterprises and ultimate wealth holders.

With these interpretations of the variables, equation (7), with w excluded, can be regarded as symbolizing the business demand for money and, as it stands, symbolizing aggregate demand for money, although with even more serious qualifications about the ambiguities introduced by aggregation.

5. The Keynesian Challenge to the Quantity Theory

The income-expenditure analysis developed by John Maynard Keynes in his *General Theory* (Keynes 1936) offered an alternative approach to the interpretation of changes in nominal income that emphasized the relation between nominal income and investment or autonomous expenditures rather than the relation between money income and the stock of money.

Keynes's basic challenge to the reigning theory can be summarized in three propositions that he set forth:

1. As a purely *theoretical* matter, there need not exist, even if all prices are flexible, a *long-run equilibrium* position characterized by "full employment" of resources.

2. As an *empirical* matter, prices can be regarded as rigid—an institutional datum—for *short-run economic fluctuations;* that is, for such fluctuations, the distinction between real and nominal magnitudes that is at the heart of the quantity theory is of no importance.

3. The demand function for money has a particular empirical form —corresponding to absolute liquidity preference—that makes velocity highly unstable much of the time, so that changes in the quantity of money would, in the main, simply produce changes in V in the opposite direction. This proposition is critical for both propositions (1) and (2), though the reasons for absolute liquidity preference are different in the long run and in the short run. Absolute liquidity preference at an interest rate approaching zero is a necessary though not a sufficient condition for proposition (1). Absolute liquidity preference at the "conventional" interest rate explains why Keynes regarded the quantity equation, though perfectly valid as an identity, as largely useless for policy or for predicting short-run fluctuations in nominal and real income (identical by proposition [2]). In its place, Keynes put the income identity supplemented by a stable propensity to consume.

a) Long-Run Equilibrium

The first proposition can be treated summarily because it has been demonstrated to be false. Keynes's error consisted in neglecting the role of wealth in the consumption function—or, stated differently, in neglecting the existence of a desired stock of wealth as a goal motivating savings.[5] All sorts of frictions and rigidities may interfere with the attainment of a hypothetical long-run equilibrium position at full employment; dynamic changes in technology, resources, and social and economic institutions may continually change the characteristics of that equilibrium position; but there is no fundamental "flaw in the price system" that makes unemployment the natural outcome of a fully operative market mechanism.[6]

b) Short-Run Price Rigidity[7]

Alfred Marshall's distinction among market equilibrium, short-period equilibrium, and long-period equilibrium was a device for analyzing

[5] Keynes, of course, verbally recognized this point, but it was not incorporated in his formal model of the economy. Its key role was pointed out first by Haberler (1941, pp. 242, 389, 403, 491–503) and subsequently by Pigou (1947), Tobin (1947), Patinkin (1951), and Johnson (1961).

[6] This proposition played a large role in gaining for Keynes the adherence of many noneconomists, particularly the large band of reformers, social critics, and radicals who were persuaded that there was something fundamentally wrong with the capitalist "system." There is a long history of attempts, some highly sophisticated, to demonstrate that there is a "flaw in the price system" (the title of one such attempt [Martin 1924]), attempts going back at least to Malthus. In modern times, one of the most popular and persistent is the "social credit" doctrine of Major C. H. Douglas, which even spawned a political party in Canada that captured control (in 1935) of the government of one of the Canadian provinces (Alberta) and attempted to implement some of Major Douglas's doctrines. This policy ran into legal obstacles and had to be abandoned. The successor party now (1969) controls Alberta and British Columbia. But, prior to Keynes, these attempts had been made primarily by persons outside of the mainstream of the economics profession, and professional economists had little trouble in demonstrating their theoretical flaws and inadequacies.

Keynes's attempt was therefore greeted with enthusiasm. It came from a professional economist of the very highest repute, regarded, and properly so, by his fellow economists as one of the great economists of all time. The analytical system was sophisticated and complex, yet, once mastered, appeared highly mechanical and capable of yielding far-reaching and important conclusions with a minimum of input; and these conclusions were, besides, highly congenial to the opponents of the market system.

Needless to say, the demonstration that this proposition of Keynes's is false, and even the acceptance of this demonstration by economists who regard themselves as disciples of the Keynes of *The General Theory*, has not prevented the noneconomist opponents of the market system from continuing to believe that Keynes proved the proposition, and continuing to cite his authority for it.

[7] We are indebted to a brilliant book by Leijonhufvud (1968) for a full ap-

the dynamic adjustment in a particular market to a change in demand or supply. This device had two key characteristics. One, the less important for our purposes, is that it replaced the continuous process by a series of discrete steps—comparable with approximating a continuous function by a set of straight-line segments. The second is the assumption that prices adjust more rapidly than quantities, indeed, so rapidly that the price adjustment can be regarded as instantaneous. An increase in demand (a shift to the right of the long-run demand curve) will produce a new market equilibrium involving a higher price but the same quantity. The higher price will, in the short run, encourage existing producers to produce more with their existing plants, thus raising quantity and bringing prices back down toward their original level, and, in the long run, attract new producers and encourage existing producers to expand their plants, still further raising quantities and lowering prices. Throughout the process, it takes time for output to adjust but no time for prices to do so. This assumption has no effect on the final equilibrium position, but it is vital for the path to equilibrium.

This Marshallian assumption about the price of a particular product became widely accepted and tended to be carried over unthinkingly to the price level in analyzing the dynamic adjustment to a change in the demand for or supply of money. As noted above, the Cambridge cash-balances equation lends itself to a demand-supply interpretation along Marshallian lines (Pigou 1917). So interpreted, a change in the nominal quantity of money (a once-for-all shift in the supply schedule) will require a change in one or more of the variables on the right-hand side of equation (6)—k, or P, or y—in order to reconcile demand and supply. In the final full equilibrium, the adjustment will, in general, be entirely in P, since the change in the nominal quantity of money need not alter any of the "real" factors on which k and y ultimately depend.[8] As in the Marshallian case, the final position is not affected by relative speeds of adjustment.

There is nothing in the logic of the quantity theory that specifies the dynamic path of adjustment, nothing that requires the whole adjustment to take place through P rather than through k or y. It was widely recog-

---

preciation of the importance of this proposition in Keynes's system. This sub-section and the one that follows, on the liquidity preference function, owe much to Leijonhufvud's penetrating analysis.

[8] The "in general" is inserted to warn the reader that this is a complex question, requiring for a full analysis a much more careful statement of just how the quantity of money is increased. However, these more sophisticated issues are not relevant to the point under discussion and so are bypassed.

nized that the adjustment during what Fisher, for example, called "transition periods" would in practice be partly in k and in y as well as in P. Yet this recognition was not incorporated in formal theoretical analysis. The formal analysis simply took over Marshall's assumption. In this sense, the quantity theorists can be validly criticized for having "assumed" price flexibility—just as Keynes can be validly criticized for "assuming" that consumption is independent of wealth, even though he recognized in his asides that wealth has an effect on consumption.

Keynes was a true Marshallian in method. He followed Marshall in taking the demand-supply analysis as his framework. He followed Marshall in replacing the continuous adjustment by a series of discrete steps and so analyzing a dynamic process in terms of a series of shifts between static equilibrium positions. Even his steps were essentially Marshall's, his short-run being distinguished from his long-run by the fixity of the aggregate capital stock. However, he tended to merge the market period and the short-run period, and, true to his own misleading dictum, "in the long run we are all dead," he concentrated almost exclusively on the short run.

Keynes also followed Marshall in assuming that one variable adjusted so quickly that the adjustment could be regarded as instantaneous, while the other variable adjusted slowly. Where he deviated from Marshall, and it was a momentous deviation, was in reversing the roles assigned to price and quantity. He assumed that, at least for changes in aggregate demand, quantity was the variable that adjusted rapidly, while price was the variable that adjusted slowly,[9] at least in a downward direction. Keynes embodied this assumption in his formal model by expressing all variables in wage units, so that his formal analysis—aside from a few passing references to a situation of "true" inflation—dealt with "real" magnitudes, not "nominal" magnitudes (Keynes 1936, pp. 119, 301, 303). He rationalized the assumption in terms of wage rigidity arising partly from money illusion, partly from the strength of trade unions. And, at a still deeper level, he rationalized wage rigidity by proposition (1): under conditions when there was no full-employment equilibrium, there was also no equilibrium nominal price level; something had to be brought in from outside to fix the price level; it might as well be institutional wage rigidity. Put differ-

[9] I have referred to "quantity," not "output," because I conjecture that Keynes, if pressed to distinguish the market from the short-run period, would have done so by regarding quantity available to purchase as adjusting rapidly in the market period largely through changes in inventories, and in the short-run period through changes in output.

ently, flexible nominal wages under such circumstances had no economic function to perform; hence they might as well be made rigid.

However rationalized, the basic reason for the assumption was undoubtedly the lack of concordance between observed phenomena and the implications of a literal application of Marshall's assumption to aggregate magnitudes. Such a literal application implied that economic fluctuations would take the form wholly of fluctuations in prices with continuous full employment of men and resources. Clearly, this did not correspond to experience. If anything, at least in the decade and a half between the end of World War I and the writing of *The General Theory*, economic fluctuations were manifested to a greater degree in output and employment than in prices. It therefore seemed highly plausible that, at least for aggregate phenomena, relative speeds of adjustment were just the reverse of those assumed by Marshall.[10]

Keynes explored this penetrating insight by carrying it to the extreme: all adjustment in quantity, none in price. He qualified this statement by assuming it to apply only to conditions of underemployment. At "full" employment, he shifted to the quantity-theory model and asserted that all adjustment would be in price—he designated this a situation of "true inflation." However, Keynes paid no more than lip service to this possibility, and his disciples have done the same; so it does not misrepresent the body of his analysis largely to neglect the qualification.

Given this assumption, a change in the nominal quantity of money means a change in the real quantity of money. In equation (6) we can divide through by P, making the left-hand side the real quantity of money. A change in the (nominal and real) quantity of money will then be matched by a change in k or in y.

Nothing up to this point seems to prevent Keynes from having a purely monetary theory of economic fluctuations, with changes in M being reflected entirely in y. However, this conflicted with Keynes's interpretation of the facts of the Great Depression, which he regarded, I believe erroneously, as showing that expansive monetary policy was ineffective in stemming a decline (Friedman 1967). Hence, he was inclined to interpret changes in M as being reflected in k rather more

[10] I do not mean to suggest that Marshall's assumption is always the best one for particular markets. On the contrary, one of the significant advances in recent years in relative price theory is the development of more sophisticated price adjustment models that allow the rates of adjustment of both price and quantity to vary continuously between instantaneous and very slow adjustment. However, these developments are not directly relevant to the present discussion, although they partly inspire section 12 below.

than in y. This is where his proposition (3) about liquidity preference enters in.

Indeed, in the most extreme, and I am tempted to say purest, form of his analysis, Keynes supposes that the whole of the adjustment will be in k. And, interestingly enough, this result can also be regarded as a direct consequence of his assumption about the relative speed of adjustment of price and quantity. For k is not a numerical constant but a function of other variables. It embodies liquidity preference. In Keynes's system, the main variable it depends on is the interest rate. This too is a price. Hence, it was natural for Keynes to regard it as slow to adjust, and to take, as the variable which responds, the real quantity of money people desire to hold.

If changes in M do not produce changes in y, what does? Keynes's answer is the need to reconcile the amount some people want to spend to add to the stock of productive capital with the amount the community wants to save to add to its stock of wealth. Hence Keynes puts at the center of his analysis the distinction between consumption and saving, or more fundamentally, between spending linked closely to current income and spending that is largely independent of current income.

As a result of both experience and further theoretical analysis, there is hardly an economist today who accepts Keynes's conclusion about the strictly passive character of k, or the accompanying conclusion that money (in the sense of the quantity of money) does not matter, or who will explicitly assert that P is "really" an institutional datum that will be completely unaffected even in short periods by changes in M (Friedman 1968, 1970b).

Yet Keynes's assumption about the relative speed of adjustment of price and quantity is still a key to the difference in approach and analysis between those economists who regard themselves as Keynesians and those who do not. Whatever the first group may say in their asides and in their qualifications, they treat the price level as an institutional datum in their formal theoretical analysis. They continue to regard changes in the nominal quantity of money as equivalent to changes in the real quantity of money and hence as having to be reflected in k and y. And they continue to regard the initial effect as being on k. The difference is that they no longer regard interest rates as institutional data, as Keynes in considerable measure did. Instead, they regard the change in k as requiring a change in interest rates which in turn produces a change in y. Hence, they attribute more significance to changes in the quantity of money than Keynes and his disciples did in the first decade or so after the appearance of *The General Theory*.

A striking illustration is provided in a recent Cowles Foundation Monograph, edited by Donald Hester and James Tobin, on *Financial Markets and Economic Activity* (Hester and Tobin 1967). A key essay in that book presents a comparative static analysis of the general equilibrium adjustment of stocks of assets. Yet the distinction between nominal and real magnitudes is not even discussed. The entire analysis is valid only on the implicit assumption that nominal prices of goods and services are completely rigid, although interest rates and real magnitudes are flexible.[11]

The National Bureau series of monetary studies illustrates the other side of the coin—the approach of those of us who do not regard ourselves as Keynesians. Many of the questions discussed in these monographs would not have appeared to be open questions, and large parts of them would never have been written, had we, implicitly or explicitly, accepted Keynes's assumption that prices are an institutional datum.

c) Absolute Liquidity Preference

Keynes gave a highly specific form to equation (6) or (7). The quantity of money demanded, he argued, could be treated as if it were divided

---

[11] See Tobin and Brainard (1967). A specific example documenting this statement is that Tobin and Brainard explicitly assume that central banks can determine the ratio of currency (or high-powered money) to total wealth including real assets (Hester and Tobin 1967, pp. 61–62). If prices are flexible, the central bank can determine only nominal magnitudes, not such a real ratio.

Other papers in Monograph 21, notably the paper by Brainard, "Financial Institutions and a Theory of Monetary Control" (Brainard 1967), make the same implicit assumptions. The word "prices" does not appear in the cumulative subject index of this monograph and of two companion volumes, Monographs 19 and 20.

Still another more recent example is a paper by the same authors, "Pitfalls in Financial Model Building" (Tobin and Brainard 1968), in which they present a simulation of a "fictitious economy of our construction." In this economy, the replacement value of physical assets is used as the numeraire of the system, and all prices are expressed relative to the replacement value. The result is that the system—intended to illuminate the problems of monetary analysis—takes the absolute price level as determined outside the system. The Central Bank is implicitly assumed to be able to determine the *real* and not merely the *nominal* volume of bank reserves.

Another striking example is Gramley and Chase (1965). In this article, the assumption about price rigidity is explicit and presented as if it were only a tentative assumption made for convenience of analysis. Yet the empirical significance Gramley and Chase attach to their results belies this profession.

See also the econometric study by Goldfeld (1966), which concentrates on real forms of the functions estimated because of "the superiority of the deflated version" (p. 166).

Evidence for a somewhat earlier period is provided by Holzman and Bronfenbrenner (1963). Theories of inflation stemming from the Keynesian approach stress institutional, not monetary, factors.

into two parts, one part, M_1, "held to satisfy the transactions- and precautionary-motives," the other, M_2, "held to satisfy the speculative-motive" (Keynes 1936, p. 199). He regarded M_1 as a roughly constant fraction of income. He regarded the (short-run) demand for M_2 as arising from *"uncertainty* as to the future of the rate of interest" and the amount demanded as depending on the relation between current rates of interest and the rates of interest expected to prevail in the future (Keynes 1936, p. 168; italics in original). Keynes, of course, emphasized that there was a whole complex of interest rates. However, for simplicity, he spoke in terms of "the rate of interest," usually meaning by that the rate on long-term securities that involved minimal risks of default—for example, government bonds. The key distinction to Keynes was between short-term and long-term securities, not between securities fixed in nominal value and those that were not. The latter distinction was rendered irrelevant by his assumption that prices were rigid.

The distinction between short-term and long-term securities was important to Keynes because it corresponded to differences in risk of capital gain or loss as a result of changes in interest rates. For short-term securities, changes in interest rates would have little effect. For long-term securities, the effect is important. Leijonhufvud has argued, and we believe correctly, that Keynes used the term "money" as referring not only to currency and deposits narrowly defined but to the whole range of short-term assets that provided "liquidity" in the sense of security against capital loss arising from changes in interest rates.[12] Needless to say, Keynes also regarded other kinds of risks, such as risks of default, as highly relevant, but, consistent with his proposition (2), he almost entirely disregarded risks arising from changes in the price level of goods and services (Leijonhufvud 1968, chap. 2).

It is therefore somewhat misleading to regard Keynes, as most of the literature does, as distinguishing between "money" and "bonds." Nonetheless, we shall continue to follow current practice and use that terminology. One justification for doing so is that Keynes did treat the short-term assets he labeled "money" as yielding no interest return. (It is well to recall that he was writing at a time when short-term interest rates were extremely low both absolutely and relative to long-term rates. His procedure would seem highly unrealistic today.)

[12] In this respect, the Radcliffe Committee is faithful to Keynes in treating "liquidity" broadly defined as the relevant monetary aggregate rather than "money" narrowly defined.

To formalize Keynes's analysis in terms of the symbols we have used so far, we can write his demand function as

$$\frac{M}{P} = \frac{M_1}{P} + \frac{M_2}{P} = k_1 y + f(r - r^*, r^*), \qquad (8)$$

where r is the current rate of interest, r^* is the rate of interest expected to prevail, and k_1, the analogue to the inverse of income velocity of circulation of money, is treated as determined by payment practices and hence as a constant at least in the short run.[13] The current interest rate, r, is an observed magnitude. Hence it will be the same for all holders of money, if, like Keynes, we abstract from the existence of a complex of interest rates. The expected rate, r^*, is not observable. It may differ from one holder to another and, for each holder separately, is to be interpreted as the mean value of a probability distribution, not as a single value anticipated with certainty. For an aggregate function, r^* should strictly speaking be interpreted as a vector, not a number. Though I have introduced P into the equation for consistency with my earlier equations, Keynes omitted it because of his proposition (2), which meant that P, or, more precisely, the wage rate, was taken to be a constant.

In a "given state of expectations," that is, for a given value of r^*, the higher is the current rate of interest, the lower will be the amount of money people would want to hold for speculative motives. The cost of holding money instead of securities would be greater in two ways: first, a larger amount of current earnings would be sacrificed; second, it would be more likely that interest rates would fall, and hence security prices rise, and so a larger amount of capital gains would be sacrificed.

Although expectations are given great prominence in developing the liquidity function expressing the demand for M_2, Keynes and his followers generally did not explicitly introduce them, as I have done, into that function. For the most part, Keynes and his followers in practice treated the amount of M_2 demanded simply as a function of the current interest rate, the emphasis on expectations serving only as a reason for their attribution of instability to the liquidity function.[14]

The reason for this omission is their concentration on the short-run demand function. For that function, they regarded r^* as fixed, so that the speculative demand was a function of r alone. I have introduced

[13] Later writers in this tradition have argued that k_1 too should be regarded as a function of interest rates. See Baumol (1952), and Tobin (1956). However, this issue is not relevant to the present discussion.

[14] A notable exception is Tobin (1958, pp. 65–86).

r^* in order to distinguish between the different reasons that are implicit in Keynes's analysis for absolute liquidity preference in the short run and the long run.

Keynes's special twist was less expressing the demand function in the general form described by equation (8) than the particular form he gave to the function $f(r - r^*, r^*)$. For given r^*, he believed that this function would be highly elastic at $r = r^*$, the degree of elasticity at an observed numerical value of r depending on how homogenous the expectations of different holders of money are and how firmly they are held.[15] Let there be a substantial body of holders of money who have the same expectation and who hold that expectation firmly, and f will become perfectly elastic at that current interest rate. Money and bonds would become perfect substitutes; liquidity preference would become absolute. The monetary authorities would find it impossible to change the interest rate because speculators holding these firm expectations would frustrate them.

Under such circumstances, if the monetary authorities sought to increase the amount of money by buying bonds, this would tend to raise bond prices and lower the rate of return on bonds. Even the slightest lowering would, Keynes argued, lead speculators with firm expectations to absorb the additional money balances and sell the bonds demanded by the holders of money. The result would simply be that the community as a whole would be willing to hold the increased quantity of money; k would be higher and V lower. Conversely, if the monetary authorities decreased the amount of money by selling bonds, this would tend to raise the rate of interest, and even the slightest rise would induce the speculators to absorb the bonds offered. (In Keynes's analysis, the result would be the same if the amount of money were increased or decreased by operations that added to or subtracted from total wealth, rather than by substituting one form of wealth for another, because he assumed that wealth had no direct effect on spending.)

Or, again, suppose there is an increase in nominal income for whatever reason. That will require an increase in M_1, which can come out of M_2 without any further effects. Conversely, any decline in M_1 can be added to M_2 without any further effects. The conclusion is that *under circumstances of absolute liquidity preference* income can change without a change in M or in interest rates and M can change without

[15] Tobin (1958) presents an excellent and illuminating analysis of this case. Because he assumes that shifts into or out of securities involve commitments for a finite period equal to the unit of time in terms of which the interest rate is expressed, his critical value is not $r = r^*$ but $r = r^*/(1 + r^*)$, current income on the securities compensating for an expected capital loss.

a change in income or in interest rates. The holders of money are in metastable equilibrium, like a tumbler on its side on a flat surface; they will be satisfied with whatever the amount of money happens to be.

For the long-run demand schedule, the reason for liquidity preference is different. In long-run equilibrium, r must equal r^*, so $f(r - r^*, r^*)$ reduces to a function of r^* alone. Let there be a deficiency of investment opportunities, the kind of situation envisaged in Keynes's proposition (1), so that r^* becomes very low. The lower the rate, the lower the return from capital assets other than money—whether these be bonds, equities, or physical assets (recall that because of the assumption that the price level is rigid, Keynes did not regard the distinction among these as important). Accordingly, the lower r^*, the lower the cost of holding money. At a sufficiently low, yet finite rate, the extra return from holding nonmoney assets would only just compensate for the extra risks involved. Hence at that rate, liquidity preference would be absolute. The "market rate" of interest could not be indefinitely low; a bottom limit was set by the widespread desire to substitute money for other assets at low interest rates.

This conclusion was a key element in Keynes's proposition (1). One way to summarize his argument for that proposition is in terms of a possible conflict between the "market" and the "equilibrium" rate of interest. If investment opportunities were sparse, yet the public's desire to save were strong, the "equilibrium" rate of interest, he argued, might have to be very low or even negative to equate investment and saving. But there was a floor to the "market rate" set by liquidity preference. If this floor exceeded the "equilibrium rate," he argued, there was a conflict that could only be resolved by unemployment that frustrated the public's thriftiness. The fallacy in this argument is that the introduction of money not only introduces a floor to the "market rate"; it also sets a floor to the "equilibrium rate." And, in the long run, the two floors are identical. This is the essence of the so-called Pigou effect (Friedman 1962, pp. 262–63).

Neither Keynes himself, nor most of his disciples and followers, distinguished as sharply as I have between the short-run and long-run liquidity traps. They tended to merge the two and, in line with the general emphasis on the short run, to stress elasticity with respect to current, not expected, interest rates.[16]

Keynes regarded absolute liquidity preference as a strictly "limiting case" of which, though it "might become practically important in

[16] Tobin makes an explicit distinction of this kind, though not in connection with a liquidity trap as such.

future," he knew "of no example . . . hitherto" (Keynes 1936, p. 207). However, he treated velocity as if in practice its behavior frequently approximated that which would prevail in this limiting case.

Absolute liquidity preference is no longer explicitly avowed by today's economists—the failure of central banks in their attempts to peg interest rates at low levels have made that proposition untenable. Yet, like absolutely rigid prices, it still plays an important role in the theorizing of many an economist. It is implicit in the tendency to regard k or velocity as passively adjusting to changes in the quantity of money. It is explicit in the tendency to regard the demand for money as "highly" elastic with respect to interest rates.

Consider again equation (6). Let there be a change in M. Economists in the Keynesian tradition continue, as noted earlier, to regard P as an institutional datum and so unaffected. They must therefore regard the change in M as affecting either k or y or both. With absolute liquidity preference, k can absorb the impact without any change in the interest rate. Since they take the interest rate as the only link between monetary change and real income, the whole of the change would then be absorbed in k with no effect on y. If liquidity preference is not absolute, k can change only through a change in the interest rate. But this has effects on y through investment spending. The more elastic is the demand for money, the less interest rates will have to change. The more inelastic are investment spending and saving with respect to the interest rate, the less will any given change in the interest rate affect y. Hence the tendency for these economists to regard k as absorbing the main impact of changes in M means that implicitly or explicitly they regard the demand for money as highly elastic with respect to the interest rate and investment spending and saving as highly inelastic.

The tendency on the part of many economists to assume implicitly that prices are an institutional datum and that the demand for money is highly elastic with respect to the interest rate underlies some of the criticisms that have been directed against earlier work by myself and associates. We have been interpreted, wrongly, we believe, as saying that k is completely independent of interest rates (Friedman 1966). In that case, changes in M need not be reflected at all in k. If, also, P is taken as an institutional datum, all of the effect will be on y. This is the implicit source of the criticism leveled against us, that we regard the quantity of money as determining the level of economic activity. Not only, say our critics, do we believe that money matters, we believe that money is all that matters (Okun 1963; Tobin 1965a, p. 481).

If P is not regarded as an institutional datum, and we have not so regarded it, then even if we supposed k to be completely insensitive to interest rates and to anything else that might be affected by changes in M (such as the rate of change in P or in y) and so to be an absolute constant, aside from random disturbances, something other than the quantity of money would have to be brought into the analysis to explain how much of the change in M would be reflected in P and how much in y (see section 12, below).

We have always tried to qualify our statements about the importance of changes in M by referring to their effect on *nominal* income. But this qualification appeared meaningless to economists who implicitly identified nominal with real magnitudes. Hence they have misunderstood our conclusions.

We have accepted the quantity-theory presumption, and have thought it supported by the evidence we examined, that changes in the quantity of money as such *in the long run* have a negligible effect on real income, so that nonmonetary forces are "all that matter" for changes in real income over the decades and money "does not matter." On the other hand, we have regarded the quantity of money, plus the other variables (including real income itself) that affect k as essentially "all that matter" for the long-run determination of nominal income. The price level is then a joint outcome of the monetary forces determining nominal income and the real forces determining real income (Friedman 1958, pp. 242–46; Friedman and Schwartz 1963*b*, p. 695).

For shorter periods of time, we have argued that changes in M will be reflected in all three variables on the right-hand side of equation (6): k, P, and y. But we have argued that the effect on k is empirically not to absorb the change in M, as the Keynesian analysis implies, but often to reinforce it, changes in M and k frequently affecting income in the same rather than opposite directions. Hence we have emphasized that changes in M are a major factor, though even then not the only factor, accounting for short-run changes in both nominal income and the real level of activity (y). I regard the description of our position as "money is all that matters for changes in *nominal* income and for *short-run* changes in real income" as an exaggeration but one that gives the right flavor of our conclusions. I regard the statement that "money is all that matters," period, as a basic misrepresentation of our conclusions (Friedman 1958, pp. 246–51; Friedman and Schwartz 1963*a*, pp. 38–39, 45–46, 55–64; Friedman and Schwartz 1963*b*, p. 678).

Another, more subtle, difference between the approach of the economists in the Keynesian tradition and the approach that we have adopted has also contributed to much misunderstanding. This difference is in the transmission mechanism that is assumed to connect a change in the quantity of money with a change in total nominal income (= total spending). The Keynesians regard a change in the quantity of money as affecting in the first instance "the" interest rate, interpreted as a market rate on a fairly narrow class of financial liabilities. They regard spending as affected only "indirectly" as the changed interest rate alters the profitability and amount of investment spending, again interpreted fairly narrowly, and as investment spending, through the multiplier, affects total spending..Hence the emphasis they give in their analysis to the interest elasticities of the demand for money and of investment spending. We, on the other hand, stress a much broader and more "direct" impact on spending, saying, as in section 1 above, that individuals seeking "to dispose of what they regard as their excess money balances . . . will try to pay out a larger sum for the purchase of securities, goods and services, for the repayment of debts, and as gifts than they are receiving from the corresponding sources."

The two approaches can be readily reconciled on a formal level. The transmission mechanism that we have stressed can be described as operating "through" the balance sheet and "through" changes in interest rates. The attempt by holders of money to restore or attain a desired balance sheet after an unexpected increase in the quantity of money will tend to raise the prices of assets and reduce interest rates, which will encourage both spending to produce new assets and spending on current services rather than on purchasing existing assets. This is how an initial effect on balance sheets gets translated into an effect on income and spending.

The difference between us and the Keynesians is less in the nature of the process than in the range of assets considered. The Keynesians tend to concentrate on a narrow range of marketable assets and recorded interest rates. We insist that a far wider range of assets and interest rates must be taken into account—such assets as durable and semi-durable consumer goods, structures and other real property. As a result, we regard the market rates stressed by the Keynesians as only a small part of the total spectrum of rates that are relevant (Friedman 1961, pp. 461–463; Friedman and Meiselman 1963, pp. 217–222; Friedman and Schwartz 1963a, pp. 59-63; Friedman 1970b, pp. 24–25; Brunner 1970, pp. 3–5).

This difference in the assumed transmission mechanism is largely a by-product of the different assumptions about price. The rejection of absolute liquidity preference forced Keynes's followers to let the interest rate be flexible. This chink in the key assumption that prices are an institutional datum was minimized by interpreting the "interest rate" narrowly, and market institutions made it easy to do so. After all, it is most unusual to quote houses, automobiles, let alone furniture, household appliances, clothes and so on, in 'terms of the "interest rate" implicit in their sales and rental prices. Hence the prices of these items continued to be regarded as an institutional datum, which forced the transmission process to go through an extremely narrow channel. On our side, there was no such inhibition. Since we regarded prices as flexible, though not "perfectly" flexible, it was natural for us to interpret the transmission mechanism in terms of relative price adjustments over a broad area rather than in terms of narrowly defined interest rates.

6. A Simple Common Model

We can summarize the key points of the preceding sections of this paper, and lay a groundwork for the final sections, by setting forth a highly simplified aggregate model of an economy that encompasses both a simplified quantity theory and a simplified income-expenditure theory as special cases. In interpreting this model, it should be kept in mind that the same symbols can have very different empirical counterparts, so that the algebraic statement can conceal a difference as fundamental as that described in the preceding four paragraphs.

For the purpose of this summary, we can neglect foreign trade, by assuming a closed economy, and the fiscal role of government, by assuming that there are neither government expenditures nor government receipts. We can also neglect stochastic disturbances. What I shall concentrate on are the division of national income between induced and autonomous expenditures and the adjustment between the demand for and supply of money.

The simple model is given by six equations:

$$\frac{C}{P} = f\left(\frac{Y}{P}, r\right); \tag{9}$$

$$\frac{I}{P} = g(r); \tag{10}$$

$$\frac{Y}{P} = \frac{C}{P} + \frac{I}{P} \ \left(\text{or, alternatively, } \frac{S}{P} = \frac{Y - C}{P} = \frac{I}{P}\right); \tag{11}$$

$$M^D = P \cdot l\left(\frac{Y}{P}, r\right); \tag{12}$$

$$M^S = h(r); \tag{13}$$

$$M^D = M^S. \tag{14}$$

The first three equations describe the adjustment of the flows of savings and investment; the last three, of the stock of money demanded and supplied. Equation (9) is a consumption function (Keynes's "marginal propensity to consume") expressing real consumption (C/P) as a function of real income $(Y/P = y)$ and the interest rate (r). For simplicity, wealth is omitted, although, if the model were to be used to illustrate Keynes's proposition (1), and why it is fallacious, wealth would have to be included as an argument in the function.

Equation (10) is an investment function (Keynes's marginal efficiency of investment) which expresses real investment (I/P) as a function of the interest rate. Here again, consistent with both Keynes and subsequent literature, both the total stock of capital and real income could be included as arguments. However, in Keynes's spirit, the model refers to a short period in which the capital stock can be regarded as fixed. For a longer-period model, the capital stock would have to be included and treated as an endogenous variable, presumably defined by an integral of past investment. The inclusion of income in the equation, as an independent variable, would confuse the key point of the distinction between C and I. As a theoretical matter, the relevant distinction is not between consumption and investment but between expenditures that are closely linked to current income ("conditional" on income would, from this point of view, be a better mnemonic for C than consumption, though the term usually used is "induced") and expenditures that are autonomous, that is, independent (a better mnemonic for I than investment), of income. The identification of these categories with consumption and investment is an empirical hypothesis. For theoretical purposes, any part of investment spending that is conditional on current income should be included with C.

Equation (11) is typically referred to as the income identity. As the parenthetical transformation makes clear, it can also be regarded as a market-clearing or adjustment equation specifying that saving is to be equal to investment.

Equation (12) is the demand function for nominal money balances (Keynes's liquidity preference function). It is simply equation (6) or (7) rewritten in simplified form and expresses the real quantity of money demanded (M^D/P) as a function of real income and the interest rate. Here again, as in equation (9), wealth could properly be included but is omitted for simplicity.

Equation (13) is the supply function of nominal money. To be consistent with the literature, the interest rate enters as a variable. However, no purpose for which we shall use the model would be affected in any way by treating M^s as simply an exogenous variable, determined, say, by the monetary authorities.[17]

Equation (14) is the counterpart of equation (11), a market-clearing or adjustment equation specifying that money demanded shall equal money supplied.

These six equations would be accepted alike by adherents of the quantity theory and of the income-expenditure theory. On this level of abstraction, there is no difference between them. However, while there are six equations, there are seven unknowns: C, I, Y, r, P, M^D, M^s. There is a missing equation. Some one of these variables must be determined by relationships outside this system.[18]

7. The Missing Equation: Three Approaches

The difference between the quantity theory and the income-expenditure theory is the condition that is added to make the equations determinate.

The simple income-expenditure theory adds the missing equation in one form. Different versions of the quantity theory add it in two other forms. Of these, the missing equation that has been generally regarded in the literature as defining the simple quantity theory is discussed in this section. The missing equation supplied by an alternative version of the quantity theory that is implicit in much recent literature but has not heretofore been made explicit is discussed in the following section. I shall designate the alternative version of the quantity theory as the monetary theory of nominal income.

The simple quantity theory adds the equation

$$\frac{Y}{P} = y = y_0; \tag{15}$$

that is, real income is determined outside the system. In effect, it appends to this system the Walrasian equations of general equilibrium, regards

[17] This would be consistent with Cagan's findings about the absence of any significant effect of changes in the interest rate on the supply of money. However, to be consistent with his findings, income or some other indicator of business cycles would have to be included as a variable, as has been done in some empirical studies of the supply of money. See Cagan (1965, pp. 150, 228–32) and Hendershott (1968).

[18] Of course, this is speaking figuratively. It is not necessary that a single variable be so determined. What is required is an independent relation connecting some subset of the seven endogenous variables with exogenous variables, and that subset could in principle consist of all seven variables.

them as independent of these equations defining the aggregates, and as giving the value of Y/P, and thereby reduces this system to one of six equations determining six unknowns.[19]

The simple income-expenditure theory adds the equation[20]

$$P = P_0; \tag{16}$$

that is, the price level is determined outside the system, which again reduces the system to one of six equations in six unknowns. It appends to this system a historical set of prices and an institutional structure that is assumed either to keep prices rigid or to determine changes in prices on the basis of "bargaining power" or some similar set of forces. Initially, the set of forces determining prices was treated as not being incorporated in any formal body of economic analysis. More recently, the developments symbolized by the "Phillips curve" reflect attempts to bring the determination of prices back into the body of economic analysis, to establish a link between real magnitudes and the rate at which prices change from their initial historically determined level (Phillips 1958).

For the quantity theory specialization, given that $Y/P = y_0$, equations (9), (10), and (11) become a self-contained set of three equation in three unknowns: C/P, I/P, and r. Substituting (9) and (10) into (11), we have

$$y_0 - f(y_0, r) = g(r), \tag{17}$$

or a single equation which determines r. Let r_0 be this value of r. From equation (13), this determines the value of M, say M_0 which, using equation (14), converts equation (12) into

$$M_0 = P \cdot l(y_0, r_0), \tag{18}$$

which now determines P.

[19] This is the essence of what has been called the classical dichotomy. Strictly speaking, the division between consumption and investment and the rates of exchange between current and future goods or services (the set of "real" or "own" interest rates) are also determined in a Walrasian "real" system, one which admits of growth, which is why quantity theorists have tended to concentrate only on equations (12), (13), and (14). On this view, equations (9), (10), and (11) are a summarization or aggregation or subset of the Walrasian system.

[20] Keynes distinguished between the price level of products and the wage rate and allowed for a change in the ratio of the one to the other as output changed, even before the point of full employment. However, this change in relative prices plays no important role in the aspects of his theory that are relevant to our purpose, so I have simplified the model by taking prices rather than wages as rigid—a simplification that has been widely used. However, explicit reference to this simplification should have been made in an earlier paper (Friedman 1970). I am indebted to an unpublished paper by Paul Davidson for recognition that the earlier exposition on this point may have been misleading.

Equation (18) is simply the classical quantity equation, as can be seen by multiplying and dividing the right-hand side by y_0 and replacing $l(y_0,r_0)/y_0$ by its equivalent, $1/V$. If we drop the subscripts, this gives,

$$M = \frac{Py}{V}, \qquad (19)$$

or

$$P = \frac{MV}{y}. \qquad (20)$$

For the income-expenditure specialization, setting $P = P_0$ does not in general permit of a sequential solution. Substituting equations (9) and (10) into equation (11) gives

$$\frac{Y}{P_0} - f\left(\frac{Y}{P_0}, r\right) = g(r), \qquad (21)$$

an equation in two variables, Y and r. This is the *IS* curve of Hicks's famous *IS–LM* analysis (Hicks 1937). Substituting equations (12) and (13) into equation (14) gives

$$h(r) = P_0 \cdot l\left(\frac{Y}{P_0}, r\right), \qquad (22)$$

a second equation in the same two variables, Y and r. This is Hicks's *LM* curve. The simultaneous solution of the two determines r and Y.

Alternatively, solve equation (21) for Y as a function of r, and substitute in equation (22). This gives a single equation which determines r as a function of the demand for and supply of money. This can be regarded as the Keynesian parallel to equation (18), which determines P as a function of the demand for and supply of money.

A simpler sequential analysis, faithful to many textbook versions of the analysis and to Keynes's own simplified model, is obtained by supposing either that Y/P is not an argument in the right-hand side of equation (12) or that absolute liquidity preference holds so that equation (12) takes the special form:

$$M^D = 0 \text{ if } r > r_0 \qquad (12a)$$

$$M^D = \infty \text{ if } r < r_0.$$

In either of these cases, equations (12) or (12a), (13), and (14) determine the interest rate, $r = r_0$ (just as in the simple quantity approach, equations [9], [10], and [11] do); substituting the interest rate in equation (10) determines investment, say at $I = I_0$ and in equation (9) makes consumption a function solely of income, so that real income must then be determined by the requirement that it equate saving with investment.

If we approximate the function $f(Y/P, r_0)$ by a linear form, say,

$$\frac{C}{P} = C_0 + C_1 \frac{Y}{P}, \tag{23}$$

substitute equation (23) in equation (11), and solve for Y/P, we get

$$\frac{Y}{P} = \frac{C_0 + I_0}{1 - C_1}, \tag{24}$$

or the simple Keynesian multiplier equation, with $C_0 + I_0$ equalling autonomous expenditure and $1/(1 - C_1)$ equalling the multiplier.

8. The Missing Equation: The Third Approach Examined

A third form of the missing equation involves bypassing the breakdown of nominal income between real income and prices and using the quantity theory to derive a theory of nominal income rather than a theory of either prices or real income.

a) Demand for Money

As a first step, assume that the elasticity of the demand for money with respect to real income is unity. We can then write (12) in the equivalent form:

$$M^D = Y \cdot l(r), \tag{12b}$$

where the same symbol l is used to designate a different functional form. This enables us to eliminate prices and real income separately from the equations of the monetary sector.

This assumption cannot, so far as I am aware, be justified on theoretical grounds. There is no reason why the elasticity of demand for money with respect to per capita real income should not be either less than one or greater than one at any particular level of income, or why it should be the same at all levels of real income. However, much empirical evidence indicates that the income elasticity is not very different from unity. The empirical evidence seems to me to indicate that the elasticity is generally larger than unity, perhaps in the neighborhood of 1.5 to 2.0 for economies in a period of rapid economic development, and of 1.0 to 1.5 for other circumstances. Other scholars would perhaps set it lower. More important, the present theory is for short-term fluctuations during which the variation in per capita real income is fairly small. Given that the elasticity is unlikely to exceed 2.0, no great error can be introduced for such moderate variations in income by approximating it by unity.[21]

b) Savings and Investment Functions

As a second step, it is tempting to make a similar assumption for the savings and investment functions, i.e., to write:

$$C = Y \cdot f(r), \tag{9a}$$

or,

$$C = Y \cdot f(r, Y), \tag{9b}$$

and

$$I = Y \cdot g(r), \tag{10a}$$

which would eliminate any separate influence of prices and real income from the savings-investment sector also. However, this is an unattractive simplification on both theoretical and empirical grounds. Theoretically, it dismisses Keynes' central point: the distinction between expenditures that are independent of current income (autonomous expenditures) and expenditures dependent on current income (induced expenditures). Empirically, much evidence suggests that the ratio of consumption to income over short periods is not independent of the level of measured income [equation (9a)], or of the division of a change in income between prices and output [equation (9b)]. The extensive literature on the consumption function rests on this evidence.

c) Interest Rates

A more promising route is to combine a key idea of Keynes' with a key idea of Irving Fisher's.

The idea that we take over from Keynes is that the current market interest rate (r) is largely determined by the rate that is expected to prevail over a longer period (r^*) (see section 5c above) [Leijonhufvud 1968, pp. 158, 405, 411].

Carrying this idea to its limit gives:

$$r = r^*. \tag{25}$$

---

[21] Of course, considerations such as these can at most be suggestive. The real test of the usefulness of this, and the later assumptions, is in the success of the resulting theory in predicting the behavior of nominal income.

The idea that we take over from Fisher is the distinction between the nominal and the real rate of interest:

$$r = \rho + \left(\frac{1}{P}\frac{dP}{dt}\right),\tag{26}$$

where ρ is the real rate of interest and $(1/P)(dP/dt)$ is the percentage change in the price level. If the terms r and $(1/P)(dP/dt)$ refer to the observed nominal interest rate and observed rate of price change, ρ is the realized real interest rate. If they refer to "permanent" or "anticipated" values, which we shall designate by attaching an asterisk to them, then ρ^* is likewise the "permanent" or "anticipated" real rate.

Combine equation (25) and the version of (26) that has asterisks attached to the variables. This gives:

$$r = \rho^* + \left(\frac{1}{P}\frac{dP}{dt}\right)^*,\tag{27}$$

which can be written as:

$$r = \rho^* + \left(\frac{1}{Y}\frac{dY}{dt}\right)^* - \left(\frac{1}{y}\frac{dy}{dt}\right)^* = \rho^* - g^* + \left(\frac{1}{Y}\frac{dY}{dt}\right)^*\tag{28}$$

where $g^* = [(1/y)(dy/dt)]^* =$ "permanent" or "anticipated" rate of growth of real income, i.e., the secular or trend rate of growth.

Let us now assume that

$$\rho^* - g^* = k_o,\tag{29}$$

i.e., that the difference between the anticipated real interest rate and the anticipated rate of real growth is determined outside the system. This equation is the counterpart of the full employment and rigid price assumptions [equations (15) and (16)] of the simple quantity theory and the simple Keynesian income-expenditure theory.

There are two ways that assumption (29) can be rationalized: (1) that over a time interval relevant for the analysis of short-period fluctuations, ρ^* and g^* can separately be regarded as constant; (2) that the two can be regarded as moving together, so the difference will vary less than either. Of course, in both cases, what is relevant is not absolute constancy, but changes in $\rho^* - g^*$ that are small compared to changes in $[(1/P)(dP/dt)]^*$, and hence in r.

(1) The stock of physical capital, the stock of human capital, and the body of technological knowledge are all extremely large compared to annual additions. Physical capital is, say, of the order of three to five years' national income; annual net investment is of the order of

$\frac{1}{10}$ to $\frac{1}{5}$ of national income or 2 to 8 per cent of the capital stock. Let the capital *stock* be subject even to very rapidly diminishing returns and the real yield will not be much affected in a few years time. Similar considerations apply to human capital and technology.

If we interpret g^* as referring to growth potential, then a roughly constant yield on capital, human and nonhuman, and a slowly changing stock of capital imply a slowly changing value of g^* as well.

Empirically, a number of pieces of evidence fit in with these assumptions. We have interest rate data over very long periods of time, and these indicate that rates are very similar at distant times, if the times compared have similar price behavior (Gupta 1964). More recently, the Federal Reserve Bank of St. Louis has been estimating the "real rate," and their estimates are remarkably stable despite very large changes in nominal rates.

Similarly, average real growth has differed considerably at any one time for different countries—compare Japan in recent decades with Great Britain—but for each country has been rather constant over considerable periods of time.

(2) Let $s^* =$ the fraction of permanent income which is invested. Then the permanent rate of growth of income as a result of this investment alone will be equal to $s^* \rho^*$. Empirically, the actual rate of growth tends to be larger than this product, if s^* refers only to what is recorded as capital formation in the national income accounts. One explanation, frequently suggested, is that recorded capital formation neglects most investment in human capital and in improving technology and that allowance for these would make the relevant s^* much higher than the 10 or 20 per cent that is the fraction estimated in national income accounts, both because it would increase the numerator of the fraction (investment) and decrease the denominator (income) by requiring much of what is commonly treated as income to be treated as expenses of maintaining human capital and the stock of technology. In the limit, as s^* approaches unity, ρ^* approaches g^*, so $\rho^* - g^* = 0$.[22] Without going to this extreme,

$$\rho^* - g^* = (1 - s^*)\rho^*. \tag{30}$$

The preceding argument suggests that ρ^* is fairly constant, and subtracting g^* decreases the error even further.

[22] An argument justifying this equality on a purely theoretical level has been developed ingeniously and perceptively by Stephen Friedberg in some unpublished papers that take Frank H. Knight's capital theory as their starting point. This equality is also a key implication of Von Neumann's general equilibrium model (Von Neumann 1945, p. 7).

Empirically, it does seem to be the case that ρ^* and g^* tend to vary together, though in the present state of evidence, this is hardly more than a rough conjecture.

(d) The Alternative Model

If we substitute equation (12b) for equation (12), keep the original equations (13) and (14), and substitute equation (29) in equation (28) to replace the remaining equations of the initial simple model, we have the following system of four equations:

$$M^D = Y \cdot l(r) \tag{12b}$$

$$M^S = h(r) \tag{13}$$

$$M^D = M^S \tag{14}$$

$$r = k_o + \left(\frac{1}{Y}\frac{dY}{dt}\right)^*. \tag{31}$$

At any point of time, $[(1/Y)(dY/dt)]^*$, the "permanent" or "anticipated" rate of growth of nominal income is a predetermined variable, presumably based partly on past experience, partly on considerations outside our model. As a result, this is a system of four equations in the four unknowns, M^D, M^S, Y, and r.

Prices and quantity do not enter separately, so the set of equations constitutes a model of nominal income.

It will help to clarify the essence of this third approach to simplify it still further by assuming that the nominal money supply can be regarded as completely exogenous, rather than a function of the interest rate,[23] and to introduce time explicitly in the system. Let $M(t)$ be the exogenously determined supply of money. We then have from equations (12b), (13), and (14)

$$Y(t) = \frac{M(t)}{l(r)}, \tag{32}$$

or

$$Y(t) = V(r) \cdot M(t), \tag{33}$$

where V stands for velocity of circulation. This puts the equation in standard quantity theory terms, except that it does not try to go behind

---

[23] Alternatively, we could write equation (13) as

$$M^S = H \cdot m(r),$$

where H is high-powered money and $m(r)$ is the money multiplier.

nominal income to prices and quantities. Equations (31) and (33) then constitute a two-equation system for determining the level of nominal income at any point in time. To determine the path of nominal income over time, there is needed in addition some way to determine the anticipated rate of change of nominal income. I shall return to this below.

Although the symbolism in the demand equation for money [(12b) or (33)] is the same as in the two other specializations of the general model, there is an important difference in substance. Both the simple quantity theory and the income-expenditure theory implicitly define equilibrium in terms of a stable price level, hence real and nominal interest rates are the same. The third approach, based on a synthesis of Keynes and Fisher, abandons this limitation. The equations encompass "equilibrium" situations in which prices may be rising or falling. The interest rate that enters into the demand schedule for money is the nominal interest rate. So long as we stick to a single interest rate, that rate takes full account of the effect of rising or falling prices on the demand for money.

(e) The Saving-Investment Sector

What about equations (9) to (11), which we have so far completely bypassed? Here the interest rate that is relevant, if a single rate is used, is clearly the real not the nominal rate. If we replace r by ρ, these equations become

$$\frac{C}{P} = f\left(\frac{Y}{P}, \rho\right) \tag{9}'$$

$$\frac{I}{P} = g(\rho) \tag{10}'$$

$$\frac{Y}{P} = \frac{C}{P} + \frac{I}{P}. \tag{11}$$

If we were to accept a more restricted counterpart of equations (25) and (29), namely

$$\rho = \rho^* = \rho_o, \tag{34}$$

i.e., the realized real rate of interest is a constant, then these equations would be a self-contained consistent set of five equations in the five variables, C/P, I/P, Y/P, ρ, ρ^*. Equations (34) would give the real interest rate. Equation (10)' would give real investment and equations

(9)' and (11), real income. The price level would then be given by the ratio of the nominal income obtained from equations (31) and (33) to the real income given by equations (9)', (10)', (11), and (34). The two sets of equations combined would be a complete system of seven equations in seven variables determining both real and nominal magnitudes.

Such a combination, if it were acceptable, would be intellectually very appealing. Over a decade ago, during the early stages of our comparison of the predictive accuracy of the quantity theory and the income-expenditure theory, my hopes were aroused that such a combination might correspond with experience. Some of our early results were consistent with the determination of the real variables by the multiplier, and the nominal variables by velocity. However, later results shattered the hope for this outcome (Friedman and Meiselman 1963). The unfavorable empirical findings, moreover, are reinforced by theoretical considerations.

The major theoretical objections are twofold. First, it seems entirely satisfactory to take the anticipated real interest rate (or the difference between the anticipated real interest rate and the secular rate of growth) as fixed for the demand for money. There, the real interest rate is at best a supporting actor. Inflation and deflation are surely center stage. Suppressing the variations in the real interest rate (or the deviations of the measured real rate from the anticipated real rate) is unlikely to introduce serious error. The situation is altogether different for saving and investment. Omitting the real interest rate in that process is to leave out Hamlet. Second, the consumption function (9)' is highly unsatisfactory, especially once we take inflation and deflation into account. Wealth, anticipations of inflation, and the difference between permanent and measured income are too important and too central to be pushed off stage completely.

Hence for both empirical and theoretical reasons, I am inclined to reject this way of marrying the real and the nominal variables and to regard the saving-investment sector as unfinished business, even on the highly abstract general level of this paper.

9. Some Dynamic Implications of the Monetary Theory of Nominal Income

In equation (31), which determines r, we have so far taken $[(1/Y)(dY/dt)]^*$ as a predetermined variable at time t and not looked closely at its antecedents. It is natural to regard it as determined by past history. If it is, we can write equation (33) as

$$Y(t) = V[Y(T)] \cdot M(t), \ T < t, \tag{35}$$

where V is now a functional of the past history of income, $Y(T)$ for $T < t$. However, the past history of income in its turn is a function of the past history of money, thanks to equation (33) for earlier dates. Hence, we can also write equation (33) as

$$Y(t) = F[M(T)] \cdot M(t), \ T < t, \tag{36}$$

where F is a functional of the past history of money. There is also imbedded in these equations the value k_0, i.e., the assumed fixed value of the difference between the anticipated real interest rate and the secular rate of growth of output. So equations (35) and (36) must be interpreted as depicting the movements of nominal income around a long-term trend on which k_0, and its components, ρ^* and g^*, adjust to more basic long-term forces—fundamentally for both, changes in the quantity of resources available (human and nonhuman) and in technology.

A specific example may help to bring out the dynamic character of this simple model. Take logarithms of both sides of equation (33) and differentiate with respect to time. This gives

$$\begin{aligned}
\frac{1}{Y}\frac{dY}{dt} &= \frac{1}{V}\frac{dV}{dt} + \frac{1}{M}\frac{dM}{dt}. \\
&= \frac{1}{V}\frac{dV}{dr}\frac{dr}{dt} + \frac{1}{M}\frac{dM}{dt}.
\end{aligned} \tag{37}$$

Replace $(1/V)(dV/dr)$ by s (to stand for the slope of the regression of $\log V$ on r), and dr/dt by the derivative of the right-hand side of equation (31):

$$\frac{1}{Y}\frac{dY}{dt} = s \cdot \frac{d}{dt}\left[\frac{1}{Y}\frac{dY}{dt}\right]^* + \frac{1}{M}\frac{dM}{dt}. \tag{38}$$

Assume that the anticipated rate of growth of income is determined by a simple adaptive expectations model:

$$\frac{d}{dt}\left[\frac{1}{Y}\frac{dY}{dt}\right]^* = \beta\left[\frac{1}{Y}\frac{dY}{dt} - \left(\frac{1}{Y}\frac{dY}{dt}\right)^*\right]. \tag{39}$$

Substitute equation (39) in equation (38) and solve for $(1/Y)(dY/dt)$. The result is

$$\frac{1}{Y}\frac{dY}{dt} = \left(\frac{1}{Y}\frac{dY}{dt}\right)^* + \frac{1}{1-\beta s}\left[\frac{1}{M}\frac{dM}{dt} - \left(\frac{1}{Y}\frac{dY}{dt}\right)^*\right]. \tag{40}$$

Subtract $(1/M)(dM/dt)$ from both sides, and equation (40) can also be written

$$\frac{1}{V}\frac{dV}{dt} = \frac{\beta s}{1 - \beta s}\left[\frac{1}{M}\frac{dM}{dt} - \frac{1}{Y^*}\frac{dY^*}{dt}\right]. \tag{41}$$

Assume that $0 < \beta s < 1$.[24] Equations (40) and (41) give a very simple and appealing result. If the rate of change of money equals the anticipated rate of change of nominal income, then nominal income changes at the same rate as money—we are in the simple quantity equation world. If the rate of change of money exceeds the anticipated rate of change of nominal income, so will the actual rate of change of nominal income, which will also exceed the rate of change of money—velocity is increasing in a "boom." Conversely for a "contraction" or "recession," interpreted as a slower rate of growth in the actual than in the anticipated rate of growth of income.

Note that this way of introducing a procyclical movement in velocity is an alternative or complement to the approach I suggested in an earlier article (Friedman 1959 and 1969). There the procyclical movement of velocity was explained by the difference between measured and permanent income. The two approaches are not mutually exclusive—as I indicated in my earlier article, when I left room for interest rate effects on velocity (Friedman 1969, pp. 130–136). In the present context, the simplest way to introduce both effects would be to rewrite (12b) as

$$M^D = Y^* l(r), \tag{12c}$$

where Y^* is permanent nominal income. To complete the system, equation (14) must be replaced with a more sophisticated adjustment mechanism involving Y—otherwise the system, with Y^* treated as determined by the past history of Y, would be overdetermined. Such a more sophisticated mechanism is discussed in section 12 below.

In summary, the key elements of the monetary theory of nominal income are:

(a) A unit elasticity of the demand for money with respect to real income.

(b) A nominal market interest rate equal to the anticipated real rate plus the anticipated rate of change of prices, kept at that level by speculators with firmly held anticipations.

(c) A difference between the anticipated real interest rate and the real secular rate of growth determined outside the system.

[24] This is the condition for dynamic stability of the system. See Cagan 1956.

(d) Full and instantaneous adjustment of the amount of money demanded to the amount supplied.

These elements are borrowed mostly from Irving Fisher and John Maynard Keynes. Together they yield a simple two-equation system that determines the time path of nominal income but has nothing to say directly about the division of changes in nominal income between prices and quantity.

This simple model for analyzing short-term economic fluctuations seems to me more satisfactory than either the simple quantity theory which takes real output as determined outside the system and regards economic fluctuations as a mirror image of changes in the quantity of money or the simple Keynesian income-expenditure theory which takes prices as determined outside the system and regards economic fluctuations as a mirror image of changes in autonomous expenditures.

10. Comparison of the Three Approaches

None of the three simple theories—the simple quantity theory, the simple income-expenditure theory, the simple monetary theory of nominal income—professes to be a complete, fully worked out analysis of short-term fluctuations in aggregate economic magnitudes. All are to be interpreted rather as frameworks for such analyses, establishing the broad categories within which further elaborations will proceed.

The simple quantity theory puts in center stage the relation at each point in time between a particular flow—the flow of spending or income—and a particular stock—the quantity of money. The simple income-expenditure theory emphasizes the relation at each point in time between two components of the flow of income—autonomous and induced spending. The simple monetary theory of nominal income emphasizes the relation between the flow of income at each point in time and the past history of the quantity of money.

The simple quantity theory and the simple income-expenditure theory have six common elements, in addition to sharing the same six-equation model, that deserve emphasis because they indicate what are the main unresolved problems.

1. Both analyze short-run adjustments in terms of shifts from one static equilibrium position to another.

2. Both implicitly regard each equilibrium position as characterized by a stable *level* of prices or output. Neither explicitly introduces changing prices or changing output into the formal theoretical analysis.

The recent proliferation of formal growth models and the even more recent introduction of monetary change into them are attempts to fill this gap.[25]

3. Both regard interest rates as adjusting instantaneously to a new equilibrium level—in the quantity theory, to equate saving and investment; in the income-expenditure theory, to equate quantity of money demanded and supplied. This is a retrogression from Irving Fisher's earlier work.

4. Neither model gives any explicit role to anticipations about economic magnitudes. The income-expenditure theory comes closer to doing so in terms of the role that Keynes assigned to expectations about long-term interest rates, which could be incorporated in equation (12), as we did in equation (8). Here again, there has been much recent work directed at filling this gap.[26]

5. Both fill in the missing equation by an assumption that is not part of the basic theoretical analysis. This is less blatant, in one sense, for the quantity theory, since at least there is a well-developed economic theory, summarized in the Walrasian equations of general equilibrium, that explains what determines the level of output, so that the equations chosen for analysis can be regarded as a subset of a complete system. That is why, as agreement has been reached on the fallaciousness of Keynes's proposition (1), essentially all economic theorists, whatever model they prefer for short-run analysis, accept the quantity-theory model, completed by the Walrasian equations, as valid for long-run equilibrium.[27] The rigid price assumption of Keynes is, in this sense, much more arbitrary. It is entirely a *deus ex machina* with no underpinning in economic theory. Moreover, given that the price level in the long run is determined by the quantity-theory model, there is no theoretical link between the short-run model and the long-run model, no way of connecting the one to the other.

6. One aspect of the preceding point is so important that it deserves to be stated explicitly and separately. Neither theoretical model has anything to say about the factors that determine the proportions in which a change in nominal income will, in the short run, be divided between price change and output change. One theory *asserts* that the change in nominal income will all be absorbed by price change; the other, that it

[25] Some of the more important items are Solow (1956), Mundell (1965), Tobin (1965), Johnson (1967a, 1967b), Uzawa (1966), Sidrauski (1967a, 1967b), Levhari and Patinkin (1968), and Friedman (1969, chap. 1).

[26] Some of the more important items are Koyck (1954), Cagan (1956), Friedman (1957), Nerlove (1958), Muth (1960), Solow (1960), Allais (1966).

[27] See, for example, the model in Bailey (1962, pp. 33–36, 40–42).

will all be absorbed by quantity change. In my opinion, this is the central common defect of the two approaches as theories of short-run change.

The third approach differs significantly in regard to the elements that are common to the simple quantity theory and simple income-expenditure theory.

1. It does not, as they do, analyze short-run adjustments in terms of shifts from one static equilibrium position to another. It embodies a dynamic adjustment process.

2. It does not, as they do, regard each equilibrium position as characterized by a stable *level* of prices or output. It encompasses steady growth in prices or output as long-run equilibrium positions.

3. It does not regard interest rates as adjusting instantaneously to a new equilibrium level because it allows for a change in interest rates along with a change in the anticipated rate of change of prices. However, it does neglect the effect of other factors on interest rates (the saving-investment process stressed by the quantity theory; the effect of changes in the nominal quantity of money stressed by the income expenditure theory) except as they affect the course of nominal income and, in consequence, the anticipated rate of change of prices.

4. It does, unlike the other approaches, give an explicit role to anticipations about economic magnitudes. The differences between anticipated and actual magnitudes are the motive force behind the short-run fluctuations.

5. Like the others, it fills in the missing equation by an assumption that is not part of the basic theoretical analysis. The assumption (that speculators determine the interest rate in accord with firmly held anticipations, and that the difference between the permanent real interest rate and the secular growth of output can be taken as a constant for short period fluctuations) is intermediate between the others in its link to economic theory. It is not as clearly linked to a well-developed body of theory as the simple quantity approach is to the Walrasian equations of general equilibrium, yet it has more of a link to theory than does the rigid price assumption of Keynes. Further, like the quantity approach and unlike the income-expenditure approach, there is a theoretical link between the short-run model and the long-run model.

6. The chief defect that this model shares in common with the other two is that none of the three has anything to say about the factors that determine the proportions in which a change in nominal income will, in the short run, be divided between price change and output change—the topic with which section 12 below deals. The one advantage in this

respect of the third approach is that it does not make any assertion about this division as both the others do. It is, as it were, orthogonal to that issue and can therefore be more easily linked to alternative theories about that division.

11. Correspondence of the Monetary Theory of Nominal Income with Experience

I have not before this written down explicitly the particular simplification I have labelled the monetary theory of nominal income—though Meltzer has referred to the theory underlying our *Monetary History* as a "theory of nominal income" (Meltzer 1965, p. 414).[28] But once written down, it rings the bell, and seems to me to correspond to the broadest framework implicit in much of the work that I and others have done in analyzing monetary experience. It seems also to be consistent with many of our findings. I do not propose here to attempt a full catalogue, but wish to suggest a number, and, more important, to indicate the chief defect that I find in the framework.

One finding that we have observed is that the relation between changes in the nominal quantity of money and changes in nominal income is almost always closer and more dependable than the relation between changes in real income and the real quantity of money or between changes in the quantity of money per unit of output and changes in prices.[29] This result has always seemed to me puzzling, since a stable demand function for money with an income elasticity different from unity led us to expect the opposite. Yet the actual finding would be generated by the monetary approach outlined in this paper, with the division between prices and quantities determined by variables not explicitly contained in it.

Another broad finding is the procyclical pattern of velocity, which can be rationalized either by the distinction between permanent and measured income or, as in the monetary approach, by the effect of changes in the anticipated rate of change in prices.

[28] However, he referred to it as a "long-run theory of nominal income," whereas the theory outlined in section 8 above is intended to be a short-run theory. We accept much of what Meltzer says about the theory underlying our *Monetary History,* but also disagree with much of it; in particular, the way he introduces real income and changes in real income into the analysis. This is strictly *ad hoc* and renders the asserted theory a logically open and underdetermined theory.

[29] However, Walters reports a different result for Britain for the period since the end of World War I—a closer relation with prices in the interwar period and with real output in the post-World War II period (Walters, 1970, p. 52).

On still another level, the approach is consistent with much of the work that Fisher did on interest rates, and also the more recent work by Anna Schwartz and myself, Gibson, Kaufman, Cagan, and others. In particular, the approach provides an interpretation of the empirical generalization that high interest rates mean that money has been easy, in the sense of increasing rapidly, and low interest rates, that money has been tight, in the sense of increasing slowly, rather than the reverse.

Again, the approach is consistent with the importance we have been led to attach to *rates of change* in money rather than levels, and, in particular, to changes in the rate of change in explaining short-term fluctuations.

The approach is consistent also with the success of the equations constructed by Andersen and Jordan at St. Louis relating changes in nominal income to current and past changes in the quantity of money (Andersen and Jordan 1968).

The chief defect of the approach is that it does not give a satisfactory explanation of the lags in the reaction of velocity and interest rates at turning points in monetary rates of change.[30] These lags are significant for cyclical analysis. They are less relevant for a study of monetary trends. Because of this defect, the movements of velocity and interest rates in the first nine months or so after a distinct change in the rate of

[30] We know, for example, that when the rate of growth of the quantity of money declines, the rate of change of income will not show any appreciable effect for something like six to nine months (for the United States) on the average. During this interval, interest rates typically continue to rise, indeed generally at an accelerated pace. After the interval, both velocity and interest rates start to decline.

This result is not necessarily inconsistent with the monetary approach outlined here. Suppose that prior to the decline in the rate of monetary growth the system was not in full equilibrium, so that the actual rate of growth of nominal income $(1/Y)(dY/dt)$ was higher than the anticipated rate of growth $[(1/Y)(dY/dt)]^*$. Then, even the new rate of monetary growth could be higher than the anticipated rate, implying from equation (41) a further rise in velocity, from equation (40), a larger actual than anticipated rise in nominal income, from equation (39), a further rise in the anticipated rate, and from equation (31), a further rise in the nominal interest rate. These would continue until the anticipated rate had risen to equality with the new rate of monetary growth.

However, this reaction would imply a slower rate of rise in velocity and interest rates than prior to the monetary turning point, whereas our impression is that the opposite often occurs. More important, even if the system is not in full equilibrium prior to a decline in the rate of monetary growth, the decline in monetary growth, if large enough, will make the new rate of monetary growth less than $[(1/Y)(dY/dt)]^*$. In that case, equations (41), (40), (39), and (31) would produce a decline in velocity and in interest rates contemporaneous with the decline in the rate of monetary growth. Yet the lag in reaction is highly consistent and, in particular, seems to be independent of the size of the change in the rate of monetary growth.

monetary growth cannot be satisfactorily explained by the monetary theory of nominal income. If these periods were cut out of the historical record, my impression is that the model would fit the rest of the record very well—not of course without error but with errors that are on the modest side as aggregate economic hypotheses go.

Periods just after turning points can, I believe, be explained best by incorporating two elements so far omitted. The first is a revision of equation (14) to allow for a difference between actual and desired money balances, as in equation (48), below. The second is a weakening of equation (25) to permit a stronger liquidity effect on interest rates.

12. The Adjustment Process

The key need to remedy the defects common to all the models I have sketched is a theory that will explain (a) the short-run division of a change in nominal income between prices and output, (b) the short-run adjustment of nominal income to a change in autonomous variables, and (c) the transition between this short-run situation and a long-run equilibrium.[31]

In the rest of this paper, the central idea I shall use in sketching the direction in which such a theory might be developed is the distinction between actual and anticipated magnitudes or, to use a terminology that need not be identical but that I shall treat for this purpose as if it is, between measured and permanent magnitudes. At a long-run equilibrium position, all anticipations are realized, so that actual and anticipated magnitudes, or measured and permanent magnitudes, are equal.[32]

I shall regard long-run equilibrium as determined by the earlier quantity-theory model plus the Walrasian equations of general equilibrium. In a full statement, the earlier model should be expanded by including wealth in the consumption and liquidity-preference functions,

[31] Still other parts of the theoretical framework are developed more fully in the course of the empirical analysis of some of the issues raised in the other chapters of the book from which this paper is abstracted.

[32] Note that the equality of actual and anticipated magnitudes is a necessary but not a sufficient condition for a long-run equilibrium position. In principle, actual and anticipated magnitudes could be equal along an adjustment path between one equilibrium position and another. The corresponding proposition is more complicated for measured and permanent magnitudes and depends on the precise definition of these terms. However, since we shall be considering a special case in which the stated condition is treated as both necessary and sufficient for long-run equilibrium, these complications can be bypassed.

and the capital stock in the investment function, and by allowing for steady growth in output and prices.

I shall regard short-run equilibrium as determined by an adjustment process in which the rate of adjustment in a variable is a function of the discrepancy between the measured and the anticipated value of that variable or its rate of change, as well as, perhaps, of other variables or their rates of change. Finally, I shall let at least some anticipated variables be determined by a feedback process from past observed values.

a) Division of a Change in Nominal Income between Prices and Output

It seems plausible that the division of a change in nominal income between prices and output depends on two major factors: anticipations about the behavior of prices—this is the inertia factor stressed by Keynes—and the current level of output or employment compared with the full-employment (permanent) level of output or employment—this is the supply-demand response stressed by quantity theorists. We can express this in general form as:

$$\frac{dP}{dt} = f\left[\frac{dY}{dt}, \left(\frac{dP}{dt}\right)^*, \left(\frac{dy}{dt}\right)^*, y, y^*\right], \tag{42}$$

$$\frac{dy}{dt} = g\left[\frac{dY}{dt}, \left(\frac{dP}{dt}\right)^*, \left(\frac{dy}{dt}\right)^*, y, y^*\right], \tag{43}$$

where an asterisk attached to a variable denotes the anticipated value of that variable and where the form of equations (42) and (43) must be consistent with the identity

$$Y = Py, \tag{44}$$

so that only one of equations (42) and (43) is independent.

To illustrate, a specific linearized version of equations (42) and (43) might be

$$\frac{d \log P}{dt} = \left(\frac{d \log P}{dt}\right)^* + \alpha\left[\frac{d \log Y}{dt} - \left(\frac{d \log Y}{dt}\right)^*\right]$$
$$+ \gamma[\log y - (\log y)^*]; \tag{45}$$

$$\frac{d \log y}{dt} = \left(\frac{d \log y}{dt}\right)^* + (1 - \alpha)\left[\frac{d \log Y}{dt} - \left(\frac{d \log Y}{dt}\right)^*\right]$$
$$- \gamma[\log y - (\log y)^*]. \tag{46}$$

The sum of these is exactly the logarithm of equation (44), differentiated with respect to time, provided the anticipated variables also satisfy a corresponding identity,[33] so the equations satisfy the specified conditions.

The simple quantity theory assumption, that all of the change in income is in prices, and that output is always at its permanent level, is obtained by setting $\alpha = 1$ and $\gamma = \infty$. An infinite value of γ corresponds to "perfectly flexible prices" and assures that $y = y^*$. The unit value of α assures that prices absorb any change in nominal income, so that real income grows at its long-term rate of growth.[34]

The simple Keynesian assumption, that all of the change in income is in output, so long as there is unemployment, and all in prices, once there is full employment, is obtained by setting $[(d \log P)/(dt)]^* = 0$, and $\alpha = \gamma = 0$ for $y < y^*$, and then shifting to the quantity theory specification of $\alpha = 1$, $\gamma = \infty$ for $y \geq y^*$. The zero value of $[(d \log P)/dt]^*$ assures that anticipations are for stable prices and, combined with the zero values of α and γ, that $(d \log P)/(dt) = 0$. It would be somewhat more general, and perhaps more consistent with the spirit rather than the letter of Keynes's analysis, and even more that of his modern followers, to let $[(d \log P)/(dt)]^*$ differ from zero while keeping $\alpha = \gamma = 0$ for $y < y^*$. This would introduce the kind of price rigidity relevant to Keynes's short-period analysis, yet could be regarded as capturing the phenomenon that his modern followers have emphasized as cost-push inflation.

The simple monetary theory of nominal income is of course consistent with these equations in their general form since it does not specify anything about the division of a change in nominal income between prices and output.

In their general form, equations (45) and (46) do not by themselves specify the path of prices or output beginning with any initial position. In addition, we need to know how anticipated values are formed. Presumably these are affected by the course of events so that, in response to a disturbance which produces a discrepancy between actual and anticipated values of the variables, there is a feedback effect that brings the actual and anticipated variables together again (see

[33] This also explains why $[(d \log y)/(dt)]^*$ does not appear explicitly in equation (45), or $[(d \log P)/(dt)]^*$ in equation (46), as they do in equations (42) and (43). They are implicitly included in $[(d \log Y)/(dt)]^*$.

[34] With γ infinity, and $\log y = \log y^*$, the final expression in equations (45) and (46) is $\infty \cdot 0$, or technically indeterminate. The product can be taken to be zero in general, except possibly for a few isolated points at which $\log y$ deviates from $\log y^*$, a deviation closed instantaneously by infinite rates of change in $\log P$ and $\log y$.

below). If this process proceeds rapidly, then the transitory adjustments defined by equations (45) and (46) are of little significance. The relevant analysis is the analysis which connects the asterisked variables.

b) Short-Run Adjustment of Nominal Income

For monetary theory, the key question is the process of adjustment to a discrepancy between the nominal quantity of money demanded and the nominal quantity supplied. Such a discrepancy could arise from either a change in the supply of money (a shift in the supply function) or a change in the demand for money (a shift in the demand function). The key insight of the quantity-theory approach is that such a discrepancy will be manifested primarily in attempted spending, thence in the rate of change in nominal income. Put differently, money holders cannot determine the nominal quantity of money (though their reactions may introduce feedback effects that will affect the nominal quantity of money), but they can make velocity anything they wish.

What, on this view, will cause the rate of change in nominal income to depart from its permanent value? Anything that produces a discrepancy between the nominal quantity of money demanded and the quantity supplied, or between the two rates of change of money demanded and money supplied. In general form

$$\frac{dY}{dt} = f\left[\left(\frac{dY}{dt}\right)^*, \frac{dM^S}{dt}, \frac{dM^D}{dt}, M^S, M^D\right], \qquad (47)$$

where M^S refers to money supplied, M^D refers to money demanded, and the two symbols are used to indicate that the two are not necessarily equal. That is, equation (47) replaces the adjustment equation (14), $M^D = M^S$, common to all the simple models, as well as the special adjustment equation (41) derived from the monetary theory of nominal income.

To illustrate, a particular linearized version of equation (47) would be

$$\frac{d \log Y}{dt} = \left(\frac{d \log Y}{dt}\right)^* + \Psi\left(\frac{d \log M^S}{dt} - \frac{d \log M^D}{dt}\right) + \Phi(\log M^S - \log M^D). \quad (48)$$

Unlike equations (45) and (46), the two final adjustment terms on the right-hand side do not explicitly include any asterisked magnitudes. But implicitly they do. The amount of money demanded will depend on anticipated permanent income and prices as well as on the anticipated rate of change in prices.

The three simple models considered earlier all require setting $\Phi = \infty$ in equation (48) to assure that $M^S = M^D$. However, once this is done, the rest of the equation provides no information on the adjustment process, since the final term, which is of the form $\infty \cdot 0$ is indeterminate. Hence, even though $M^S = M^D$ implies that

$$\frac{d \log M^S}{dt} = \frac{d \log M^D}{dt}, \tag{49}$$

so that the second term on the right-hand side of equation (48) is zero for any finite value of Ψ, it does not follow that

$$\frac{d \log Y}{dt} = \left(\frac{d \log Y}{dt}\right)^*. \tag{50}$$

The requirement (49) leads to the equation

$$\frac{d \log Y}{dt} = \frac{d \log M}{dt} \tag{51}$$

for the simple quantity theory since, with real income and the interest rate fixed, the quantity of money demanded is proportional to prices and hence to nominal income. This equation says that a change in money supply is reflected immediately and proportionately in nominal income.

For the simple Keynesian theory, equation (49) leads, from equation (22), to

$$\frac{d \log M}{dt} = \left[\frac{\partial \log l}{d \log Y} + \frac{\partial \log l}{\partial r} \frac{dr}{d \log Y}\right] \frac{d \log Y}{dt} \tag{52}$$

where $dr/d \log Y$ is to be calculated from equation (21), the IS curve. In the special case of absolute liquidity preference $\partial \log l/\partial r = \infty$; in the special case of completely inelastic investment and saving functions, $dr/d \log Y = \infty$. In either of these cases, equation (52) implies that, for $d \log M/dt$ finite, $d \log Y/dt = 0$; i.e., a change in the supply of money has no influence on income. In the more general case, equation (52) says that a change in money supply is reflected immediately, but not necessarily proportionately, in nominal income.

For the monetary theory of nominal income, equation (49) implies, as we have seen earlier, equation (41), which allows for a delayed adjustment of permanent income to measured income, but not for any discrepancy between M^S and M^D.

In its general form, equation (48) allows for changes in both supply of money and demand for money. It also implicitly allows for the forces emphasized by Keynes, shifts in investment or other autonomous expenditures, through the effect of such changes on M^s and M^D. For example, an autonomous rise in investment demand will tend to raise interest rates. The rise in interest rates will tend to reduce M^D, introducing a discrepancy in one or both of the bracketed expressions on the right-hand side of equation (48), which will cause $(d \log Y)/(dt)$ to exceed $[(d \log Y)/(dt)]^*$.

c) Money Demand and Supply Functions

As this comment indicates, in order to complete the theory of the adjustment process, it is necessary to specify the functions connecting M^D and M^s with other variables in the system, and also to provide relations determining any additional variables—such as interest rates—entering into these functions. Sections 3 and 4 above discuss the demand and supply functions for money that we regard as relevant for this purpose, so only a few brief supplementary comments are required for present purposes.

First, in much of our empirical work we have taken M^s itself as an autonomous variable and have not incorporated in the analysis any feedback from other adjustments. A major reason that we have done so is our judgment that the supply function has varied greatly from time to time.

Second, in the notation we have been using in this section, the variables y and $(1/P)(dP/dt)$ in equation (7) should have asterisks attached to them.

Third, the function specifying M^D might in principle include a transitory component. That is, there is nothing inconsistent with the theory here sketched and distinguishing between a short-run and long-run demand for money, as some writers have done (Heller 1965; Chow 1966; Konig 1968).

d) Determination of Interest Rates

Given that interest rates enter into the demand function for money (equation [7]) and also, presumably, into the supply function, a complete model must specify the factors determining them. Our long-run model determines their permanent values. So what is needed is an analysis of the adjustment process for interest rates comparable with that for prices and nominal income discussed above—provided, as seems reasonable, that measured as well as permanent values of interest rates enter into the money demand and supply functions.

The monetary theory of nominal income incorporates one possible adjustment process—via the anticipated rate of price change. We have not worked out the formal theory of a more sophisticated adjustment process in any detail. The one aspect we have considered is the effect of changes in M^s on interest rates.[35] In that analysis, we have in effect regarded interest rates as adjusting very rapidly to clear the market for loanable funds, the supply of loanable funds as being possibly linked to changes in M^s, and the demand for and supply of loanable funds expressed as a function of the nominal interest rate as depending on Y and $[(1/P) (dP/dt)]^*$ along with other variables.

In some of our empirical work, we have treated interest rates as exogenous.

e) Determination of Anticipated Values

The transition between the short-run adjustment process and long-run equilibrium is produced by an adjustment of anticipated values to measured values in such a way that, for a stable system, a single disturbance will set up discrepancies that will in the course of time be eliminated. To put this in general terms, we must have

$$\left[\frac{d \log P}{dt} (t)\right]^* = f\left[\frac{d \log P}{dT} (T)\right], \tag{53}$$

$$\left[\frac{d \log Y}{dt} (t)\right]^* = g\left[\frac{d \log Y}{dT} (T)\right], \tag{54}$$

$$y^*(t) = h[y(T)], \tag{55}$$

$$P^*(t) = j[P(T)], \tag{56}$$

where t stands for a particular point in time and T for a vector of all dates prior to t.

A disturbance of long-term equilibrium, let us say, introduces discrepancies in the two final terms in parentheses on the right-hand side of equation (48). This will cause the rate of change in nominal income to deviate from its permanent value, which through equations (45) and (46) produces deviations in the rate of price change and output change from their permanent values. These may in turn re-enter equation (48) but whether they do or not, they will, through equations (53)–(56), produce changes in the anticipated values that will, sooner or later and perhaps after a cyclical reaction process, eliminate the discrepancies between measured and permanent values.

[35] See chapter 7 in the forthcoming book from which this paper is abstracted.

These anticipation equations are in one sense very general, in another, very special. They require that anticipations be determined entirely by the past history of the particular variable in question, not by other past history or other currently observed phenomena. These equations deny any "autonomous" role to anticipations. These equations, or preferable alternatives to them, are not directly related to the monetary issues that are the main concern of this paper, which is why I have treated them so summarily. Their only function here is to close the system.

One subtle problem in this kind of a structure, in which we have identified the absence of a discrepancy between actual and anticipated values as defining long-period equilibrium, is to assure that the feedback relations defined by equations (53)–(56), as well as the other functions, are consistent with the expanded system of Walrasian equations which specify the long-term equilibrium values. At least some values are implicitly determined in two ways: by a feedback relation such as equations (53) and (56), and by the system of long-run equilibrium equations. The problem is to assure that at long-run equilibrium these two determinations do not conflict.

In our empirical work, we have generally used a particular form of anticipated function, namely, one which defines the anticipated values as a declining weighted average of past observed values. For example, a specific form of equation (55) is

$$y^*(t) = \beta \int_{T=-\infty}^{t} e^{(\beta-\alpha)(t-T)} y(T) dT, \qquad (57)$$

where α and β are parameters, α defining the long-term rate of growth, and β, the speed of adjustment of anticipations to experiences (Friedman 1957, pp. 142–47).

13. An Illustration

It may help to clarify the general nature of this theoretical approach if we apply it to a hypothetical monetary disturbance.

Let us start with a situation of full equilibrium with stable prices and full employment and with output growing at, say, 3 percent per year. For simplicity, assume that the income elasticity of demand for money is unity, so that the quantity of money is also growing at the rate of 3 percent per year. Assume also that money is wholly non-interest-bearing fiat money and that its quantity can be taken as autonomous.

Assume that there is a shift at time $t = t_0$ in the rate of growth of the quantity of money from 3 percent per year to, say, 8 percent per year and that this new rate of growth is maintained indefinitely. Figure 1 shows the time path of the money stock before and after time t_0. These figures are not drawn strictly to scale. For emphasis, they exaggerate the difference in the slopes of the lines before and after t_0.

a) Long-Run Equilibrium

Let us first ask what the long-run equilibrium solution will be. Clearly, after full adjustment, nominal income will be rising at 8 percent per year. If, for the moment, we neglect any effect of this monetary change on real output and the rate of growth of output, this means that prices would be rising at 5 percent per year. It might therefore seem as if the equilibrium path of nominal income would duplicate that of the quantity of money in figure 1 (redrawn as the solid plus dashed line in fig. 2). But this is not the case. With prices rising at the rate of 5 percent per year and, at equilibrium, with this price rise fully anticipated by everyone, it is now more costly to hold money. As a result, equation (7)

FIGURE 1

Time Path of Money Stock Before and After Time t_0

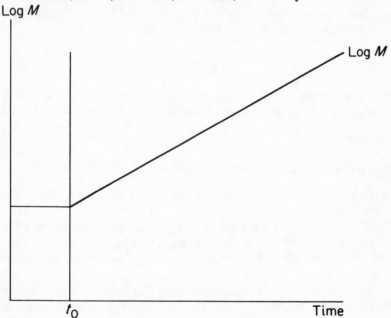

would indicate a decline in the real quantity of money demanded relative to income, that is, a rise in desired velocity. This rise would be
achieved by a rise in nominal income over and above that required to
match the rise in the nominal quantity of money. The equilibrium path
of nominal income would be like the solid line in figure 2 rather than
the dashed line.

If equilibrium real output and the rate of growth of real output were
unaffected by the monetary change, as I have so far assumed, the
equilibrium path of prices would be the same as that of nominal income,
except that it would have a slope of 3 percent per year less, to allow
for the growth in real income. However, equilibrium real output will not
be unaffected by this monetary change. The exact effect depends on just
how real output is measured, in particular whether it includes or excludes the nonpecuniary services of money. If it includes them, as in
principle it should, then the level of real output will be lower after the
monetary change than before. It will be lower for two reasons: first,
the higher cost of holding cash balances will lead producers to substitute
other resources for cash, which will lower productive efficiency; second,

FIGURE 2

Equilibrium Path of Nominal Income Before and After Time t_0

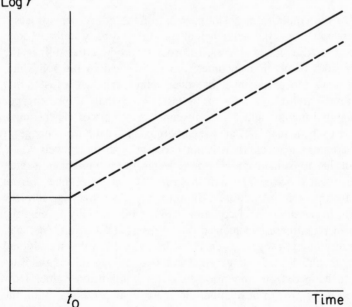

Log Y

t_0

Time

the flow of nonpecuniary services from money will be reduced (Friedman 1969, pp. 14–15). For both reasons, the price level of output will have to rise more than nominal income—a solid line and a dashed line like those for nominal income in figure 2 would be farther apart vertically for prices of final products than for nominal income.

It is harder to be precise about the equilibrium rate of growth, since that depends on the particular growth model. What is clear is that the aggregate stock of nonhuman capital, including money, will be lower relative to human capital, but that the aggregate stock of physical (non-money) capital will be higher, so that the real yield on capital (essentially our r_e of equation [7]) will be lower. The nominal interest rate (the r_b of equation [7]) will equal this real yield plus the rate of change in prices, so it will be higher. If these changes have any effect on the rate of growth of real output, they will tend to reduce it, so that the equilibrium price level of final products will not only be higher relative to its initial value than the equilibrium level of nominal income; it may also rise more rapidly (Stein 1966; Johnson 1967a, 1967b; Marty 1968). For simplicity, I shall neglect this possibility and assume that the equilibrium rate of rise in prices is 5 percent per year.

b) The Adjustment Process

So much for the equilibrium position. What of the adjustment process?

This description of the equilibrium position already tells us one thing about the adjustment process. In order to produce the shift in the equilibrium path of nominal income from the dashed to the solid line, nominal income and prices must rise over some period at a faster rate than the final equilibrium rate—at a faster rate than 8 percent per year for nominal income and 5 percent per year for prices. There must, that is, be a cyclical reaction, an overshooting, in the rate of change in nominal income and prices, though not necessarily in their levels.

How will this adjustment process be reflected in my theoretical sketch of the adjustment process? The shift in $(d \log M^s)/(dt)$ at time t_0 from 3 percent to 8 percent introduces a discrepancy of positive sign into the second term in parentheses of equation (48), while initially leaving the third term in parentheses unchanged. As a result, $(d \log Y)/(dt)$ will increase, exceeding $[(d \log Y)/(dt)]^*$, which, viewed in this transitional process as an anticipated value rather than as a long-run equilibirum value, is unchanged from the prior long-run equilibrium value. How rapidly the rate of growth of nominal income rises depends partly on the value of Ψ, the coefficient indicating speed of adjustment, and partly on the demand function for money. If the latter depends only on anticipated values (that is, if all the variables in equation [7] have asterisks), $(d \log M^D)/(dt)$ will initially be unchanged, so everything will depend on Ψ, which might have any value, from zero, meaning no adjustment, to a value higher than unity, meaning that nominal income would rise initially by more than 5 percent per year.[36]

Whatever the rate of rise in nominal income, it will be divided into a rise in prices and in output, in accordance with equations (45) and (46). If α is less than unity, both real output and prices will start rising, their relative rates depending on the size of α.

The rising prices and nominal income will start affecting anticipated rates of change, through equations (53) and (56), feeding back into (48) and (45) and (46).

All of this is so at time t_0, with no effect on the levels of any of the variables. However, as the process continues, the levels start being affected. In equation (48), $\log M^S$ comes to exceed $\log M^D$, so the second term of equation (48) adds to the upward pressure on $(d \log Y)/(dt)$, making for a speeding up in the expansion of nominal income. In equations (45) and (46), $\log y$ comes to exceed $\log y^*$, thus increasing the fraction of income increase absorbed by prices and reducing the fraction absorbed by output. The changed levels of y and P feed into equations (55) and (56) and so start altering y^* and P^*.

The changes in all of the variables now start affecting the demand functions for money, both directly, as these variables enter the demand functions, and indirectly, as they affect other variab'es, such as interest rates, which in turn enter the demand functions. As a result, $(d \log M^D)/(dt)$ and M^D in equation (48) start to change. The process will, of course, finally be completed when the relevant measured variables are all equal to their permanent counterparts and these equal the long-run equilibrium values discussed above.

It is impossible to carry much farther this verbal statement of the solution of an incompletely specified system of simultaneous differential equations. The precise adjustment path depends on how the missing elements of the system are specified and on the numerical values of the parameters, but perhaps this much is enough to give the flavor of the kind of adjustment process they generate, and to indicate why this process is necessarily cyclical.

What is the reflection in these equations of the point made in the second paragraph of this section, namely, that $(d \log Y)/(dt)$ and $(d$

[36] The model briefly sketched in the final two paragraphs of Friedman (1959) implicitly has an initial value of Ψ which is much higher than unity.

log $P)/(dt)$ must, during the transition, average higher than their final long-term equilibrium values? Consider equation (48). Suppose that over a period the *average* value of $(d \log Y)/(dt)$ and $(d \log P)/(dt)$ had been 8 percent per year and 5 percent per year, respectively. Suppose the anticipations functions (53) and (56) were such that this was fully reflected in anticipated values. Then, as we have seen, although M^s would have risen at the rate of 5 percent per year, M^D would not have; so the final term in equation (48) would not be zero, even though the middle term on the right-hand side might be. Hence, $(d \log Y)/(dt)$ would exceed $[(d \log Y)/(dt)]^*$, which by assumption is at its long-run equilibrium value; so full equilibrium would not have been attained.

Figure 3 summarizes various possible adjustment paths of $(d \log Y)/(dt)$ consistent with the theory sketched. The one common feature of all of them is that the area above the 8 percent line must exceed the

FIGURE 3

Possible Adjustment Paths of Rate of Change in Nominal Income

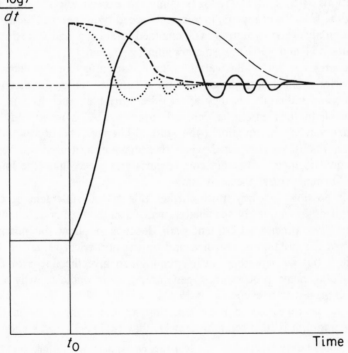

area below. In principle, of course, still other paths are possible. For example, it is conceptually possible for the adjustment to be explosive rather than damped. Restricting ourselves to damped paths is an empirical judgment.

14. Conclusion

In concluding this discussion of a theoretical framework, it may be worth stating that it is not a framework special to me or to those economists who view the operation of the economy in terms of the quantity theory either in its simple form or in the form of the monetary theory of nominal income. No doubt other economists would expand the framework differently, stress different parts of it, elaborate points I have skimmed over, and skim over points I have elaborated. But almost all economists would accept the framework, and this is true even, I believe, of the least thorough part, the sketch of the adjustment process in the preceding two sections.

One purpose of setting forth this framework is to document my belief that the basic differences among economists are empirical, not theoretical: How important are changes in the supply of money compared with changes in the demand for money? Are transactions variables or asset variables most important in determining the demand for money? How elastic is the demand for money with respect to interest rates? With respect to the rate of change in prices? When changes in demand or supply occur that produce discrepancies between the quantity of money that the public holds and the quantity it desires to hold, how rapidly do these discrepancies tend to be eliminated? Does the adjustment impinge mostly on prices or mostly on quantities? Is the adjustment process cyclical or asymptotic? Is the adjustment to sharp changes over short periods different in kind or only in degree from the adjustment to slower changes over longer periods? How long does it take for people to alter their anticipations in light of experience?

Much of the controversy that has swirled about the role of money in economic affairs reflects, in my opinion, different implicit or explicit answers to these empirical questions. The reason such differences have been able to persist is, I believe, that full adjustment to monetary disturbances takes a very long time and affects many economic magnitudes. If adjustment were swift, immediate, and mechanical, as some earlier quantity theorists may have believed, or, more likely, as was attributed to them by their critics, the role of money would be clearly and sharply etched even in the imperfect figures that have been available. But, if the adjustment is slow, delayed, and sophisticated, then crude evidence may be misleading, and a more subtle examination of the record may be needed to disentangle what is systematic from what is random and erratic. That, not the elaboration of the theory, is the primary aim of the monograph from which this paper is adapted, as well as of the other monetary studies of the National Bureau.

Friedman's Monetary Theory

Karl Brunner and Allan H. Meltzer

None of the participants in the current discussion of monetary or macrotheory has contributed more than Milton Friedman to the revival of monetary theory and its development as a lively, perhaps the liveliest, area of active research in economics. Evidence of the revived interest is the much greater attention now given by economists, politicians, speculators, and even journalists to changes in the stock of money and its growth rate. A cross section of the views that Friedman and others have espoused constitutes the core of "monetarism," a set of propositions that has been called the "central issue that is debated these days in connection with macroeconomics" (Samuelson 1969, p. 7). We, therefore, welcome the opportunity provided by this symposium to discuss some of the issues in Friedman's paper that, we take it, summarize and synthesize his current views on the role of money in monetary theory. Crosscurrents, ambiguities, and differences frequently arise in a field developing as rapidly as monetary theory, so we welcome, also, the opportunity to compare our view of monetary theory with his.

No serious scholar can fail to be influenced and stimulated by the many contributions that Friedman has made, alone and in collaboration with Mrs. Schwartz. The very quantity, quality, and importance of their work stimulated us (Meltzer 1965; Brunner 1968) and others (Andersen and Carlson 1970) to attempt either to state a theory that provided some analytic underpinning for Friedman's brand of monetarism or to develop alternative "monetarist" theories. For us, and perhaps for many others, the absence of an explicitly stated theory capable of generating the propositions that have been supported by empirical investigation has impeded the further development of monetary theory. The very success of Friedman's insightful comments and conjectures when tested against alternative conjectures increases the benefits that we expected to obtain

We gratefully acknowledge the financial support of the National Science Foundation.

from the development of an explicit theory capable of generating the empirical regularities that support "monetarism."[1]

Friedman's statement of monetary theory does not seem to us an adequate underpinning for monetary theory or a particularly useful basis for empirical work. In the following section we discuss six of the points at which we differ. Because we believe the issues are important and resolvable, we present an alternative framework elsewhere (Brunner and Meltzer 1972). The alternative framework generates the principal conjectures that distinguish our version of monetarism from Friedman's and from the standard paradigm.

The Missing Equations and Variables

One difficulty in interpreting some of Friedman's statements arises because he tells us very little about timing and speed of adjustment or the length of run to which his models apply. If Friedman's assumption of fixed real output is replaced by a linear homogeneous production function as a better statement of the constraint on real resources, we can accept one version of the framework he presents as a restatement of the *IS-LM* model found in textbooks such as Bailey (1962) or Patinkin (1965). The problem is that the analysis in Bailey or Patinkin is a comparative statics equilibrium analysis while Friedman suggests at several points that he is concerned with questions of timing and adjustment. For example, he points out that differences between observed and expected speeds of adjustment of prices and output were the principal reasons that economists rejected pre-Keynesian monetary theory and accepted the Keynesian framework (pp. 16–21). He then notes that "the relative speed of adjustment of price and quantity is still a key to the difference in approach and analysis between those economists who regard themselves as Keynesians and those who do not" (p. 20).[2] There is no mention of Fisher's

---

[1] A prevalent view among economists is that hypotheses involving empirical regularities must be "supported" by a higher-level theory from which the lower-level proposition can be derived. We do not share this view; in fact, we dissent strongly and so does the modern literature of the philosophy of science. However, if theories generate useful empirical conjectures—such as the empirical work on the demand for money and the relation of money to income (Andersen and Jordan 1968; Keran 1969)—the expected gain from more discriminating tests derived from more fully developed hypotheses increases.

[2] For Friedman, either $p = p_0$ or $y = y_0$ characterizes a short-period equilibrium. We have difficulty relating these restrictions to the separate adjustment hypothesis introduced later in the paper. The adjustment hypothesis bears no clear relation to the static framework. Friedman explicitly rejects the attempt to characterize the framework underlying his work with Mrs. Schwartz as a "long-run theory of nominal income" and describes as "ad hoc" the way in which one of us (Meltzer 1965) introduced income and changes in income into a statement of his framework (p. 46, n. 28). Yet his adjustment equations (pp. 51–55) explain the deviation of actual from expected or permanent income in a way that seems no less "ad hoc" and no more useful than the one attributed to them.

"transition periods" that were expected to last as long as ten years (Fisher 1920, p. 70) and no reference to his earlier conclusion that the lag of output behind money is "long and variable." The only explicit statement about timing mentions a six- to nine-month lag in the adjustment of interest rates at turning points (p. 47, n. 30). The impression he conveys is that he expects his theory or theories to predict adequately except at the turning points of business cycles.

We can *more readily* accept Friedman's statements of monetary theory and his version of the "common framework" as a theory of price fluctuation around the long-run position of an economy that has constant output, $y = y_0$, than as a short run theory.[3] A short-run theory with $y = y_0$ and real rates of return held constant has limited applicability and holds little interest. With $p = p_0$, the framework is unacceptable as either a long- or a short-run theory, since it cannot explain long-run persistent inflation or the frequently observed short-run combination of inflation and unemployed resources.

Our disagreements with Friedman's analysis of the short run are partly, but only partly, disagreements about research strategy and particularly about the possibility of developing an empirically verifiable "common framework" applicable to both short- and long-run processes and capable of generating testable implications for short- and long-run positions of aggregate variables. We believe it is undesirable and unnecessary to divide macroeconomic problems into two sets—unemployment in which prices are fixed *or* inflation in which output is fixed. Further, we believe it is ambiguous and misleading to characterize the problem of underutilized resources as "Keynesian" and inflation as "non-Keynesian." An economist as astute and knowledgeable as Harry Johnson (Johnson 1971) is led by arguments such as Friedman's to conclude that monetarist analysis applies only to inflation, and that "Keynesian problems" must be analyzed with Keynesian theory and treated with Keynesian remedies. Such conclusions, and the arguments that suggest them, obscure the issue that we regard as Keynes's main challenge to economics and economists.

Keynes clearly recognized that the price theory of his day did not, and could not, explain unemployment. Two alternatives were available: one a reformulation of price theory, the other a framework that separated macro- and microtheory. Keynes chose the latter, not completely and not without qualification. Careful readers from Hicks (1937) to Leijonhufvud (1968) have been able to find substantial portions of price theory

---

[3] One item missing from "the common model" as presented (pp. 29-31) is the distinction between market rates and real rates. Friedman partly removes this gap by introducing the rate of price change, but, as he notes, he holds the growth rate of output and the real rate of interest constant throughout.

remaining in the *General Theory*. Despite the attempts by early Keynesians to obliterate these elements—to make the "Keynesian special case" into the general case—some price-theoretic elements survived. The "new price theory" (Phelps et al. 1970) develops the alternative that Keynes neglected. Friedman does not discuss these developments or their relevance to the missing equations in his or Keynes's theory.[4]

The reformulated price theory—incorporating costs of search, adjustment, and the acquisition of information—has developed out of attention to the problem posed by inflation and unemployment. The implication of these studies is that macrotheories that seek to explain underutilization of resources must take account of changes in relative prices, including but not limited to changes in interest rates. Of the six points discussed in the remainder of this paper, five involve variables which cannot be incorporated without extending the "common framework" to analyze relative price changes. On our reading of the evidence, the five missing variables and equations must be part of any hypothesis seeking to explain short-run changes in output, employment, and the price level. Including these variables and equations, however, takes us beyond the "common framework" discussed by Friedman.

The Quantity Theory or Theories

The opening theme is familiar to Friedman's readers. The quantity theory is presented as the theory of the demand for money, just as in his earlier work (Friedman 1956), and the demand for money is assumed to depend on asset prices or relative returns and wealth or income. For Friedman, the problem is one of showing how a theory of the (stable) demand for money can become a theory of prices and output.

Friedman resolves the problem by postulation. The "key insight of the quantity-theory approach is that . . . a discrepancy [between the nominal quantity of money demanded and the nominal quantity supplied] will be manifested primarily in attempted spending, thence in the rate of change in nominal income" (p. 51). Since the demand for money is a stable function of a few key variables, the quantity demanded changes in response to changes in the determinants. It follows that "substantial

[4] Friedman's discussion (pp. 17–21) makes clear that we hold a similar interpretation of Keynes's problem and the reasoning that led Keynes to regard price theory as irrelevant for the analysis of unemployment.

[*sic*] changes in prices or nominal income are almost invariably the result of changes in the nominal supply of money" (p. 3).

In the monetary theories of Keynes (1936) and Patinkin (1965) and in Metzler's classic article (1951), "the quantity theory" is a proposition about the effects of a change in money in a fully employed economy where capital stock, real output, and employment remain unchanged. Metzler's article makes clear that the effect on prices is not invariant to the way in which the stock of money is changed. Different types of changes produce different permanent responses in interest rates, in monetary velocity, and in real cash balances.

The issues raised in Metzler's analysis involve the roles of debt or real capital and money and the effect of changes in money on relative prices. A main point of the analysis is to show that open-market operations and fiat changes in the stock of money have different consequences for relative prices. The existence of a stable demand for money does not discriminate between alternative monetary theories that assign more rather than less importance to the effect on interest rates and other relative prices of changes in the public's real stock of interest-bearing government debt, or more rather than less importance to the relative price changes expected to result from open-market operations. Friedman does not show how the existence of a stable demand for money settles these issues or discriminates between "quantity theories" and nonquantity theories. The aura of quaint and rather irrelevant memories surrounding the term "quantity theory" obstructs the useful application of this term to current issues. We see no reason to resurrect "the quantity theory" but much usefulness in building on the ideas and conjectures of Thornton, Wicksell, Fisher, Keynes, and Friedman and attempting to combine major portions of their analysis in an analytical framework that also exploits the developments in economic theory during the past decade.

An additional objection to Friedman's "quantity theory" is that he bypasses a question of central importance and one on which there has been considerable discussion: Why (or how) do changes in the nominal stock of money induce households or firms to purchase more goods and services? Friedman assigns limited importance to the real balance effect in the short run, and his differential equations describing the adjustment of output contain neither real balances nor relative prices (including interest rates). The way to repair this deficiency, we believe, is to expand the analysis to include some of the variables and equations that Friedman neglects. Doing so forces the development of an alternative theory in which the adjustment of relative prices becomes a key element in the adjustment of output and the price level.

Fiscal Policy

One of the more striking features of Friedman's analysis is that in sixty-two pages of text, much of it devoted to short-run or short-term adjustments, the fiscal role of government is mentioned only once and only to be dismissed (p. 29). Changes in government expenditure and taxes, apparently, have so little effect that they can be ignored entirely.

We know of no evidence to support this conclusion. The empirical work done by Friedman and Meiselman (1963), Keran (1969), Andersen and Jordan (1968), and others frequently identified as "monetarists" provides no evidence that changes in the government expenditure and taxation have no effect on output. On the contrary, many of their regression equations show that tax changes have a larger effect on GNP than government expenditure, contrary to the implication of the standard Keynesian model, contrary also to the implications of Friedman's model.[5] These findings are supported in the retests by DeLeeuw and Kalchbrenner (1969) and in other studies. We see no way to get from the proposition that an equal change in government expenditure and taxation has a negative effect on GNP, found in these studies, to the proposition that the government's budget has no systematic effect.

One result of neglecting fiscal policy is that Friedman is able to neglect the effect of fiscal variables on interest rates and of interest rates on velocity and the demand for money during cycles. He does not fail to mention some of these effects; on the contrary, he refers to the effect of interest rates on the demand for money several times, but neither interest rates nor other relative prices appear in his adjustment equations (eq. [52] was not in Friedman [1970a]), and he never mentions any effect of fiscal variables on real rates. Instead, he assumes that real rates are constant and that market rates adjust rapidly to changes in anticipations (pp. 35–36, 53). We know of no empirical evidence supporting these propositions for the short periods, National Bureau half-cycles or cycles, to which Friedman elsewhere applies his analysis.

To bring out the problem, suppose that a war such as World War II, the Korean, or even the Vietnam War had been financed entirely by taxes

---

[5] Friedman never explicitly states that fiscal policy variables have no effect on output, prices, or other variables. His formal analysis implies that these variables either have no effect in the short run or cannot be separated reliably from other random factors.

instead of partly by issuing debt and money. Would there have been no short- or long-term effects on the economy? Would the real rates of return—anticipated and realized—during and immediately after each of the wars have been the same if each of the wars had been financed entirely by taxes? Would not interest rates, other relative prices, the distribution of expenditure, and even the appropriate rate of monetary growth have differed if war expenditures had been tax financed? We believe that, in each case, the answer is yes, and that this is one essential difference between our version of monetarism, Friedman's, and the standard Keynesian theory.

In Keynesian theory, fiscal policies change income flows and induce reliable, predictable responses in real variables via the multiplier-accelerator mechanism. Relative price changes have limited, and often zero, effect on the outcome. Interest rates enter only, if at all, as the costs of borrowing, and as such have minimal effect because spending is said to be relatively insensitive to changes in market interest rates, that is, borrowing costs (Smith 1970). Many, and probably most investigations of the process set off by changes in fiscal (or monetary) policy are conditioned by this view. The clear conclusion is that even if fiscal policy affects interest rates, the effect of interest rates on aggregate expenditure is small, so that the effect of fiscal changes on expenditure is diminished only slightly by a change in interest rates. The evidence to support this conclusion is usually a recitation of the effect on various expenditure categories of changes in borrowing costs. The role of interest rates as the relative price of future consumption is neglected.

By dismissing fiscal policy and ignoring the effects of tax changes on interest rates, relative prices, and output, Friedman avoids developing an alternative to the Keynesian analysis of the "transmission mechanism" with its emphasis on borrowing costs. Equally important and related, neglecting fiscal variables is one of several ways in which Friedman avoids any explicit role for relative price changes and the application of price theory to aggregative analysis.

Government Debt

Analysis of the aggregate effect of fiscal policy involves more than the usual Keynesian treatment of government expenditure and taxation. Changes in taxes on income from labor services relative to the taxes on income from capital affect resource allocation by changing relative prices and relative rates of return. These, in turn, change short-run expenditures. In a multiple tax system, the real value of the outstanding stock of publicly held government securities is not equal, in general, to the discounted present value of future tax liabilities. Changes in debt induce changes in interest rates, in expenditure, and in desired borrowing or lending. Evidence has now been presented showing that changes in the stock of government debt have more than a negligible effect on market interest rates (Brunner and Meltzer 1968; Eckstein and Feldstein 1970; Zwick 1971).

In Friedman's framework as in the Keynesian framework, there is no market in which the outstanding stock of government securities is bought and sold, no market in which owners of existing securities can attempt to unload or increase their liabilities, and no way in which changes in the outstanding stock of government securities can affect relative prices, interest rates, velocity, and the rate of spending. For the nonbank public, selling outstanding government securities to banks is an alternative to borrowing from banks; for banks, acquiring outstanding government securities is a principal alternative to lending. In the process of redistributing the outstanding stock of securities, the banks and the public (proximately) determine the level of market interest rates. For the aggregate nonbank public, purchasing or selling government securities is part of the process of adjusting to current and anticipated changes in prices, output, and rates of return.

Friedman hints at some of these points in his discussion of the demands for money by households and business (pp. 14–15). He asserts that household demand depends on expected income or wealth; business demand does not, at least not to the same extent. Businesses seek to maximize returns, and they "can acquire additional capital through the capital market" (p. 14). A more complete analysis would note that households maximize utility subject to a constraint that includes the returns from holding securities. Although households do not enjoy perpetual life and do not generally sell equities, they can borrow from banks or lend to the government. By borrowing or lending, and buying or selling securities, a household can change its debtor-creditor position; by saving, a household can change its net wealth. Households, like businesses, must adjust their balance sheets as part of the process of obtaining an optimum. For both households and businesses, the choice of an optimum balance sheet position is a consequence of maximizing behavior —utility maximizing in one case, maximizing present value in the other.

If Friedman had pursued his analysis of the demand for money we believe he would have been led to distinguish between money and bank credit. Making the latter distinction forces an analysis of the public's desired indebtedness, the market processes distributing the stock of government debt and determining the equilibrium stocks of money and bank credit. Including the market for bank credit in his analysis of the markets for money and output would have taken Friedman beyond the *IS-LM* framework and the Keynesian paradigm.

Keynes avoided discussion of the bank credit market by identifying "bonds" and "debt" with real capital and by treating the Walrasian money market as a market for both "credit" and real capital. Given the stock of money, the quantity of money demanded determined (proximately) the interest rate on financial assets and the price of real capital. This interpretation of Keynes receives its clearest formulation in Metzler (1951) and in several of Tobin's papers, most recently in Tobin (1969*a*). The Keynesians substantially changed Keynes's analysis by treating interest rates as borrowing costs. On their interpretation, a constant, maintained deficit financed by increasing government securities has no effect on interest rates via the credit market. Increases or decreases in the stock of securities raise or lower interest rates only by changing wealth and thereby raising or lowering desired money balances and real consumption. Many and perhaps most Keynesians deny any effect of this kind by denying any effect of wealth on the demand for money, by identifying the effect of wealth on consumption with the "real-balance" effect, and by minimizing the empirical significance of the real-balance effect.

The evidence showing that the stock of securities affects interest rates poses a problem for Friedman, Keynes, and the Keynesians. Each dismisses (or minimizes) the role of existing securities. Several of Tobin's portfolio models separate debt and money and analyze the effects on real rates and relative prices. But so far as we know, no one has extended these results by analyzing the effect of relative prices on current output and expenditure.

The Money-Supply

Friedman also ignores any effect of prices, output, or interest rates on the stock of money. The money stock is treated as autonomous. At one point, the justification for doing so is that "the supply function has varied greatly from time to time" (p. 53). At another, the supply depends on interest rates, but the point is dismissed as of no importance for his analysis (p. 30), and the money stock is said to be "independent of any changes in demand" (pp. 3, 51).

We believe that the first argument is incorrect, the second largely correct but misleading. There is now considerable evidence showing that the stock of money can be expressed as a function of a few variables. The evidence for such money-supply functions is no worse than the evidence in support of demand functions for money.[6] We conclude from the available empirical evidence that the first argument must be rejected.

However, despite numerous plausible arguments to the contrary, there is very little evidence that, with the monetary base given, current or recent income or current interest rates have any sizable effect on money. Nor is there evidence of any substantial effect of current income on the base. If Friedman's second argument means that the "feedback" from current market interest rates, wealth, or income to money is small relative to the effect of interest rates and income or wealth on the demand for money, we concur.[7] The part of his argument that we find misleading is the stress he places on the independence of monetary changes. Friedman's argument suggests that strict independence is a necessary condition for "monetarism" (Tobin 1969b). The two issues are separate. The conclusion that monetary impulses are relatively important for the determination of aggregate income does not require that the stock of money be independent of income or interest rates. The monetarist hypothesis should not be presented in the way that permits the hypothesis to be rejected for irrelevant reasons.

The Transmission Mechanism

In the *IS-LM* framework, the effect of monetary policy on income depends on the slope or elasticity of the *IS* curve. The more interest elastic the *IS* curve, the larger the effect of a given dollar or a given percentage change in money or income. With real resources fixed, prices eventually rise or fall until equilibrium is restored at a higher or lower price level, unchanged stock or real money balances, and unchanged interest rate. Friedman's acceptance of the *IS-LM* framework and this view of the transmission mechanism (pp. 26–27) brings him into general agreement with the neo-Keynesians about the transmission of monetary policy (Bailey 1962; Samuelson 1969; Goodhart 1970).

We regard Friedman's discussion as either misleading or a complete reversal of his often stated position. In the *IS-LM* analysis, interest rates

---

[6] Several of these items are cited in Brunner (1968, p. 12, n. 9) and in Brunner and Meltzer (1968). The evidence to the contrary is based on National Bureau methods (Cagan 1965) and not on multivariate analysis.

[7] If the monetary authority follows a "money market" strategy, a rise in market interest rates leads to an increase in the base. If the monetary authority follows a rainy day strategy, changes in weather cause changes in the base. In both cases, the central bank controls the base in the short run, and the consequences of its actions are important for macrotheory, the reasons for choosing particular strategies much less so.

are generally taken as measures of borrowing costs. There is no distinction between market and real rates in the usual statement or in Friedman's restatement. No mention is made of interest rates as a proxy for relative prices of assets and output as in Hicks's (1937) paper formulating the *IS-LM* model. There is nothing in the model as presented capable of explaining the fact—driven home for all of us in recent years by Friedman—that market interest rates generally rise during periods of economic expansion and fall during contractions. There is nothing in his statement of the *IS-LM* model capable of raising expenditure or interest rates above their initial equilibrium positions following a monetary expansion or pushing them below the initial equilibrium following a contraction. The reason is that there is no variable capable of shifting the *IS* curve in the short run and no reason for the *LM* curve to overshoot the initial equilibrium.

We do not know of any evidence showing that the *IS* curve remains fixed in the short run.[8] By keeping real rates constant, ignoring fiscal variables, and relative prices, Friedman's "common model" neglects the variables that, we believe, explain many of the short-run changes in expenditure and market interest rates.

Friedman recognizes that the short-run explanation of income and interest rates, obtained from the "common model," is incomplete. He resolves the problems in two different ways. In both, real rates are assumed constant, as discussed earlier. Changes in nominal income, or in real income and prices, are made dependent in one case (pp. 49–53) on the difference between actual and expected income and prices and ultimately on (1) the expected rate of change of nominal income, (2) the deviation of desired from actual money balances, and (3) the difference between the growth rates of actual and desired money balances. In an alternative approach (pp. 41–42), the deviation of nominal income from its growth path depends only on the difference between the rates of change of money and nominal income. All other factors have been impounded in (constant?) coefficients. In the alternate version, interest rates rise in periods of expansion and fall in contraction if changes in the rate of inflation are anticipated by speculators (p. 45).

Friedman's first approach to short-run adjustment has no clear connec-

---

[8] Like Friedman (p. 16), we believe that the real-balance effect is one of several explanations of long-run changes in the *IS* curve. We agree, also, that the short-run importance of the real-balance effect is small enough to neglect in most developed economies where real balances are a small part of wealth. In our analysis the size of the traditional real-balance effect depends on the proportion of money to total nonhuman wealth, a factor that is less than .05 for the United States.

tion to the "common model." The level of income is determined by one process, the rate of income change by another.[9] No doubt a set of postulates can be introduced to reconcile the two, but only at the cost of eliminating interest rates and the negatively sloped *IS* curve from the "common model" or including interest rates in the adjustment equation. If the *IS* curve has a negative slope, interest rates change with changes in income and money, and these changes must be explainable by the same process explaining changes in income. Friedman is unprepared to make the required assumptions but unable to "express this case in any simple fashion."[10]

The adjustment equations that Friedman uses express many of the conjectures about the role of money that one of us has called the "strong monetarist hypothesis" (Brunner 1968). Many of these conjectures are familiar to Friedman's readers. The solution equations that express the conjectures can be derived, however, only by introducing postulates that eliminate any effect of changes in the composition of wealth, in taxes, or in other variables that change the relative prices of assets and output.

Inflation or Real Output

Friedman offers "common models" that determine real income, or the price level, or nominal income, but not all three. To get the time rates of change of income and the price level, he does not differentiate the equations of one or another of the models. He either introduces some new equations that have no clearly specified relation to the "common model" or disregards the division between prices and income and concentrates on nominal income. In these ways Friedman attempts to overcome the inconvenience of having a theory from which (at least) one equation is "missing."

We believe that more than one equation is missing. Relative prices, real rates of return, the outstanding stock of government debt, and the government budget are additional "missing" variables. Without better

[9] The differential equations expressing the adjustment are of interest for several reasons, not the least of which is the implied modification of a position—the Friedman rule—that has long been identified with the Simons-Friedman tradition. The rate of change of nominal income depends on both the level and the rate of change of the nominal stock of money. Hence, the rate of growth of income is not independent of initial conditions, represented by the existing nominal stock, and the appropriate rate of growth of money is no longer a constant but a variable dependent on past monetary policy.

[10] This quotation and the sentence of which it is a part were in the version on which we commented (Friedman 1970*a*, p. 226) but do not appear in the NBER version.

evidence for the model than has been provided, we do not accept the framework as a useful statement of short-run macrotheory. Too many familiar features of cycles are omitted or ignored.

Conclusion

Friedman's unpublished critiques of standard macroeconomic analysis developed over two decades with substantial benefit to monetary and economic theory. Until recently, however, his many contributions did not include a detailed analytic statement of the framework guiding his research, connecting his empirical findings, or providing a foundation for the policies he advocated. Without such a statement, it was often impossible to separate valid implications of an empirically tested framework from less well supported conjectures. Frequently, his work left unclear the extent to which he accepted the *IS-LM* paradigm as a short-run framework and rejected only the particular version known as the Keynesian special case, or accepted only that part of the framework called the "classical" special case or the strong monetarist position. Friedman's paper helps to make his position clear. In principle, he accepts the *IS-LM* common framework as a short-run theory; however, to explain observed short-run changes in prices or output, he offers a theory that eliminated any effect of changes in relative prices, interest rates, government expenditure, tax rates, or the stock of securities.

We offer four types of criticisms of Friedman's approach. (1) The restrictions that he imposes on the standard theory to remove any short-term effect of changes in interest rates, fiscal variables, and the stock of securities are not well supported by evidence. (2) The framework does not imply some of the main propositions that have been developed in recent years as a result of the empirical work done by Friedman and others. For example, there is no mention of the variability of the lag in monetary policy. The gradual adjustment of the price level following the adjustment of real output is either assumed (1970) or is not obtained at all. (3) The framework ignores some main developments in economic theory during the past ten years that have important bearing on the issues discussed. Keynes's observations during the twenties and thirties suggested to him that the long recession and most of the observed unemployment could not be explained by standard price theory. Cost of acquiring information, cost of search, and adjustment have been introduced to remove some of the main problems that led Keynes to this conclusion. None of Friedman's hypotheses builds on these new developments toward a theory of prices and output that removes the deficiency noted by Keynes. (4) The explanation of fluctuations in prices and output has very little relation to the static theory of prices and output.

Our criticisms of Friedman's monetary theory lose much of their force if his "common framework" represents the best that economists can do. We believe that our criticisms obligate us to state an alternative framework that is richer in implications and one that captures some main developments in the economic theory of the past ten years, developments stimulated and in some cases carried forward by the important contributions of Milton Friedman. Elsewhere[11] we attempt to sketch such a theory and to develop a few of its implications for cycles and for theories of cycles.

[11] In Brunner and Meltzer (1972) we state our alternative and attempt to resolve the main problems common to Friedman's work and the work of his other critics. We believe discussion has reached the point at which further debate within the confines of the *IS-LM* paradigm does little to clarify the disputed issues. Friedman's statement on p. 28 recognizes that increases in money affect output by raising the prices of existing assets and lowering interest rates, thereby encouraging both "spending to produce new assets and spending on current services rather than on purchasing existing assets." Unlike Friedman's common model, our alternative to the *IS-LM* framework develops from this starting point.

Friedman's Theoretical Framework

James Tobin

Milton Friedman has earned our gratitude by setting forth his theoretical framework. He has certainly facilitated communication by his willingness to express his argument in a language widely used in macroeconomics, the Hicksian *IS-LM* apparatus. He undoubtedly hoped that use of a common theoretical apparatus would reduce the controversy about the roles of monetary and fiscal policies to an econometric debate about empirical magnitudes. If the monetarists and the neo-Keynesians[1] could agree as to which values of which parameters in which behavior relations imply which policy conclusions, then they could concentrate on the evidence regarding the values of those parameters. I wish that this contribution had brought us closer to this goal, but I am afraid it has not. I have been very surprised to learn what Professor Friedman regards as his crucial theoretical differences from the neo-Keynesians.

Money, Income, and Prices in Short-Run Equilibrium

First, let me explain what *I* thought the main issue was. In terms of the Hicksian language of Friedman's article, I thought (and I still think) it was the shape of the *LM* locus. This locus is for given stock of money M and price level p, the combinations of real income Y and interest rate r that satisfy $M/p=L(Y, r)$.[2] It will be vertical if the demand for money is

[1] I do not know what to call those of us who take an eclectic nonmonetarist view. "Neo-Keynesian" will do, I guess, but so would "neoclassical." The synthesis of the last twenty-five years certainly contains many elements not in the *General Theory* (Keynes 1936). Perhaps it should be called Hicksian, since it derives not only from his *IS-LM* article but, more importantly, from his classic paper on money (Hicks 1935). One thing the nonmonetarists should *not* be called is "fiscalists." The debate is not symmetrical. Whereas neo-Keynesians believe that *both* monetary and fiscal policies affect nominal income, monetarists believe that only monetary policies do so. At least, I *think* that is the distinctive and characteristic message that monetarists have been conveying to the profession and the public. Friedman agrees that this gives "the right flavor of our conclusions."

[2] To minimize misunderstanding, I should point out that imagining an *LM* curve in (Y, r) space for a given price level p does *not* mean that p is taken to be an exogenous variable in

wholly insensitive to interest rates. This assumption leads to the following characteristic monetarist propositions:

a) Y can be changed only if M/p is changed. Or, if one prefers a relation between nominal magnitudes, pY can be changed only if M is changed. The link may or may not be one of proportionality, and it may of course involve lags and leads and stochastic terms.

b) In particular, a shift of the IS locus, whether due to fiscal policy or to exogenous change in consumption and investment behavior, cannot alter Y.

c) If Y is supply-determined, then M/p is determined and both the price level p and money income pY are proportionate to M.

The neo-Keynesian view is that the LM locus is upward sloping, because $L/\partial Y$ is positive and $\partial L/\partial r$ is not zero but negative. Assuming that there is also some interest sensitivity of investment and/or consumption, we have the following characteristic neo-Keynesian propositions:

d) If Y is not uniquely determined by the supply equations of the system, it can be changed *either* by shifts in the IS curve, whether they stem from policy or other exogenous shocks, *or* by shifts in the LM locus, whether due to monetary policy or exogenous shocks.

e) In particular, an increase in the nominal stock of money M will be absorbed partly in an increase in Y, partly in an increase in p, and partly in a reduction in velocity due to a decline in the interest rate r.

f) Even with Y supply-determined, price level and money income are not uniquely related to the nominal money supply M. They also depend on the interest rate and thus on fiscal policy. For example, an expansionary fiscal policy or any other upward shift in the IS locus will raise r, lower the stock of real balances demanded, and raise the price level corresponding to any nominal money stock.[3]

---

the complete system of which the LM relation is only a part. Even if M is exogenously given, there is a whole family of LM curves, one for each possible value of p. (Indeed, there may be other endogenous variables, including actual or expected rate of change of p, which help to determine the position of the LM curve.) In system-wide equilibrium, the economy must be on that LM curve which corresponds to a value of p that satisfies the other relations of the system, notably including those that describe the labor market. The crucial issue is the shape of a typical member of the LM family. Because of the way in which p enters the equation $M/p=L$, all members of the family have essentially the same shape, which depends on the partial derivatives of the demand for money function L. The monetarist-Keynesian differences listed in the text depend on whether $\partial L/\partial r$ is zero, so that a typical LM curve is vertical, or negative, so that a typical LM curve has positive slope.

[3] None of these propositions depends on absolute liquidity preference (the trap) or, Friedman to the contrary, on any "tendency to regard k or velocity as passively adjusting to changes in the quantity of money" (p. 26).

All this is the stuff of macroeconomics courses all over the country. Friedman, however, explicitly disavows belief that the demand for money is independent of interest rates and denies that his propositions depend on any such assumption. May we, therefore, assume that he accepts propositions *d, e,* and *f* and rejects *a, b,* and *c?*

Friedman shifts attention to the supply side of the model, the short-run relation of *Y* and *p*. I was certainly amazed to find this relationship—which he calls the "missing equation"—identified as the crux of the controversy. I had thought that both monetarists and neo-Keynesians agreed that short-run variations of money income (*pY* or *MV*), however caused, were generally divided between changes in output and changes in price. The common view, I thought, was that the proportions in which an increment in aggregate nominal demand go into output increase and price increase depend on the degree of pressure on existing labor and capital resources. There is plenty of qualitative empirical evidence for such a proposition, though plenty of theoretical and statistical doubt about its precise specification.

Anyway, it is a caricature of the monetarist position to identify it with the notion that *Y* is wholly supply-determined in the short run. We know that Friedman himself has not assumed that. He summarizes his own view as follows: "I regard the description of our position as 'money is all that matters for changes in *nominal* income and for *short-run* changes in real income' as an exaggeration but one that gives the right flavor of our conclusions."[4]

It is equally a caricature of the neo-Keynesian view to say that *p* is an "institutional datum" in the short run. Keynes certainly did not make this assumption, nor did Hansen—and neither has any careful version of a complete neo-Keynesian macroeconomic model.[5] Nor is it at all necessary

[4] Friedman goes on to say that " 'money is all that matters, period' is a basic misrepresentation of our conclusions." When I tried to clarify the debate by distinguishing among the three propositions "money does not matter," "it does too matter," and "money is all that matters," the context was perfectly clear. It was what matters in the determination of money income. In the same paragraph, "money is all that matters" is translated into "the stock of money [is] the necessary and sufficient determinant of money income" (Tobin 1965*a*). There has been no basic misrepresentation. No one has accused Friedman and his colleagues of claiming that money is all that matters for the determination of *real* income in the long or short run, to the neglect of supply factors—or all that matters for the cold war, or for the rotation of the planets. They have been represented as claiming exactly what he now agrees "gives the right flavor of our conclusions."

[5] At some stage during the various discussions of the papers here combined, Friedman learned that Keynes could at worst be charged with assuming a constant value of the money wage rate (p. 32, n. 20). Since Keynes also assumed increasing marginal labor and user cost, a constant money wage implies a price level that rises with nominal income. But Keynes did not even assume a constant money wage; see his discussion (Keynes 1936, p. 285) of "the

for proposition d. As long as Y is not wholly supply-determined, as long as prices are not completely flexible in the short run, the monetary authorities can change the *real* supply of money, not just the nominal stock. As long as Y is not wholly supply-determined, any analysis of the consequences of changes in the real supplies of monetary assets is relevant and legitimate.[6] Once again, just as in the debate over the shape of the money demand function, Friedman has tried to saddle his opponents and critics with an extreme assumption and to claim the entire middle ground for himself. In both cases, the truth is that it is his propositions, not theirs, which depend on a special polar case.

His "third approach" model in section 8 is, if possible, even more surprising than the preceding parts of the paper. The "missing equation" —apportioning changes in money income between price and output—is

---

elasticity of money-wages in response to changes in effective demand in terms of money." See also Hansen (1949, p. 136), where fig. 18 shows both prices and wages as increasing (and concave upward) functions of nominal effective demand. Keynesian theory does not require money wage rate rigidity, only stickiness in the sense that, in the short run, labor supply varies directly with the money wage for any given real wage.

[6] Friedman (p. 21, n. 11) attacks papers by me and my colleague William Brainard on the ground that "the entire analysis is valid only on the implicit assumption that nominal prices of goods and services are completely rigid." This is not true, as Friedman's own footnote of explanation makes clear. An example of our crime, it turns out, is to "assume that central banks can determine the ratio of currency (or high-powered money) to total wealth including real assets. . . . If prices are flexible, the central bank can determine only nominal magnitudes, not such a real ratio." To believe that the central bank can affect real magnitudes as well as nominal quantities, it is not necessary to assume that prices are rigid. What assumption is necessary depends on whether there is only one or more than one exogenous asset denominated in the monetary unit of account. In some of our models, there is more than one exogenous asset denominated in the monetary unit of account. In addition to having a monetary debt, the government has obligations not payable on demand. Unless the government is constrained always to change the nominal quantities of its n types of monetary obligations in the same proportion, it must be capable of altering the real quantities of at least $n-1$ of them. Far from requiring an assumption of price rigidity, this proposition is obviously true even if prices are completely flexible. Open market operations, as observed in the final section of this paper, will have real consequences. In particular, they will alter interest rates and the demand for money. If there is only one exogenous monetary asset, currency or high-powered money, it is still not necessary to assume rigid prices. It is necessary only to assume that prices are not perfectly flexible, that output is not perfectly rigid. Some further observations on Friedman's attack are in order: (a) The papers he is criticizing did not pretend to provide complete macroeconomic models. Their objective was to refine and generalize the "LM" sector. Given this limited focus, we did not feel obligated to elaborate all other macrorelations, including those connecting p and Y. We did not think it would be controversial to attribute to the monetary authorities some real effects in the short run. After all, that is what Friedman believes, too. (b) Even if Y were supply-determined and prices were completely flexible, the structure of the demand sectors of the macroeconomy (IS and LM) is still of interest. Our system of "LM" equations could be solved for the commodity price level and the structure of interest rates, given the level of real income, the real rate of return on capital, and the nominal values of exogenous monetary quantities.

no longer the crux of the matter. Instead, we are asked to assume that in the short run both the real interest rate and the nominal interest rate are fixed. The real rate, which is relevant to real investment and saving decisions, is identified with the net marginal productivity of capital along a normal growth path.[7] This yield changes very slowly, if at all. The nominal rate is simply the real rate plus the aniticipated rate of inflation, which is taken to be firmly predetermined by past experience and other considerations.

Friedman invokes the memory of Keynes, as well as that of Fisher, as inspiration for this construction. The Keynesian touch is that speculators keep the actual nominal rate at its proper value. But it is important to note that these are not Keynesian "liquidity preference" speculators between money and bonds. They are Fisherian speculators between goods, or equities in goods, and bonds. The nominal interest rate is not in a liquidity trap. There is indeed, for every M/p, a normally shaped LM curve in the nominal interest rate and real income. But the only point on it that matters is the one that corresponds to the exogenously determined interest rate.

The level of real income is determined wholly by the IS (or multiplier) equations, once the real rate of interest is given. Given $M/p = L(r, Y)$, the fixing of both r and Y determines M/p and leads to a short-run quantity theory of both price level and money income.

The system is illustrated in figure 1. Given the $(IS)_0$ locus and the real rate ρ^*, the equilibrium E_0 is determined with real income Y_0. The nominal rate is measured on the right-hand vertical axis, displaced from the left-hand, real rate, axis by the expected rate of inflation. There is a family of LM curves, connecting real income and the nominal rate, of which two are shown: $(LM)_1$ corresponds to a greater real stock of money M/p than $(LM)_0$. The only LM locus that can coexist with $(IS)_0$ is $(LM)_0$. If the authorities try to shift $(LM)_0$ to the right by increasing M, their efforts will be frustrated by an offsetting rise in p.

Fiscal policy, however, can control real income. Indeed, an increase in real government purchases will have the full multiplier effect—for example, shifting the IS locus to $(IS)_1$ and real income to Y_1. The LM curve will follow along, shifting to $(LM)_1$; this will require a reduction of p if the

[7] The real interest rate is constant, ρ^*, in a neoclassical golden age. So also, of course, is its difference from the long-run rate of growth, g^*, as indicated in eq. (29). But Friedman's eq. (30), which implies $\rho^* = g^*/s^*$, is puzzling to those of us who would have expected $\rho^* = (\alpha^* g^*)/s^*$. Here s^* and α^* are the equilibrium proportions of saving and of capital income, respectively, in net national product. Friedman is assuming that $\alpha^* = 1$, that all productive resources are reproducible capital endogenously supplied.

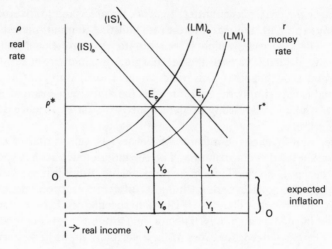

Fig. 1

nominal stock of money is kept constant or increased insufficiently.[8] So deficit spending increases output and employment and lowers prices and money wages. Prices are completely flexible, not because output is supply-determined but because it is multiplier-determined.

As this result suggests, the model is bizarre, and it is hard to imagine that it is seriously intended. Critics have complained that the constant-velocity assumption of monetarism ignores interest-rate effects on the demand for money. It is indeed difficult to persist in maintaining that they are negligible while simultaneously stressing the importance of the rate of price inflation both for nominal interest rates and for velocity. So here is a model that acknowledges the interest sensitivity of the demand for money but preserves the quantity theory by the simple expedient of fixing interest rates. But the cost of this expedient is to concede fiscal policy more control over output and employment than virtually any Keynesian would claim.

The author himself offers this model as tentative and expresses serious doubts. He doubts that the real rate should really be regarded as a constant in the short run, and he is surely justified. The rate of investment depends, on the one hand, on estimates of the future stream of quasi-rents from the ownership of capital and, on the other, on the discount rate at

[8] The model is reminiscent of Mundell's *IS-LM* analysis of fiscal and monetary policy in a small open economy with complete international mobility of capital and fixed exchange rate. There, too, the interest rate is externally given and the *LM* curve floats to whatever equilibrium the *IS* equations determine.

which this stream is converted to present value for comparison with the cost of capital goods. Both of these determinants are subject to short-run changes connected with departures from the long-run growth path of the economy. Securities markets provide a somewhat exaggerated index of these fluctuations, in the ratio of the market value of claims on business income to the reproduction cost of business assets. The sensitivity of this ratio to short-run changes in business activity and the sensitivity of investment to this ratio are important determinants of the short-run stability or instability of the economy.

Friedman finds it easy to accept the assumption of his model that the only short-run fluctuations of nominal interest rates relevant to the demand for money are those associated with the inflation premium. This is not consistent with his acknowledgment that real rates relevant for investment and saving decisions vary in the short run. Nor is it consistent with the ample empirical evidence of rapid interest-rate gyrations. When the Treasury bill rate falls 350 basis points and the corporate bond rate 150 basis points in seven months, as happened July 1970–February 1971, it strains credulity to attribute the decline to a change in inflationary expectations, the more so when inflation continued unabated and when in any case Friedman has taught us that these expectations are a slowly changing derivative of past experience.

The Dynamics of Price and Income

Friedman's ostentatious discovery of the problem of "the missing equation" may give innocent readers the idea that macroeconomics has neglected or fudged an important relationship, without which its models are logically and empirically incomplete. This is not true. Keynes certainly included in his system a relationship between real output and the price level, derived from a theory of labor demand and supply. All careful expositions, mathematical or verbal, of the Keynesian model have done likewise. In postwar macroeconomics, the price variable has slipped one derivative, and the "missing equation" is the complex of price-wage-employment-output relations summarized partially in "Okun's law" and partially in "Phillips curves" for wages and prices. A large fraction of the profession is preoccupied with theoretical and empirical investigations of these matters.

Friedman's particular proposal is simply a Phillips trade-off which vanishes in the long run. Characteristically, his long-run equilibrium relations connect expected or normal values of output, nominal income, wage, and price—both levels and rates of change. These normal values are moving averages of past actual values. Disequilibrium relations apply to surprises, that is, to deviations of the actual values of these variables from expected values. In particular, surprises in the growth rate of nominal income are divided, for unexplained reasons, between deviations in the growth rates of price and real output. Moreover, deviations in the level of real output contribute to positive deviations in the rate of price inflation. Friedman's equation for the rate of inflation, as derived from equations (44)–(46), is:

$$\frac{\dot{p}}{p} = \frac{\dot{p}^*}{p^*} + \frac{a}{1-a}\left(\frac{\dot{y}}{y} - \frac{\dot{y}^*}{y^*}\right) + \frac{\gamma}{1-a} \; (\log y - \log y^*),$$

where p is price level, y is real income, and the starred symbols represent expected values; a, $1-a$, and γ are all positive. The parameter a measures the price proportion of a deviation in the growth rate of nominal income; $1-a$ is the output share. The equation will be recognized as a standard price Phillips curve. The variable

$$\frac{\dot{y}}{y} - \frac{\dot{y}^*}{y^*}$$

is related to the change in unemployment, and the variable $\log y/y^*$ to its level. That the long-run Phillips curve is vertical is ensured by entering expected price change $\dot{p}^*/p^*$ with a coefficient of 1; y^* corresponds to the natural rate of unemployment.

This is not the place to discuss the natural rate hypothesis. I will merely record my view that there is a great deal more to the short-run interrelations of wages, prices, employment, and output than can be captured by a model of universally agreed expectations and deviations from them. Aggregation is always risky, but it seems particularly inappropriate to pretend that aggregate variables obey the relationships that would be expected in a single homogeneous product and labor market.

In the architecture of Friedman's theoretical framework, nominal income is the keystone. The "missing equation" dynamics just reviewed are designed to explain the division of changes of nominal income between price and output. The other side of the arch is the dynamic dependence of nominal income on money supply. Apparently, it is now doctrine that the link of these two variables is the same regardless of the split of changes in nominal income between price and output. It was not always so: in Friedman's earlier permanent income model of the demand for money, both price and income histories were determinants of velocity.

The dynamic link of nominal income to money is only suggestively sketched. The basic idea is that, in moving equilibrium, the growth rate of the money supply and the expected growth rate of money income are equal. As usual, the expected growth rate of money income is a slowly changing moving average of actual growth rates in the past. When money supply grows faster than the equilibrium rate, money income does likewise. This is the dynamic proposition.

However, Friedman is interested in establishing a stronger proposition, namely, that the income velocity of money rises when the growth rate of the money stock exceeds the expected growth rate of money income. In the past, he offered his permanent income theory of money demand as an explanation of this phenomenon.[9] He now offers an alternative or complementary explanation (pp. 41-42). This relates the procyclical movement of velocity to the procyclical movement of interest rates— superficially, at least, the orthodox Keynesian interpretation which Friedman has so stubbornly resisted for so long. In Friedman's version, it is true, interest rates rise during a money-generated boom in nominal income only because the boom in actual income raises expectations of income and price inflation.[10] But the camel's nose is in the tent.

The Long-Run Quantity Theory

Friedman begins with an exposition of the "quantity theory." The phrase has, it turns out, a number of different meanings: (1) emphasis on the distinction between the real and the nominal quantity of money, and on the fact that what matters to rational individuals is the real quantity; (2) use of the quantity identity, $MV=PQ$ or some variant, as an organizing framework for macroeconomic analysis; (3) belief that the central equation of macroeconomics is that of the demand for money to a largely exogenous supply; (4) interest in the determinants of the demand for money, and the size and direction of their effects; (5) assertion that in the short run, nominal income is proportional to the supply of money, although changes in nominal income may affect output as well as prices; (6) assertion that real magnitudes are in long-run equilibrium independent of the nominal quantity of money, so that nominal magnitudes— prices, money incomes—are simply proportional to the nominal quantity of money.

---

[9] See Tobin (1970) for criticism of this explanation. Although it is consistent with observed procyclical fluctuations of velocity, it is not consistent with Friedman's own evidence on the cyclical timing of money and income peaks and troughs.

[10] Incidentally, Friedman's Phillips curve does not justify his assumption that price and money income expectations always move together. Nor does his "monetary theory of nominal income" imply that all changes in money income, inflation expectations, and interest rates are induced by changes of money supply. Within his own framework, the determination of velocity is a good deal more complex than he suggests.

Version 1 is not in dispute and does not imply any other quantity theory proposition. Versions 2 and 3 concern the language in which substantive arguments are expressed, not the substance of the arguments. Keynes could have cast his arguments in the language of the quantity equation, just as Friedman could convey his message in *IS-LM* diagrams. In monetarist language, all influences on nominal income other than the stock of money are dumped into velocity (or its Cambridge reciprocal). This may be awkward, but it is not impossible. Of course, the roster of determinants of velocity may include more than one endogenous variable. If so, the demand-supply equation for money cannot constitute a complete model of nominal income in Chicago or anywhere else. This brings us to version 4 and to the observation that nonmonetarists as well as monetarists fill the journals with studies of the demand for money in its several definitions. The fifth assertion has been the subject of the first part of my comment.

The sixth proposition is the neutrality of money in long-run equilibrium: absolute prices and other nominal quantities are proportional to the stock of money; real magnitudes and ratios of prices (including interest rates) are independent of the stock of money.

It is important to stress that this quantity theorem—which should be called the "quantity of money" theory of prices rather than the quantity theory of money—is not in general implied by rationality, by the absence-of-money illusion. True, no self-respecting theorist believes that de Gaulle made any real economic difference when he cut two zeros off the franc, thus reducing the supply of money in the unit of account to one-hundredth its former amount.

The fallacy of misplaced concreteness is the tacit identification of every change in the supply of money, as engineered by government, central bank, and private banks, with a monetary change of the nature, if not the magnitude, of the change from old to new francs. There is a true quantity theorem, to be sure, but it is a more general proposition than the quantity-of-money theory of prices, and an emptier one.

The true quantity theorem is as follows. Consider a system of supply and demand equations for goods and services and for stocks of assets and debts denominated in the monetary unit of account. Given tastes, technologies, and certain exogenous variables, these supplies and demands will be functions of nominal prices. Among the exogenous data will be some quantities defined in the monetary unit of account, including the monetary base of currency and bank reserves, and the outstanding stocks of government debts of other kinds and maturities. Now suppose that, with a given vector of these exogenous monetary quantities, the system is solved for equilibrium commodity prices p_e. If every exogenous monetary variable is then multiplied by the same positive scalar λ, then the price vector λp_e will solve the system, with every physical quantity unchanged and every endogenous variable measured in the unit of account scaled up or down by λ. This theorem, if it should be so dignified, is a simple consequence of the "homogeneity postulate" or the absence-of-money illusion. A corollary is that the prices of various monetary assets in terms of the unit of account will be unchanged; interest rates do not depend on the quantities of these assets when they all change in the same proportion.

It should take only a moment's reflection to convince anyone that the usual operations that alter the quantity of money, in any of its usual definitions, fail to meet the conditions of the theorem. First, open market operations typically consist in changing some exogenous monetary variables in the opposite direction from others, not in moving them all in the same direction and same proportion. Second, except in the longest of runs, the list of exogenous monetary variables is very long, including individual as well as aggregate stocks and unmatured private debts contracted in the past. While a Gaullist monetary reform scales all these up or down in proportion, ordinary monetary operations do not.

The strict quantity theory applies only if there is a single exogenous monetary variable which *is* "money" except for a factor of proportionality, for example, reserve requirements. Much monetary theory, modern as well as ancient, has developed from a model in which government debt and the monetary base are one and the same. But in a model with various kinds of government liabilities, time as well as demand obligations, it is easy to show that the real equilibrium—for example, capital intensity and marginal productivity of capital—depends on the proportions in which these liabilities are supplied. Even in the long run, the real quantity of money depends on monetary policy, and accordingly monetary policy has other real consequences.

The crucial issue is whether government interest-bearing time debt is of any significance. If not, then an increase in the quantity of money has the same effect whether it is issued to purchase goods or to purchase bonds. If all kinds of debt matter, then the genesis of new money makes a difference. To borrow an overworked metaphor, is a "rain" of Treasury bills—promises to pay currency in three months or less—of no consequence for the price level, while a "rain" of currency inflates prices proportionately?

It may be true that the debt involves an expected stream of taxes equivalent to the stream of interest. But the two streams do not wash out. Bills and bonds share some of the attributes, and perform some of the functions, of the currency they promise to pay. The government has a monopoly of their issue, as it does of currency. As long as the government does not expand the supply of these assets to the point where the public no longer pays an interest premium for their advantages, they will be valued more highly than the corresponding stream of taxes. The tax liabilities forced into public balance sheets are not the same in maturity, risk, convenience, etc., as the government obligations of which they are the counterpart. The tax liabilities will be discounted at the rate appropriate for the incomes on which the taxes are levied.

Interest-bearing debt will also, in general, have important distributional effects. Some of the taxes to pay the interest may be levied on wage income. If such levies were just proportional to property income, one could argue that—risk and portifolio considerations aside—government debt is neutral. It changes neither the demand of the population for a given stream of after-tax income from nonhuman wealth nor the capacity of any given capital stock to generate such a stream. But if wage incomes are taxed to pay bond interest, after-tax human wealth is reduced while nonhuman wealth is increased. Now human wealth and nonhuman wealth are not in general perfect substitutes for each other; indeed, they are complements—the larger households' permanent labor incomes are, the greater will be their demand for nonhuman wealth. Government debt displaces some capital investment from the saving of the labor force; taxation of wages to pay bond interest also diminishes the total supply of saving. Monetization of the debt eliminates the second effect.

Friedman's "theoretical framework" does not provide monetarism, either its short-run or its long-run propositions, with strong theoretical support.

* * *

Postscript

My paper was written originally as a comment on two separate papers by Friedman, one published in the *Journal of Political Economy* in 1970 (Friedman 1970a), the other in the same *Journal* a year later (Friedman 1971). In the present version these two articles have been combined, with considerable reordering of sections, rephrasing of transitional material, and revision and rearrangement of footnotes. Most important, the four paragraphs which here conclude Friedman's section 5 were not present in the original versions. The editor has therefore invited me to comment on this new material, and my comment follows.

The new material—a return, as Patinkin observes in footnote 25 of his comment—to a previous Friedman theme—argues that monetary shocks affect demands for goods and services by setting in motion complex, interrelated chains of asset substitutions and revaluations. If portfolios are to absorb greater quantities of money, prices of other assets—not just Treasury bills and corporate bonds but equities and used cars—must change, mostly rise. Increases in the values of existing stocks of physical assets, or titles to physical assets, encourage the production of new goods of the same type or of close substitutes.

Now this scenario is quite standard. It is one which "neo-Keynesian" monetary economists have been teaching and expounding for years. It is, for example, the principal point of my own "portfolio" approach to monetary theory. Neo-Keynesian econometric models, notably the Federal Reserve-M.I.T.-Penn model, link monetary policies via financial markets and intermediaries to the markets for producer capital, houses, and durable goods.

The puzzle is how Friedman could think that his account of the transmission mechanism supports monetarist conclusions. On the contrary, emphasis on portfolio substitutions suggests, for example, (1) that there is no unique relation between any monetary aggregate and nominal income, (2) that nonmonetary events—fiscal policies, shifts in asset preferences, revisions of expectations—will also affect the attractiveness of accumulating physical assets, and (3) that the market does not automatically put full changes in inflation expectations into nominal interest rates.

Friedman stresses that he is more catholic than nonmonetarists in the list of assets he includes in portfolios—in particular his inclusion of durable goods for which there are not good organized markets. Specific asset lists are not usually presented in theoretical models, but my own conception of "capital" has always included consumer durables. I doubt that anyone disagrees with the principle that portfolio adjustments and interest rate changes will affect asset demands across a broad spectrum. But Friedman has never offered any argument, theoretical or empirical, to support the implicit claim that the existence of untraded physical assets implies strong, direct effects of the *quantity* of money, effects which bypass credit and securities markets and leave no imprint on interest rates and prices of traded assets.

It is true that the formal structure of Keynes's *General Theory* focuses on "*the* rate of interest" and concentrates on its role in substitution between money and bonds. The assumption is that capital and bonds are nearly perfect substitutes, so that *the* rate of interest is also the cost of equity capital, to which the marginal efficiency of capital is equated by investment. This could be regarded as an elliptic version of the now standard transmission scenario, not an alternative approach. In pointing out that financial and real assets are not perfect substitutes, more modern theory actually weakens the link of monetary policy to aggregate demand.

A Keynesian View of Friedman's Theoretical Framework for Monetary Analysis

Paul Davidson

In response to some critics, Professor Friedman has elaborated and made more explicit his views on "A Theoretical Framework for Monetary Analysis," a framework which he claims "almost all economists would accept" (p. 61). Undoubtedly, this new presentation will evoke wide praise and attention; and the obvious future influence of Friedman's theoretical framework on economic thinking makes a critical examination of certain key elements and assertions of his analysis important. Before the dialogue becomes immersed in a critical discussion of the many fine analytical points raised by Friedman, it is essential to begin with a statement of some of the fundamental conceptual differences between the analytical monetary structure developed by Keynes and the model presented by Friedman, for despite Friedman's numerous trenchant confrontations with "Keynesians," he has never compared his analytical framework with the "Theory of a Monetary Economy" developed by Keynes.

Friedman's claim that his discussion of "The Keynesian Challenge to the Quantity Theory" (pp. 15–29) "does not misrepresent the body of his [Keynes's] analysis" (p. 19), even though a "qualification" is neglected, is simply not true. Since Friedman has declared that a "fair-minded reader" can be misled by Tobin's criticism of a model labeled Friedmanian but which "ignores large parts of our argument" (Friedman 1970c, p. 320), and since Friedman has asserted that Tobin has given a "completely erroneous" impression via a "straw man . . . a non-Friedmanian Friedman model that produces its effects by a myopic concentration on a single element out of a complex mosaic" (Friedman 1970c, p. 327), fair play suggests that Friedman should not have attacked a straw-man version of the Keynesian system which others have, in the name of Keynes, erected,

I am grateful for helpful comments from M. Fleming, J. A. Kregel, B. J. Moore, and S. Weintraub. This paper evolves from an ongoing study on *Money and the Real World* which has been supported by a grant from the Rutgers University Research Council.

nor should he have ignored several important chapters in Keynes's *General Theory.* [1]

This is not the place either to put forth a complete Keynesian theoretical framework for analyzing the role of money in the real world or to engage in a debate as to what Keynes "really" meant;[2] space will permit only an enumeration of a few of what I believe are the more fundamental conceptual differences between Keynes's "Theory of a Monetary Economy" and Friedman's framework. These distinctions can be readily viewed by focusing upon three aspects of Friedman's theoretical framework—namely, omissions, misspecifications, and false assertions about the nature of Keynes's model.

From the Keynesian view, the basic factors Friedman omits are:

1. The essence of uncertainty, in the Knightian sense (Keynes 1936, p. 148, n. 1; pp. 293-94), so that decisions involving contractual commitments for future performance and payment are made by individuals who recognize that all anticipations cannot, and often will not, be realized.

2. The existence of particular market institutions, organizations, and constraints (for example, money contracts, the legal system, money, and sticky money-wage rates) which exist only because uncertainty is present (Keynes 1930, chap. 1; 1936, chap. 17). (Other institutions, such as the Walrasian auctioneer and flexible money wages and prices, are not applicable, even as a logical construct to define the norm or trend around which the real world monetary-production economy fluctuates, as long as plans can be, and are, disappointed. Thus these institutions cannot be used to close logically the Keynesian system; they are logically inadmissible to the Keynesian model.)

3. The existence of money which, in an uncertain world, has a dual function—namely, a medium of exchange and a store of value. In a

---

[1] Specifically chaps. 12, 17, 20, and 21. Unfortunately, Friedman is guilty of the same fault he attributes to Tobin, namely, that although he "looks at everything through different glasses. . . he [Friedman] takes it for granted that we [all economists] wear the same glasses he does " (Friedman 1970c, p. 322). Without polling all economists, it is impossible to find out how many hold theoretical views about money which differ significantly from those currently presented by Friedman and many so-called Keynesians. I would suggest that Keynes, Shackle, Clower, R. F. Kahn, Champernowne, Harrod, Minsky, Hines, J. Robinson, Kaldor, Weintraub, and I are only a few of those who have, in print, viewed monetary phenomena through different colored glasses than Friedman offers in his current article.

[2] In this symposium, I can only highlight some aspects which I believe to be critical to Keynes's theory. In 1972 I wrote a monograph, *Money and the Real World* (Davidson 1972), which develops and sets forth Keynes's entire analytical framework of the *General Theory* and the *Treatise on Money* and its implications for modern economic growth theory.

modern monetary, production, specialization economy, money has two essential properties, namely, (*a*) a zero (or negligible) elasticity of production and (*b*) a zero (or negligible) elasticity of substitution between money and any other good which has a high elasticity of production.[3] These two properties are necessary if an object is to possess liquidity (Keynes 1936, p. 241, n. 1). The existence of a money possessing these properties underlies Keynes's basic propositions that (*a*) as a purely theoretical matter, if there is uncertainty in a monetary, production economy, a long-run equilibrium position characterized by full employment of labor need not exist (Keynes 1936, pp. 30, 191, 235–36); (*b*) stickiness of the money-wage rate is necessary if money is to play its peculiar role in such an economy (Keynes 1936, pp. 238–39); and (*c*) if wages and prices are flexible, "the quantity of money is, indeed, nugatory in the long period" (Keynes 1936, p. 191).[4]

In Friedman's framework, since *all expectations* are realized (p. 48), and therefore there is no uncertainty, these essential properties are unimportant, since in such a world a rational economic man would never hold money for precautionary purposes (nor would there be any speculative motive, if, in fact, all men's expectations about the future rate of interest were always realized). If the future is uncertain, the quantity of money will be an important policy variable only if there is a *variety* of opinion about the perfidious future (Keynes 1936, p. 172); if there is a

---

[3] "A zero elasticity [of production and of substitution] is a more stringent condition than is necessarily required" (Keynes 1936, p. 236, n. 1). Those who do not believe that Keynes said these elasticities are essential properties of money should look in the index to the *General Theory* under "Money—its essential properties," where references are made to (1) the entire chap. 17 entitled "The Essential Properties of Interest and Money," and to (2) p. 293, where these properties are specifically linked to disappointed expectations. (I will leave it to the economic historians to resolve whether these properties were associated with wampum or cowrie shells; and if not, whether these trinkets actually performed the dual functions of money. Certainly, both Friedman's framework—which explicitly states that the supply of money depends "critically" on banking factors [pp. 10–11]—and Keynes's model are developed to deal primarily with bank-money economies where these elasticities are relevant. Whether either framework would deal with "wampum economies" where there were no well-organized spot markets for securities, and therefore no speculative motive, is an interesting digression, but it should not distract from the basic issues of this symposium— namely, the differences of the two frameworks for analyzing modern monetary economies.)

[4] Friedman "summarily" dismisses propositions *a* and *b* as already having been proved false while ignoring proposition *c* altogether (p. 16). The rejection of propositions *a* and *b* depends either on defining equilibrium as synonymous with market clearing instead of in the usual sense of the term that nothing changes in the system (Davidson 1967, pp. 563–64), or by assuming some variant of a Pigou effect based on expectation of future money-wage and price changes in a world where *all* expectations are realized. If, however, Friedman had analyzed the concept of money by its essential properties within a framework where expectations can be disappointed, he would have noted that a dismissal of propositions *a* and *b* is unwarranted.

variety of expectations, then some people's plans must be disappointed.

Within the Friedman framework, a Keynesian view would suggest misspecification of:

4. The demand function for money and the supply processes for altering the money supply.

Finally, from a Keynesian view, at least two of Friedman's assertions about Keynes's model are incompatible with the *General Theory*, specifically:

5. Keynes assumed that before full employment all adjustments to changes in demand take place via quantity changes (p. 19).

6. The price analysis underlying Keynes's model is "arbitrary" and has "no underpinning in economic theory" (p. 44).

Keynes versus Friedman on the Price Level

Friedman's discussion of Keynes's view about prices ignores large parts of Keynes's argument as he developed it in chapters 20 and 21 of the *General Theory*. For example, Friedman (p. 19) states, "Keynes explored this penetrating insight by carrying it to the extreme: *all adjustment in quantity, none in price. He qualified this statement by assuming it to apply only to conditions of underemployment.*" (Italics added.)

Even a cursory reading of chapters 20 and 21 of the *General Theory* would show that, in Keynes's view, money prices as well as output tended to vary with changes in demand, in the short run, at less than full employment. In these chapters, Keynes develops various elasticity concepts, such as the elasticity of output e_o, the elasticity of money prices e_p, and the elasticity of money wages e_w, which represent proportionate changes in the various variables for a given proportionate change in effective demand. The change in money prices for any given relative change in demand is given by the formula $e_p = 1 - e_o(1 - e_w)$ (Keynes 1936, p. 285). Thus, unless $e_o = 1$ and $e_w = 0$, prices will show some change for any given change in demand. Indeed, throughout the *General Theory*, Keynes maintained that at less than full employment an "increase in effective demand will, generally speaking, spend itself partly in increasing the quantity of employment and partly in raising the level of prices" (Keynes 1936, p. 296).

Therefore, Friedman is in error when he suggests that Keynes used a "rigid price assumption" which is "arbitrary. It is entirely a *deus ex machina* with no underpinning in economic theory" (p. 44). Keynes's "Theory of Prices" (Keynes 1936, chap. 21) was, of course, firmly based on those "homely and intelligible" theoretical concepts "the conditions of supply and demand; and in particular, changes in marginal cost and the elasticity of short-period supply" (Keynes 1936, p. 292). One of the explicit objectives of the *General Theory* was "to bring the theory of prices as a whole back to close contact with the theory of value" (Keynes 1936, p. 293). Keynes skillfully constructed the elasticities of output, wages, and prices from traditional price theory concepts.[5] Empirical estimates of these elasticities (see Weintraub and Habibagahi 1971) would go a long way toward answering some of the questions on the adjustment process which Friedman raises in the concluding section of his paper (p. 61). Unfortunately, such elasticity concepts are not specified at all in Friedman's framework; therefore, before economists rush off to heed Friedman's request for "a more subtle examination of the record . . . to disentangle what is systematic from what is random and erratic" (p. 62), it is essential that the relevant theoretical constructs to be estimated from the record be agreed upon.

Unlike Keynes, Friedman (p. 44) bases his quantity theory approach to price-level phenomena on the Walrasian equations. Although the Walrasian system may have a long history in the economic literature, and therefore Friedman's approach is not open to the charge of blatant arbitrariness which Friedman (p. 44) levels against Keynes,[6] the theoretical foundation underlying the Walrasian equations is, from a Keynesian

[5] Some may say that Keynes's price formula is a mere truism (derived from the definition of the Marshallian short-period supply price schedule) and that such elasticities by themselves are empty empirically and theoretically, since they involve the pure arithmetic of adding up all the components that make up the general price level. But how else can one proceed intellectually, unless one accounts for all the components of the price level? The function of a theoretical framework then is to explain the relationships between all the various components after they have been specifically identified, to indicate which components are active and which are passive, to suggest under what conditions components will change endogenously and when they will change exogenously. For example, in Keynes's model, observed changes in money wages could be either a response to change in demand if $e_w > 0$, or it could be a result of the social and political struggle to alter the relative money wage structure (Keynes 1936, pp. 13–14); consequently money-wage changes may be partly exogenous. Thus, Keynes recognized that "if there are strong social or political forces causing spontaneous changes in the money-rates of efficiency wages, the control of the price level may pass beyond the power of the banking system" (Keynes 1930, p. 351), a result which is impossible in the Friedman framework in which money wages are completely endogenous!

[6] Although Friedman's assertion about the lack of theoretical underpinning is not applicable to Keynes's analytical framework, it is pertinent to the "neoclassical synthesis" framework developed by many American "Keynesians." Friedman indicates his indebtedness to Leijonhufvud's (1968) "brilliant book" and then he disregards the main thesis of this book, namely, that there is a world of difference between the monetary economics of Keynes and that of the American "Keynesians." Keynes (1936, p. 32) would reject the assumption that the price level was determined outside the system, a postulate Friedman (p. 32) claims is a logical necessity in Keynes's analysis.

point of view, not applicable to any analysis of a monetary production economy (Keynes 1933, pp. 8–9; Clower 1965; Jaffé 1967, pp. 9–13; Hahn 1970, p. 3; 1971, p. 417).

The Crux of the Money Matter: Uncertainty, Contracts, and the Money-Wage Rate

What Friedman and so many other modern monetarists have failed to grasp is that Keynes utilized a "wage unit" and postulated the stickiness of the money-wage rate not simply, as Friedman (p. 32) claims, to logically close the system or to rationalize wage rigidity because "something had to be brought in from the outside to fix the price level; it might as well be institutional wage rigidity" (p. 18); rather, Keynes (1936, p. 239) was attempting to deal with a vital logical condition for a viable monetary system, as well as an obvious fact of life.

In a world of uncertainty where production takes time, the existence of money contracts permits the sharing of the burdens of uncertainty between the contracting parties whenever resources are to be committed to produce a flow of goods for a delivery date in the future. Such contractual commitments (for example, hire contracts and forward-offer, or supply, contracts) are, by definition, tied to such flow-supply concepts as the flow-supply price. Ultimately underlying the flow-supply price is the relationship between money-wage rates and productivity phenomena. If individuals are to utilize money as a temporary abode of purchasing power, either because they expect to accept delivery of a reproducible good in the very near future or because they desire a vehicle for transferring purchasing power to the more remote and indefinite future, then these economic units must have *confidence* that no matter how far the current spot price for any reproducible good may be momentarily displaced by spot market conditions,[7] the market price for the good will be at some anticipated level at a future date.[8] As long as the flow-supply price is sticky (that is, the annual

[7] Since Friedman (pp. 7–8) insists that the income version of the quantity theory completely excludes transactions involving existing assets, and since it is the income version which he propounds, therefore he has rejected analyzing spot prices—the only prices in the real world which might promptly change with respect to every change in demand, since these market prices are not directly related to flow-supply elasticity concepts. Thus Friedman has excluded from his analysis the main type of real world markets for which his flexible-price assumption might have some relevance.

[8] In a world of uncertainty, the forward price (which can never exceed the flow-supply price) (Kaldor 1960, p. 35) is the best estimate of the spot price at the future date (Working 1962, pp. 446–47). Thus, if production is occurring and if the flow-supply prices of goods (that is, money-wage costs plus profit margins) are sticky, then they are reliable estimates of future costs of buying such goods either spot or forward; and therefore, the flow-supply

rate of change in the money-wage rate relative to productivity is small), individuals "know" they can, whenever they desire, accept a contract offering the good at a delivered money price *not* significantly different from today's money flow-supply price, at a future date. Accordingly, the existence of money as an asset with negligible carrying costs, stickiness in the money-wage rate, and the availability of contracting in money terms for performance at future dates permit individuals, at any moment of time, to delay decisions which would necessitate exercising their currently earned claims on resources.

Keynes was not using a handy institutional rigidity which was due to a friction or a readily correctable imperfection in the labor market to close his system. A "perfect" labor market with flexible prices would be incompatible with a system where there are contracts, and money is used as a store of value, except under the most stable conditions of demand and supply where all prices remained basically unchanged over time.[9] If the number of units of money which labor is willing to buy for a given unit of effort, the money-wage rate, fluctuates rapidly every time there is a small change in demand, there will be no asset whose liquidity premium always exceeds its carrying costs[10] (a situation which Keynes [1936, p. 239] notes

---

prices are, in Friedman's language, the set of prices used in the calculation to determine the desired real quantity of money at any future date (pp. 1-2).

[9] Friedman may claim that flexibility need not imply instability as long as demand and supply functions are relatively stable over time, for then the money wage can be theoretically flexible as long as in the actual world it is really sticky. If this is Friedman's position, there is little conflict between him and Keynes about the desirability of sticky-money wages (although if, in the real world, either money wages get unstuck or involuntary unemployment occurs, Keynes and Friedman would recommend different policies to restore full-employment stability). Nevertheless, Friedman would require the further assumption that labor demand relative to labor supply (adjusted for productivity) is actually stable over time, but as indicated below (see n. 12), the existence of "false transactions" in the real world alters the parameters of any Walrasian system and thereby alters the demand and supply functions and the set of equilibrium prices. Thus, in the real world of uncertainty and false trades, it is unlikely that the demand and supply of labor in a Walrasian system which describes the trend of the actual world will be stable over any length of time.

[10] As a supplement to a sticky-money wage policy, Keynes (1936, p. 270) suggested that the authorities permit fluctuating (*not flexible*) exchange rates in order to maintain external equilibrium and prevent conditions in the foreign sector from jeopardizing the domestic economy. This policy is consistent with Keynes's views on the undesirability of flexibility in an uncertain world; Keynes was advocating that the authorities permit slow wavelike fluctuations (perhaps a crawling peg or controlled small annual rates of change?) rather than either adhering to a rigid parity policy (Keynes 1936, p. 339) or withdrawing from the exchange markets and permitting prompt changes in exchange rates to occur in response to every change, ephemeral or otherwise, in the foreign sector. *In an uncertain world,* there will only be an accidental matching of buyers and sellers in any exchange market at any point of time—no matter how well organized. Thus, unless there is an institution—a residual buyer and seller—willing to step in and make a market whenever one side or the other temporarily falls away, the exchange rate can vary violently. Such mercurial movements would add

is the "best definition" for a "non-monetary economy"). *The importance of money essentially flows from its being a link between the present and the future"* (Keynes 1936, p. 293), and this link can exist only if there is a continuity over time in contractual commitments in money units. The synchronous existence of money and money contracts over the uncertain future where change is inevitable *and* unpredictable is the basis of a monetary system whose maxim is: *"Money buys goods and goods buy money; but goods do not buy goods"* (Clower 1969).

In a neoclassical world of perfect certainty and perfect markets, with a Walrasian auctioneer assuring simultaneous equilibrium at a given point of time, it would of course be foolish to hold money as a store of value as long as other assets provided a certain positive yield (Samuelson 1947, pp. 122-24). In the absence of uncertainty, neoclassical theory has room neither for contracts nor for the store-of-value function of money. Some modern theorists—finding the real world does not possess either the perfect certainty, flexible wages and prices, complete absence of disappointment, or the ability to recontract characteristics of their theoretical norms—"resemble Euclidean geometers, in a non-Euclidean world who, discovering that in experience straight lines apparently parallel often meet, rebuke the lines for not keeping straight—as the only remedy for the unfortunate collisions which are occurring" (Keynes 1936, p. 16).

Keynes's challenge to the quantity theory as a useful analytical tool is significantly different from the "Keynesian Challenge to the Quantity Theory" which Friedman (pp. 15-29) presents. Keynes was the first important economist to accuse bluntly the neoclassical view of the nature of money as foolish. Keynes (1937*b* [1947, pp. 186-87]) wrote: "Money, it is well known, serves two principal purposes . . . it facilitates exchanges. . . . In the second place, it is a store of wealth. So we are told, without a smile on the face. But in the world of the classical economy, what an insane use to which to put it! For it is a recognized characteristic of money as a store of wealth that it is barren. . . . Why should anyone outside a lunatic asylum wish to use money as a store of wealth?"

His answer to this rhetorical question was clear and unequivocal (Keynes 1937*b* [1947, p. 187]): "Our desire to hold money as a store of wealth is a barometer of the degree of our distrust of our own calculations

---

additional uncertainty in undertaking any long-term international contractual commitments or in using foreign currencies as a temporary abode of purchasing power by multinational corporations. Hence, if foreign exchange markets do not have institutions which limit the day-to-day rate at which parities can alter, the additional uncertainty in the foreign sector would reduce the offers and acceptances of supply contracts for forward delivery and payment with foreigners, and this would create unemployment and disruption in the foreign sector.

and conventions concerning the future. . . . The possession of actual money lulls our disquietude." Distrust? Disquietude? These are states of mind[11] impossible in a world of certainty (that is, even in a world where the sum of the probabilities equals unity).

All Walrasian general equilibrium models imply worlds of certainty. The *tâtonnement* process, which is essential to the establishment of equilibrium and implies no transactions occur until equilibrium is attained (that is, recontracting is essential),[12] implies that anyone holding money either at any point in the auction or till the next market period is demented or at least economically irrational. Why hold money if it is not

[11] These states of mind emphasize the precautionary motive, and not the speculative motive, as the fundamental reason for demanding money as a store of value under uncertainty (see Keynes 1936, pp. 170–72; and n. 14 below). Friedman, on the other hand, implies that Keynes thought that the speculative motive was the only reason for demanding money because of uncertainty, and therefore Friedman puts great emphasis on "absolute liquidity preference," that is, a highly elastic speculative demand function as "the key element" in the Keynesian system (pp. 21–25). This total absorption in the shape of the speculative demand function may correctly characterize some "Keynesian" models which produce their effects by a myopic concentration on a single element out of a complex mosaic, but it is not a complete or accurate representation of Keynes's view on the demand for money as a store of value in an uncertain world.

[12] In his analysis of the Walrasian system, Jaffé (1967, p. 12) has underscored the fact that a production economy provides a "complication" for the system which can only be resolved by a complete "abandonment of reality." If some production occurs in response to nonequilibrium prices (and I assume Friedman would not deny that this does occur in the actual world) then the effect of such "false transactions" is to change the parameters of the system and thereby assure that "whatever equilibrium the market converges to—if it converges at all—must be different from the equilibrium that would result if there were no change in the original parameters" (Jaffé 1967, p. 9). This "complication" can be avoided, according to Jaffé (1967, p. 14), if it is assumed that all production and consumption plans are always realized. This assumption is, of course, explicitly utilized by Friedman (p. 48), but the use of such an assumption is, as Jaffé (1967, p. 14) has stated, simply an ingenious means for "contriving market models to elucidate mathematical systems instead of developing mathematical models to elucidate market systems."

If false transactions and disappointments are, in the actual world, continuously occurring and thereby inducing continuous changes in the parameters of any Walrasian system which purports to be representative of the long-run trend of the real world, then the resulting Walrasian system, if there is one, would fluctuate around the path of the actual world and not vice versa. It is as if every time air friction caused a falling body to fall at less than $\frac{1}{2}gt^2$ in the real world, the value of the gravitational constant for the perfect vacuum case would change!

This is, of course, precisely why Keynes (1933) indicated it was necessary to develop a "Theory of a Monetary Economy" which differed substantially from the framework of a "Real-Exchange Economy." He stressed that the differences between a "Monetary Economy" and a "Real-Exchange Economy" had been greatly underestimated and that the "machinery of thought" of the latter (in modern parlance, the Walrasian equational system) leads economists to erroneous conclusions; the belief that it is easy to adapt the conclusions of the latter "to the real world of Monetary Economics is a mistake. It is extraordinarily difficult to make the adaptation, and perhaps impossible without the aid of a developed theory of Monetary Economics" (Keynes 1933 [1963, pp. 8–9]).

needed for transactions, since in equilibrium goods trade for goods, and since the present and future values of all economic goods can be determined, at least in a probability sense, with complete certainty? The essential nature of money is disregarded in the Walrasian system, as no asset exists whose liquidity premium always exceeds its carrying costs (Davidson 1969, p. 319). As Hahn (1970, p. 3) has recently admitted, *"The Walrasian economy* that we have been considering, although one where the auctioneer regulates the terms at which goods shall exchange, *is essentially one of barter."* (Italics added.)

Friedman (p. 44) explicitly states that his quantity theory of money relies upon and is "summarized in the Walrasian equations of general equilibrium." He acknowledges that in long-run equilibrium in his view "all anticipations are realized . . . [and that he regards] long-run equilibrium as determined by the earlier quantity-theory model plus the Walrasian equations of general equilibrium" (p. 48). It is difficult to understand therefore, from a Keynesian point of view, why the resources of so many economists have been wasted on Walrasian models[13] in general, and quantity theory models in particular, where the latter make a fetish about the importance of the rate of growth of the quantity of money. If the Walrasian equations—which describe a barter economy, an economy where "money can play no essential role" (Hahn 1971, p. 417)—are the logical norm or trend around which Friedman believes the actual world fluctuates, then the quantity of money is indeed nugatory.

It is the fact that money is a means of deferring decisions about the use of claims on resources which underlies Keynes's objection to Say's law. In a world of uncertainty, he who hesitates to spend his current claims is saved to make a decision another day. A decision to save, in Keynes's view, is not a decision to "consume any specified thing at any specified date" (Keynes 1936, p. 210). Above all, individual savings decisions in a modern *monetary* economy do not involve the current purchase of newly produced consumer durables in order to obtain a stream of utility over time, as Friedman has often implied. Instead, the decision to save merely requires the individual to decide whether to hold his claims in immediate liquid command (money) or to part with command and leave it to spot market conditions at a future date to determine on what terms he can

[13] One theorist who has engaged in such activities admitted that "there is something scandalous in the spectacle of so many people refining the analysis of economic states which they give no reason to suppose will ever, or have ever, come about. . . . It must now, I fear, be admitted that the study of the Walrasian 'grouping' [*sic*] or tatonnement process has not been very fruitful" (Hahn 1970, pp. 1–2). It is indeed an astonishing intellectual achievement to be able to utilize a framework which assumes a groping process to obtain equilibrium and simultaneously assumes perfect knowledge about all future markets!

convert this deferred command back into immediate command (Keynes 1936, p. 166).[14] Consequently, as long as the spot markets for "titles" to real capital goods are better organized than the spot markets for the hire purchase of reproducible capital goods, economic units will choose titles rather than demand real capital as a vehicle for transferring purchasing power over time (see Davidson 1968, pp. 302-4; Davidson 1969, pp. 302-4). Thus, as the discussion of portfolio changes in the next section will explain, exogenous changes in the money supply will *not* directly spill over into changes in the demand for reproducible durables.

In sum, in an uncertain world, income earners will often be temporarily satiated or completely occupied with their recently purchased economic goods, or even preoccupied with noneconomic affairs, and thus may be currently unable or unwilling to predict what specific goods they will need at specific dates in the future; they may feel queasy about undertaking any contractual actions which will commit current earned claims on resources onto a path which can be altered, if future events prove necessary, only at very high costs, if at all. Recognition of this motivation to save in order to avoid the commitment of claims on resources provided Keynes the insight necessary to describe the social institutions associated with money, as well as the essential properties of anything which will fulfill the two equally important functions of money—namely, a generally accepted medium of exchange, and a store of value in a *modern, monetary, production-oriented, but uncertain world.*

The vital properties of anything which will fulfill the functional requirements of money are:

1. A zero (or negligible) elasticity of production, so that if individuals, uncertain about the future, want to defer additional commitments of resources, their increased demand for money as a mode for postponing

[14] In the absence of well-organized spot markets for durables with elasticities similar to money, Keynes (1936, p. 171) believed "liquidity preference due to the precautionary motive would be greatly increased, whereas the existence of an organized market gives an opportunity for wide fluctuations in liquidity preference due to the speculative motive." The existence of spot securities markets permits a speculative motive to interact with the basic precautionary motive. Hence, for Keynes, any event which creates uncertainty—for example, large increases in the money supply or, alternatively, rapidly falling money wages and prices (with a constant nominal money supply)—will affect the demand for money via the precautionary reason, speculative reason, or both; therefore, if such events increase the precautionary demand, they may have little effect on the rate of interest even if the speculative demand is not very elastic (see Keynes 1936, p. 172). Thus Friedman's discussion of a "Keynesian" system which virtually ignores the precautionary motive and instead emphasizes "absolute liquidity preference" in the form of a highly elastic speculative demand is a straw man, a non-Keynes Keynesian model, a perversion of Keynes's own views about liquidity preference.

action will not encourage entrepreneurs to employ additional resources in the production of additional quantities of the money commodity.

2. A zero (or negligible) elasticity of substitution between money and any other asset which has a *high* elasticity of production, so that if individuals want to preserve additional options for action for the future, the increase in the price of money induced by an increase in the demand for money as a store of value does not divert people into substituting other assets, which have high elasticities of production, as a store of value. Hence, because of these elasticities, the demand for a store of value in the form of money in an uncertain world does not generate the demand to commit resources and the virtuous interaction between supply of resources and the demand for resources, succinctly expressed via Say's law, is broken.

3. The cost of transferring money from the medium-of-exchange function to the store-of-value function, or vice versa, must be zero (or negligible) so that individuals do not find it expensive to defer decisions or to change their minds. Minimizing their transactions costs requires the existence of at least two economic institutions: (a) offer and debt contracts denominated in money units, and (b) legal enforcement of such contracts. An additional contribution to the minimizing of such transactions costs is the presence of an institution—namely, a clearing system—which permits using private debt contracts in the settlement of transactions as long as it is expected that the private debt can be promptly converted into the form of money which is enforceable in the discharge of contracts.

Thus, the main characteristic of a real world monetary economy are Uncertainty, Fallibility, Covenants, Institutions, Commerce, Finance, and Trust. These are the Seven Wonders on which the *Modern* World is based.

The Demand and Supply of Money

A Keynesian view of Friedman's theoretical framework would suggest that Friedman's demand function for money is misspecified, while some important aspects of the supply of money in a modern bank-money economy suffer from benign neglect.

The various forms of the demand-for-money function which relate the quantity of money demanded to income (Friedman's eqq. [6], [12]) are an acceptable first approximation for the correct demand-for-money relationship only if the problem being analyzed assumes there is *no change* in the aggregate demand for goods, but only a change in the quantity of goods demanded. Although Keynes (1936, p. 199) specified a similar demand-for-money function in one section of his *General Theory* as a "safe first approximation," Ohlin (1937) was quick to point out the deficiencies of such a demand function for money. Keynes (1937a, p. 667) was forced to admit that this form of the demand for money was misspecified:[15] "I allowed, it is true, for the effect of an increase in *actual* activity on the demand for money. But I did not allow for the effect of an increase in *planned* activity, which is superimposed on the former."

Keynes then retreated to his much more carefully detailed *Treatise* analysis of the demand for money, and as I have shown elsewhere, this properly specified demand—which includes the finance motive—has important ramifications for observed differences between the short-run and long-run income elasticity of demand for money (Davidson 1965, pp. 53-55), the interdependence of the real and monetary sectors (Davidson 1965, pp. 57-60), and the path of economic expansion (Davidson 1965, pp. 61-62). Thus, from a Keynesian point of view, Friedman's demand function for money which omits *planned* expenditures as a specific inde-

---

[15] In his "Third Approach" (pp. 34-40), which Friedman (in 1971) initially presented as a new and "superior" way for specifying the demand-for-money function and logically closing his theoretical system, Friedman has adopted, after years of debate and acrimony, the demand function for money specified on p. 199 of Keynes's *General Theory*. Unfortunately, this is the function which Keynes in his finance motive analysis was quick to recognize as misspecified and as such distracting economists' attention from the important role of money. Despite Friedman's recent conversion to Keynes's view about the demand for money, Friedman's "alternative model" is still deficient from a Keynesian view, for it relies on (a) a Fisherian distinction between real and monetary rates of interest which Keynes (1936, pp. 142-43) properly rejected as confusing the effect of inflationary expectations on the marginal efficiency of capital for an effect on the rate of interest; (b) an assumption that all "permanent" anticipated real values are unchanged during the period under analysis—that is, anticipations about nominal income, real growth, and the real rate of interest are either predetermined or exogenous and these anticipations are "firmly held" so that, in essence, all changes in the variables are foreseen from the beginning (inconsistent with Keynes's conception of uncertainty); and (c) the assumptions that the money supply "can be regarded as completely exogenous" and that the income elasticity of demand for money is unity (both assumptions are incompatible with Keynes's finance motive analysis) (Davidson 1965).

Even in Friedman's hands, his new "superior" monetary theory crumbles into a dichotomized model where the unknowns of the real sector (real consumption, investment, income, the realized real rate of interest) are determined by a self-contained subset of equations independent of the quantity of money—so that in this alternative version of the quantity theory, the quantity of money is indeed nugatory! (In fairness, it should be pointed out that Friedman rejects the dichotomy of the real and monetary sectors implied in his analysis and regards the marrying of the real variables with his nominal analysis as "unfinished business" [p. 40]; he admits that he "has nothing to say directly about the division of changes in nominal income between prices and quantity" [p. 45]. Since Keynes's model does make the monetary sector an integral and inseparable part of the real sector in a world of uncertainty, and since Keynes does discuss the division of changes in effective demand between prices and quantities, why not return to Keynes's original analysis?)

pendent variable can lead to wrong theoretical constructs and policy implications.[16]

On the supply side, the essential characteristic of a zero elasticity of production immediately determines the market supply behavior of producers of the money commodity in a bank-money economy. Thus, if one is to specify properly how changes in the supply of money come about, he must relate them to the relevant banking institutions and operations which bring forth money, even though the elasticity of production is zero. In the real world, Keynes (1930, p. 3) reminds us at the very beginning of his *Treatise on Money,* money "comes into existence along with debts, which are contracts for deferred payment and . . . offers of contracts for sale or purchase," that is, the supply of money, and debt and production-offer contracts are intimately and inevitably related. From a Keynesian viewpoint, money does not enter the system like manna from heaven, or dropped from the sky via a helicopter, or from the application of additional resources to the production of the money commodity. The supply of money in a modern ecomony can increase only via two distinct processes—both of which are related to contracts. It is these processes and not the shadows on the cave wall[17] of the banking institutions through which these processes operate which are the focal point of the Keynesian view about the supply of money.[18]

In the first case, which may be called the income-generating finance process, an increased desire to buy more reproducible goods per period—the finance motive—induces individuals, firms, governments, or foreigners to enter into additional debt contracts with the banking system. If these contracts are accepted by the banking system, then additional private debts of banks are issued and used to accept additional offer contracts of producers and workers.

[16] Of course, one cannot literally accuse Friedman of omitting anything from his demand-for-money function (eq. [7]), since this equation contains a portmanteau variable which is a proxy for all things that might conceivably affect the demand for money. Nevertheless, nowhere in his framework does Friedman specifically deal with the finance demand for money; and even his use of the symbol u for the portmanteau variable at the end of his equation(7) implies that Friedman views this variable as similar to an error term which results from the interaction of a very large number of independent factors, each of which has a very small effect on the dependent variable. Keynes, on the other hand, believed that the finance motive was "the coping stone" of his liquidity theory.

[17] Namely, the observed movements of high-powered money, deposits, and currency.

[18] Since Friedman defines money as including demand deposits *and* time deposits—both evidence of debt on the part of banks—he can hardly deny that the processes which change the volume of these private debt contracts are the primary mechanisms for changing the money supply in a modern economy.

In the second method, the portfolio-change process, the banking system removes assets which have a negligible elasticity of production (specifically securities) from the wealth holdings of the general public by offering private bank-debt contracts as an alternate store of value at a rate of exchange which members of the public find very favorable.[19]

In the income-generating finance process, increased desire for the hire purchase of capital goods (or even consumer durables), export purchases by foreigners, or government expenditures by legislators can provoke money demanders (money holders) to initiate the process which produces an increase in the quantity of money, as long as banks are willing to make additional bank-debt contracts available under the rules of the game (and, of course, it is in the self-interest of each banker to do so). This endogenous increase in the money supply is initially used to accept additional offer contracts (as long as some resources are idle). Depending on the supply elasticities of the various industries stimulated, and therefore the aforementioned elasticities of Keynes's price formula, changes in real income and/or prices will be observed to follow (with varying time lags) this endogenous change in the money supply.

In the portfolio-change process, on the other hand, changes in the money supply are immediately used by the general public as a substitute for securities as a vehicle for transferring purchasing power to the indefinite uncertain future. If both money and securities have zero or negligible elasticities of production, and if they are very good substitutes for each other as store of value while they exhibit very low elasticities of substitution with respect to all other goods which have high elasticities of production, then the exogenous increase in quantity of money via this process will not directly stimulate any additional demand for resource use. Thus, exogenous increases in the money supply due to open-market operations initiated by the Monetary Authority can increase the demand for resource-using reproducible capital goods only via the usual Keynesian effect of lowering the discount rate used by firms to evaluate the expected stream of future quasi-rents from potential investment projects, or by reducing the amount of credit rationing to a previously unsatisfied fringe of borrowers (or perhaps even by altering long-term expectations of quasi-rents).

---

[19] Both the income-generating finance process and the portfolio process can be reversed to alter the supply of money. If, for example, the public wishes to reduce its demand for reproducible goods, it may use some of its monetary claims to extinguish existing debts to the banking system. If the banks then do not utilize the portfolio-change process to replace the money being turned into the banking system, then the money supply available to the general public will decline as the demand for money declines.

Friedman and other monetarists, however, suggest that exogenous increases in the money supply, via open-market operations, for example, may not only operate via the traditional Keynesian interest rate mechanism on the demand for hire purchase of real capital goods, but will also increase, *pari passu,* the demand for household durables. The increased demand for consumer durables is due to (1) a real balance or wealth effect and/or (2) a portfolio balance effect. This latter effect, it is claimed, is a result of economic units finding that the proportion of their portfolio which they hold as money is excessive, and therefore they display an infinite (or very high) elasticity or substitution between money and *resource-using reproducible durables* as components of their portfolios (Friedman and Schwartz 1963a, pp. 60–61; Moore 1968, p. 228). Keynes (1936, pp. 93, 319), of course, recognized that windfall capital gains (due to the open-market operations) could affect the propensity to consume durables *and* nondurables, although there is little evidence to suggest this plays a major role in increasing the demand for consumer durables. On the other hand, Keynes would reject the implications of the portfolio-balance effect, namely, the notion that resource-using reproducible durables are a good substitute for money as a component of one's port-folio—for this would violate one of the essential properties of money. Thus, another fundamental conceptual difference between Keynes on the one hand, and Friedman and the portfolio-balance monetarists on the other, is the magnitude of the elasticity of substitution between money (and financial assets) and *resource-using reproducible durables* as vehicles for transferring purchasing power to the uncertain future.[20]

The low elasticity of substitution between financial assets including money and reproducible durable goods requires two necessary conditions: (1) a sticky money wage, so that the liquidity premium of money exceeds its carrying cost, while the contractual obligations underlying the secur-ities are safe stores of value (see Keynes 1936, p. 207; Davidson 1969, pp. 317–18); and (2) as I have demonstrated elsewhere, the existence of uncertainty and significantly greater transaction and carrying costs asso-ciated with the spot market for the hire purchase of physical goods relative to the costs associated with the spot market for titles to physical goods

[20] If consumer durables are conceived as good substitutes for money as a component of households' portfolios, it must be because consumer durables provide the service of liquidity similar to money. Such durables could conceivably provide a store of liquidity services only if there are spot markets for consumer durables available at future dates which will permit the holder to convert consumer durables back into the medium of exchange *and* the costs of trans-acting in such markets are not more than the cost of transacting in "titles" to such repro-ducible durables. (See Davidson [1968, 1969] for a further discussion of why these conditions will not be met.)

(Davidson 1968, p. 303; 1969, pp. 302–3). The lower the transactions and carrying costs in the spot market for "titles," the larger the elasticity of substitution between money and securities. Simultaneously, the lower these costs which are associated with money and securities, the closer to zero the elasticity of substitution between these financial assets and reproducible physical goods (as long as money wage rates are sticky!).

Hence, in the Keynesian system, changes in the quantity of money occurring via the income-generating finance process will be associated with, to use Friedman's symbols, changes in y, while changes in money due to the portfolio-change process will be directly associated with changes in k. Thus not only do changes in the quantity of money matter, when viewed through Keynesian glasses, but what brings about these changes are also important.

Epilogue

In sum, a view through Keynesian glasses highlights certain characteristics—uncertainty, sticky money-wage rates, contracts, carrying and transactions costs, zero elasticities of production and substitution for money—which interact to make a monetary economy function quite differently than one described by the Walrasian general equilibrium analysis which ultimately underlies Friedman's theoretical construct. In a Keynesian world, contracts and a sticky money-wage rate are essential to the viability and stability of an economic system. As Keynes (1936, p. 269) observed: "The chief result of . . . [a flexible money-wage] policy would be to cause a great instability of prices, so violent perhaps as to make business calculations futile in an economic society functioning after the manner in which we live. To suppose that a flexible wage policy is a right and proper adjunct of a system which on the whole is one of laissez-faire, is the opposite of the truth."

Thus it is obvious that Keynes's conclusions are significantly different from those which Friedman derives from his framework. In this paper, I have tried to explain what I believe are some of the conceptual differences which bring about these contrasting views. A fruitful further exchange of ideas will be enhanced if, in his rejoinder, Friedman devotes some space to:

a) indicating why his framework, which assumes a completely exogenous money supply (p. 38), is preferable to a Keynesian analysis which, when the finance motive and elasticity properties of money are included, permits money supply changes to be endogenous under certain circumstances and exogenous under others;

b) indicating why he prefers to describe the long-run norm or trend about which the actual world fluctuates via a system of Walrasian equations, since this mathematical system will describe a unique norm only if there are no false trades and no disappointments while, in the real world, disappointment and false transactions are a recognized fact of life (and are taken into account in Keynes's system);

c) indicating why a framework which determines the price level by imposing an exogenous money supply onto a logical construct of a non-monetary economy (the Walrasian equations) is preferable to Keynes's "Theory of Prices," which makes the money price level of the flow of output dependent on the Marshallian concepts of demand and flow-supply prices;

d) indicating why he prefers a framework which never deals specifically with the finance motive and instead buries it in a portmanteau variable (as if the fact that businessmen often obtain financial contractual commitments from banks before ordering investment goods is a relatively unimportant factor in the demand for money) rather than adopting the Keynesian demand for money which specifically accounts for the demand for finance (and which also specifies the precautionary motive as the basic reason for the demand for money as a store of value).

A positive response by Friedman on these aspects will lead to further discoveries and a shift of view on both sides in response to difficulties and objections. If, on the other hand, Friedman avoids these issues and instead protests that I have either misinterpreted Keynes or utilized some uncoordinate, shrewd (or wrong) side comments of Keynes which are peripheral to Keynes's "Theory of a Monetary Economy," then it will be up to fair-minded readers to judge for themselves whether Keynes's writings on the essential properties of money, the theory of prices, the finance motive, uncertainty and the precautionary motive, etc., are trivial or whether they do add up to a fundamentally different paradigm involving significantly different conclusions. Ultimately, I am sure, time rather than controversy will separate the true from the false.

*   *   *

Postscript

The above was originally written in response to Friedman's 1970 *JPE* article (Friedman 1970*a*). In the NBER paper, however, Friedman not only attempted to integrate his 1971 *JPE* article "A Monetary Theory of Nominal Income" into the theoretical framework discussion but he also made several textual changes in what was his 1970 argument; he specifically added four new paragraphs (pp. 27-29) which did not appear in either the 1970 or the 1971 article. Although Friedman suggests that these new paragraphs merely describe "another, more subtle difference between the approach of the economists in the Keynesian tradition and the [Friedman] approach" (p. 27), in reality these added paragraphs not only accentuate the difference between Keynes (but not the American Keynesians such as Tobin) and Friedman but they imply either an inconsistency or an incompatibility between Friedman's "transmission mechanism" and his view of the income version of the quantity theory framework.

This "subtle difference" between Keynes and Friedman, as discussed in these new paragraphs, involves the transmission mechanism through which an exogenous change in the quantity of money directly affects aggregate demand. Friedman's transmission mechanism involves wealth owners adjusting their portfolios. Not only do these portfolios consist of money and financial assets but they also encompass all kinds of easily reproducible real goods including "furniture, household applicances, clothes, and so on" (p. 29). Keynes's followers, on the other hand, concentrate on portfolio adjustments utilizing "only a small part of the total spectrum" (p. 28) of assets, namely, financial assets. The difference in these two views of the relevant spectrum of assets for portfolio choice is, according to Friedman, "largely a by-product of the different assumptions about price" (p. 28), for, in Friedman's view, Keynes and the Keynesians assume that commodity prices are fixed (but bond prices flexible) while Friedman assumes that all prices are flexible (p. 29).

Since money is held as a store of value in wealth owners' portfolios, any other asset which is thought to be a good substitute store of value must be a "temporary abode of purchasing power." Thus, in a monetary economy where "*money buys goods and goods buy money, but goods do not buy goods*" (Clower 1969, pp. 207-8), for any asset other than money to be used as a store of value in a wealth owner's portfolio, the asset must possess the ability to be resold, at a future date, in a well-organized spot market. If any durable cannot actually be resold (e.g., if a spot market for the durable does not exist), then the asset is illiquid and expected future changes in its notional price are irrelevant for portfolio choice, since once the purchase of the durable is made it is "permanent and indissoluble, like marriage, except for reason of death or other grave cause" (Keynes 1930, p. 160).

Accordingly, Friedman's added paragraphs describing his transmission mechanism require portfolio adjustments to include reproducible consumer durables (p. 29) as relevant substitutes for money as a store of value[21] in order for an exogenous change in the quantity of money to have a "direct

[21] Rather than consider the purchase of consumer durables such as clothing, appliances, etc., for their intrinsic use to satisfy consumer need.

impact on spending" (p. 28). This, in turn, requires households to expect to be able to readily resell such durables in well-organized spot markets in order to obtain generalized purchasing power whenever they desire it. But, at the very outset of his paper, Friedman categorically states that the "income version [of the quantity theory] excludes such transactions [in existing assets] completely" (p. 8). Hence, Friedman's income version framework which rejects spot market transactions is incompatible, or at least inconsistent, with his transmission mechanism which requires such spot market transactions.

Keynes, of course, was not as myopic as Friedman implies when Keynes emphasized a transmission mechanism which operated via "a fairly narrow class of financial liabilities" (p. 28). In the real world, exogenous changes in the money supply occur (except for occasional gold strikes—which, after all, can be sterilized) via open-market operations which directly induce wealth owners to adjust their portfolio holdings of financial assets (Keynes 1936, p. 197); and these financial assets possess elasticities of production and substitution similar to money. In Keynes's view, in the real world this portfolio adjustment behavior would never spill over into substituting easily reproducible durables for money as a store of value, for the former, having relatively high elasticities of production (by definition), could never be as liquid as money or financial assets. Rightly or wrongly, Keynes believed that "the attribute of 'liquidity' is by no means independent of the presence of these two characteristics [i.e., very low elasticities of production and substitution]. For it is unlikely that an asset, of which the supply can be easily increased or the desire for which can be easily diverted by a change in relative price, will possess the attribute of 'liquidity' in the minds of owners of wealth" (Keynes 1936, p. 241, n. 1).

Accordingly, Friedman's and Keynes's theoretical frameworks are in direct conflict on this issue of the spectrum of durables which possess liquidity and which therefore can be potential stores of value. In order for Friedman's transmission mechanism to be operative, all assets including easily reproducible consumer durables must be liquid in the sense that they can be resold in spot markets; for Keynes such a requirement is incompatible with the attribute of liquidity in the real world.

For reasons I have discussed at length in chapters 4, 6, 8, and 9 of my book *Money and the Real World*, the liquidity of most readily reproducible fixed-capital and consumer durable goods is always less than the liquidity associated with money and financial assets. Hence, the former are always inferior stores of value relative to the latter.[22] As Keynes noted: "So long as it is open to the individual to employ his wealth in hoarding or lending

[22] Working-capital goods, however, are somewhat different (see the appendix to chap. 4 of my book *Money and the Real World* [Davidson 1972]).

money, the alternative of purchasing actual capital assets cannot be rendered sufficiently attractive (especially to the man who does not manage the capital assets and knows very little about them), except by organizing markets wherein these assets can be easily realised for money"[23] (Keynes 1936, p. 160).

In an uncertain world of decentralized free markets and private property, private well-organized spot markets for readily reproducible durables have not been easy to develop. To Keynes, there were good theoretical as well as practical reasons why this is so.

In sum, it should be noted that this difference in Keynes's and Friedman's views about the spectrum of assets involved in a portfolio adjustment-transmission mechanism is based on the different assumptions as to the existence of well-organized spot markets for most reproducible durables and not, as Friedman claims, on different assumptions about the flexibility or fixity of (spot) asset prices.[24]

[23] See n. 20 above.

[24] Keynes would not deny that, if spot markets for all durables existed, the prices in these spot markets would be flexible. It is only in forward markets for reproducible durables that he argues that the (flow-supply) price should be sticky. Ultimately, Friedman can defend his transmission mechanism only by insisting that, in the long-run Walrasian norm or trend, there would be spot markets (organized by the ubiquitous auctioneer) for all durables at every future date, so that all assets, in the long run, possess liquidity. (I have already commented on the deficiencies of such a Walrasian defense for a monetary theory framework.)

Friedman on the Quantity Theory
and Keynesian Economics

Don Patinkin

> "When *I* use a word," Humpty Dumpty said, in rather a
> scornful tone, "it means just what I choose it to mean—
> neither more nor less."
> "The question is," said Alice, "whether you *can* make
> words mean so many different things."
> "The question is," said Humpty Dumpty, "which is to
> be master—that's all." [LEWIS CARROLL, *Through the
> Looking Glass*]

Milton Friedman's article on "A Theoretical Framework for Monetary
Analysis" has two concerns. The first and—from the viewpoint of the space
devoted to it—major one is the chapter in the history of monetary doctrine
which deals with the nature of—and interrelationships between—the
quantity theory and Keynesian monetary theory. The second concern is to
present an analytical framework to analyze the dynamics of monetary
adjustment. In this paper I shall concentrate primarily on the doctrinal
aspects of Friedman's paper.[1]

Clearly, questions about the history of economic doctrine are empirical
questions which can be answered only on the basis of evidence cited from

I am indebted to my colleagues Yoram Ben-Porath, Yoel Haitovsky, Giora Hanoch,
Ephraim Kleiman, and Josef May, and to Stanley Fischer of the University of Chicago for
helpful criticisms of early drafts of this paper.

[1] In the form in which Friedman's subsequent paper (Friedman 1971) was incorporated
into the version reproduced above, the "monetary theory of nominal income" described in
this paper is referred to as "an alternative version of the quantity theory" (p. 31 above). But
Friedman goes on immediately to say that this theory "is implicit in much recent literature
but has not heretofore been made explicit." And in his orginal paper, Friedman states that
the "monetary theory of nominal income is not new. It is implicit and parts of it explicit in
much work in the field of money *of the past two decades*" (Friedman 1971, p. 336; italics
added). From this I infer that Friedman does not present his monetary theory of nominal
income as a representation of the traditional quantity theory. Correspondingly, since my
major concern in the section which follows is with the true nature of this traditional theory, I
have not found it necessary to discuss Friedman's monetary theory of nominal income in this
context.

the relevant literature. Indeed, the "elementary canons of scholarship call for [such] documentation" (Friedman 1970c, p. 318). My criticism of Friedman is, accordingly, that on many occasions he has not provided such evidence; that, indeed, on some occasions he has ignored the detailed evidence which has been adduced against the views he expresses; and that on still other occasions he has indulged in casual empiricism in the attempt to support his doctrinal interpretations. These criticisms will be documented in what follows.

I. Friedman on the Quantity Theory:
The Doctrinal-History Aspects

In the paper under discussion, Friedman once again (see Friedman 1956, 1968) presents a theory of money whose central feature is a demand function for money, where this demand is treated "as part of capital or wealth theory, concerned with the composition of the balance sheet or portfolio of assets" (p. 11). Accordingly, his demand function depends on wealth and the alternative rates of return on money and other assets (pp. 11–14).

If Friedman had simply presented this as a conceptual framework to be used for monetary analysis, then few would have disagreed with him. On the contrary, most of us would have enjoyed the systematic clarity of the exposition; would have considered the suggested influence on the demand for money of the division between human and nonhuman wealth (which Friedman carries over from his well-known work on the consumption function) to be a fruitful one, well worth exploring; and would also have benefited from the insightful presentation of the rate of change of the price level as one of the alternative rates of return which affect the demand for money. For though this last factor has been referred to in both the quantity-theory and Keynesian literature (Fisher 1922, p. 63; Brown 1939, p. 34), it was not systematically integrated into our thinking until the work of Friedman and his associates, particularly Cagan (1956).

But, as indicated in my introductory remarks, Friedman is not concerned solely with substantive analytical matters but has a major concern with the doctrinal-history aspects of monetary theory. Once again, few would have disagreed if Friedman had described his conceptual framework as being a particular instance of the Keynesian liquidity-preference theory, while noting the specific contributions indicated in the preceding paragraph. This, however, is not Friedman's way. Instead he tells us that "the general theoretical framework that underlies" his empirical studies—and which has been referred to at the beginning of this section—is that of "the quantity theory of money" (p. 1). Accordingly, he presents this framework as the sequel to a fairly detailed presentation, first of Fisher's transactions equation, $MV=PT$ (which Friedman describes as being primarily concerned with "the mechanical aspects of the payments process");[2] then of the income form of this equation, $MV=Py$; and finally of the Cambridge cash-balance equation, $M=kPy$ (with which Friedman claims the closest affinity) (pp. 1-10).

What, then, does this leave as Keynes's contribution to his theoretical framework? Friedman's answer to this question is expressed in the following passage:

> J. M. Keynes's liquidity preference analysis (discussed further in section 5, below) reinforced the shift of emphasis from the transactions version of the quantity equation to the cash-balances version—a shift of emphasis from mechanical aspects of the payments process to the qualities of money as an asset.[3] Keynes's analysis, though strictly in the Cambridge cash-balances tradition, was much more explicit in stressing the role of money as one among many assets, and of interest rates as the relevant cost of holding money. [P. 11]

In his subsequent discussion of the demand function for money in section 5—entitled "The Keynesian Challenge to the Quantity Theory"—Friedman goes on to say:

> Keynes's basic challenge to the reigning theory [was in his proposition that the] . . . demand function for money has a particular empirical form—corresponding to absolute liquidity preference—that makes velocity highly unstable much of the time, so that changes in the quantity of money would, in the main, simply produce changes in V in the opposite direction. [P. 15]

Thus the picture which Friedman attempts to create is clear: namely, the conceptual framework he uses for monetary analysis is that of the quantity theory; its basic difference from the Keynesian theory lies in the fact that the latter assumed the demand function for money to become highly (infinitely) interest elastic. As against this picture, I would like to present the following one: the conceptual framework which Friedman uses to

---

[2] As a general characterization, this is somewhat unfair; for, as I have shown elsewhere, Fisher's analysis of the effects of a monetary change is actually far less mechanical than that of the Cambridge school (Patinkin 1965, pp. 166-67).

[3] From much the same viewpoint, one could say that Newton's theory reinforced the shift from Ptolemaic to Copernican astronomy.

analyze the demand for money is that of the Keynesian theory of liquidity preference—with Friedman's addendum that empirically this demand does not become highly (infinitely) elastic, and is indeed relatively inelastic. And, as important as are the policy implications of this addendum, we should not let it wag the theory.

It is obviously no criticism of Friedman—nor does it derogate from his stature as a monetary economist— to say that his analytical framework is Keynesian. All that is being criticized is Friedman's persistent refusal to recognize this is so.

Let me also say that to accept the Keynesian conceptual framework for the analysis of the demand for money does not imply that one must reject the quantity-theory conclusions about the long-run impact of monetary changes on the economy. This is a proposition which has been emphasized for many years in the literature (Modigliani 1944, sec. 14; Patinkin 1949, pp. 23–26; 1954; 1965, chaps. 10–11). But the converse of this proposition is also true: namely, that there is no need for modern-day quantity theorists to attempt to reinterpret the history of monetary doctrine so as to minimize the Keynesian nature of their analytical framework.

As I have shown elsewhere (Patinkin 1969a, pp. 58–61), there are two (related) justifications for the usual practice of treating the Keynesian theory as a distinct one, and not simply as a variation of the Cambridge cash-balance theory. The first is the different relationship of these two theories to one of the central distinctions of economic analysis—that between stocks and flows. In particular, Keynesian liquidity-preference theory is concerned with the optimal relationship between the stock of money and the stocks of other assets, whereas the quantity theory (including the Cambridge school) was primarily concerned with the direct relationship between the stock of money and the flow of spending on goods and services. Furthermore, the quantity-theory discussion of this relationship either did not make the distinction between stocks and flows—or at least was imprecise about it. This stands in sharp contrast with the Keynesian analysis of the effect of monetary changes in terms of initial balance-sheet adjustments among assets which generate changes in their relative yields, which in turn ultimately affect the flows of expenditures and receipts. Similarly, quantity theorists paid little, if any, attention to the effects on the rate of interest and other variables of shifts in the tastes of individuals as to the form in which they wish to hold their assets.

The second justification lies in the different treatment by these two theories of what continues to be[4] one of the central issues of monetary

---

[4] As attested particularly by the extensive empirical literature of the past fifteen years; see

economics—the influence of the rate of interest on the demand for money. For, though quantity theorists did frequently recognize this influence,[5] they did not fully integrate it into their thinking. Most revealingly, they failed to do so in their empirical work—which, by its very nature, confronted them with a concrete situation in which they were called upon to list the major theoretical variables which might explain the data, even if some of the variables might subsequently be rejected as statistically unimportant. It is therefore significant that the first empirical study (to the best of my knowledge) which explicitly deals with the influence of interest on the demand for money is the 1939 Keynesian-inspired study by A. J. Brown.[6]

These hallmarks of the Keynesian liquidity-preference theory also characterize Friedman's exposition. It should be said that Friedman has taken some account of criticisms and has in recent years partly acknowledged this intellectual indebtedness. Thus in his 1956 essay Friedman presented his analytical framework as one that "conveys the flavor" of the Chicago quantity-theory tradition of Simons, Mints, Knight, and Viner—and did not even mention Keynes or the liquidity-preference theory (Friedman 1956, pp. 3–4). In contrast, in his 1968 paper and the current essay he does not mention either the Chicago school or its individual members—and he describes his framework as "a reformulation of the quantity theory that has been strongly affected by the Keynesian analysis of liquidity preference" (Friedman 1968a, p. 439b).

At the same time, Friedman has not yet faced up to the implications of the fact[7] that whatever the similarities in policy proposals (and there are significant differences here too [Patinkin 1969a, p. 47]), the theoretical framework of the Chicago school of the 1930s and 1940s—a major center of the quantity theory at the time—differed fundamentally from his. In particular, the Chicago school—as exemplified especially by Henry Simons—was basically not interested in the demand function for money (Simons never even mentioned this concept!) and carried out its analysis instead in terms of Fisher's $MV=PT$ equation. Furthermore (and in marked contrast with Friedman) the basic assumption of the Chicago

---

the convenient summary in Laidler (1970, chap. 8), noting especially the questions relating to the rate of interest listed on p. 89.

[5] For specific references to the writings of Walras, Wicksell, the much-neglected Karl Schlesinger, Fisher, and the Cambridge school (Marshall, Pigou, and especially Lavington), see Patinkin (1965, p. 372 and supplementary notes C, D).

[6] For supporting documentation and fuller discussion of this and the preceding paragraph, see Patinkin (1969a, sec. 4).

For a more systematic and detailed treatment of the questions at issue here, see my paper on "Keynesian Monetary Theory and the Cambridge School" (1972b).

[7] Demonstrated in Patinkin (1969a, secs. 2, 3).

school analysis was that the velocity of circulation is unstable. Correspondingly, it considered sharp changes in this velocity to be a major source of instability in the economy.

Similarly, Friedman has not changed his basic contention that his conceptual framework is that of the quantity theory. Indeed, he includes a further misinterpretation of the nature of this theory. In particular, in his discussion of the transactions approach to the quantity theory, Friedman makes the familiar distinction between the Fisherine equation $MV=PT$ and the "income form of the quantity equation," $MV=Py$, where y is real national income and V accordingly represents the income velocity of circulation. He then goes on to say:

> Clearly, the transactions and income versions of the quantity theory involve very different conceptions of the role of money. For the transactions version, the most important thing about money is that it is transferred. For the income version, the most important thing is that it is held. This difference is even more obvious from the Cambridge cash-balances version of the quantity equation. Indeed, the income version can perhaps best be regarded as a way station between the Fisher and the Cambridge versions. [P. 8]

No evidence is given in support of this assertion about the nature of the income version of the transactions approach—which, if true, would obviously increase the possible relevance of Friedman's interpretation of the quantity theory in terms of the individual's demand to hold money as a component of a portfolio of assets. This is not the occasion to undertake a full-scale study of the development of the income-velocity form of the quantity theory. Let me only say that a brief examination of the interwar quantity-theory literature shows that the income-velocity approach was used as a variant of the transactions approach—and involved no more emphasis on the *holding* of money (as contrasted with its being *transferred*) than did the latter. The reasons for using income velocity were either considerations of data availability or the feeling that the volume of final output and/or the price level of this output were more meaningful economic variables than the gross volume of transactions and/or its price level (to use modern terms, more strategic variables). To the extent that the income-velocity approach constituted a "way station," it was one on the road between the Fisherine quantity theory and the Keynesian income-expenditure approach. It was not one on the road to the Cambridge cash-balance approach.[8]

[8] This paragraph is based on Robertson (1948, pp. 33, 38), Angell (1933, pp. 43-46), Warburton (1945, p. 161), and Chandler (1940, pp. 71-72; 1953, p. 543). I hope on some

I have so far criticized Friedman for claiming too much for the quantity theory; let me now indicate one direction in which he has claimed too little. This occurs in the context of his identification of the quantity theory with the short-run assumption that real income is constant, while only the price level changes (for details, see the next section). Here Friedman states:

> There is nothing in the logic of the quantity theory that specifies the dynamic path of adjustment, nothing that requires the whole adjustment to take place through P rather than through k or y. It was widely recognized that the adjustment during what Fisher, for example, called "transition periods" would in practice be partly in k and in y as well as in P. *Yet this recognition was not incorporated in formal theoretical analysis.* [Pp. 17–18; italics added]

The facts of the case, however, are quite different. Thus Fisher's analysis of the "transition period"—which was assumed to last ten years on the average, and during which both the level of real output and the velocity of circulation were changing—assigned a critical role to the difference between the money and real rates of interest. In this way Fisher integrated his analysis of the "transition period" into his formal theoretical analysis of the distinction between these two rates of interest—a distinction that was a basic component of his theoretical framework even before he turned to monetary problems. It might also be noted that Fisher wrote incomparably more on his monetary proposals for mitigating the cyclical problems of the "transition period" than on the long-run proportionality of prices to money. This concentration on short-run analysis was even more true of the policy-oriented Chicago quantity-theory school of the 1930s and 1940s: indeed, Simons and Mints showed little, if any, interest in the long-run aspects of the quantity theory. Again, representatives of the Cambridge school such as Lavington, Pigou, and Robertson wrote entire monographs on the problems of the "trade cycle" and of "industrial fluctuations"—and devoted substantial parts of these monographs to the analysis of the role of money in these fluctuations. Needless to say, this role was also a primary concern of Wicksell and Hawtrey. Thus, far from being a question dealt with in "asides," the systematic analysis of the short-run variations in output and velocity generated by monetary changes was a major concern of the pre-Keynesian quantity theorists.[9]

---

future occasion to deal more fully with this question, as well as the general question of the relations between the three forms of the quantity theory.

[9] See Fisher (1896; 1907; 1922, chap. 4). For a detailed description of Fisher's voluminous

In order to avoid any possible misunderstanding, I wish to emphasize that Friedman in his own application of his "modern quantity theory" obviously assigns a central role to the short-run effects of changes in the quantity of money on k and y; what I am criticizing here, however, is Friedman's contention that the traditional quantity theorists themselves did not recognize this role in their "formal theoretical analysis."

II. Friedman on the Quantity Theory: Some Analytical Issues

In the preceding section I have dealt with the history of doctrine. In the present section I shall turn briefly to analytical issues and again criticize Friedman for claiming too little: namely, for not presenting the long-run quantity theory in the most general way that one can, once one has decided to reformulate it. To a large extent, what is involved here is a question of tastes. My own are for introducing explicitly into the mathematical model the assumptions of the text—particularly when this yields (without much inconvenience) a more general model.

Friedman's presentation of the "simple quantity theory" is in terms of the following general equilibrium model which, "in Keynes's spirit, . . . refers to a short period in which the capital stock can be regarded as fixed" (p. 30):

$$f(y, \ r) + g(r) = y, \tag{1}$$

$$l(y, \ r) = \frac{M_0}{P}, \tag{2}$$

where y is real national income, r is the rate of interest, and M_0 is the fixed quantity of money; and where the left-hand side of (1) consists respectively of the consumption and investment functions, while the left-hand side of (2) consists of the demand function for money—all expressed in real terms (pp. 29–30, 32).

This is a system of two equations in three variables: y, P, and r. Hence, continues Friedman,

> there is a missing equation. Some one of these variables must be determined by relationships outside this system. . . . The simple quantity theory adds the equation

writings on his policy proposals (the main one of which was to stabilize the price level), see Reeve (1943, chap. 11). On the Chicago school, see Patinkin (1969a, secs. 2, 3). This question is discussed in greater detail in my paper "On the Short-Run Non-Neutrality of Money in the Quantity Theory" (Patinkin 1972a).

$$y = y_0; \tag{3}$$

that is, real income is determined outside the system. In effect, it appends to this system the Walrasian equations of general equilibrium, regards them as independent of these equations defining the aggregates, and as giving the value of [y], and thereby reduces this system to one of [two] equations determining [two] unknowns. [Pp. 31-32]

Equation (3) then permits "a sequential solution" of system (1)-(2). In particular, substituting from (3) into (1), we can solve for $r = r_0$. Substitution of this value into (2) then yields the "classical quantity equation"

$$M_0 = Pl(y_0, r_0) = P\frac{l(y_0, r_0)}{y_0}y_0 = \frac{Py_0}{V}, \tag{4}$$

which then determines P (pp. 32-33).

Instead of initially creating a problem of a "missing equation" which is then solved by determining y "outside the system," I would prefer including in the model from the very beginning that part of the "Walrasian equations of general equilibrium" needed to determine y endogenously. This preference is reinforced by the fact that all that need be added to the model for this purpose are the production function and the excess-demand equation in the labor market. For the assumption of wage and price flexibility (which, in the context of the quantity theory, is in any event being made) assures that the equilibrium level of employment will be achieved in the labor market. And since the capital stock is fixed, the production function then determines the equilibrium level of real output, y, corresponding to this level of employment. Indeed, this procedure has been the standard one in the literature since Modigliani (1944).

Again, in view of the crucial role that Friedman assigns to the real-balance effect in assuring the long-run equilibrium of the system (pp. 16, 25), I would prefer introducing this effect explicitly into the commodity-demand functions. This would also seem to provide an expression of Friedman's view that

> the key insight of the quantity-theory approach is that such a discrepancy [that is, between the nominal quantity of money demanded and supplied] will be manifested primarily in attempted spending. [P. 51]

It will not come as a surprise to the reader that these modifications yield a model which I have developed at length elsewhere (Patinkin 1954; 1965, chaps. 9-10). The long-run proportionality of P to M specified by the quantity theory holds true in this model even though it cannot, in Friedman's terms, be "solved sequentially" (or, to use the more usual term, it cannot be dichotomized), so as to reduce it to one equation (that for money) in one variable (the price level). Thus this model requires us to abandon the traditional single-equation form of the quantity theory which Friedman apparently prefers. On the other hand, the model has what is for me the more than compensating advantage of demonstrating that the long-run validity of the quantity theory does not (as it was at one time thought—and as might mistakenly be inferred from Friedman's presentation) depend on the restrictive assumption that the system can be dichotomized in the foregoing manner (Patinkin 1965, p. 175).

III. Friedman on Keynesian Economics

A Keynesian, according to Friedman, is one who makes the above system (1)-(2) determinate in the short run by adding the equation

$$P = P_0 \tag{5}$$

instead of equation (3), $y = y_0$ (pp. 15, 32). Thus, the contrast that Friedman tries to draw is between the quantity theorists—who assume real income constant and prices flexible, and indeed changing in direct proportion to changes in the money supply—and the Keynesians—who make the opposite assumptions about real income and prices.[10]

Let me first of all point out that this description of the quantity theory is misleading. For, though Friedman presents both of the foregoing positions as referring to the short run (pp. 15, 44), quantity theorists did not actually assume real income to remain constant—and the price level to change proportionately with the quantity of money—except in the long run. In the short run (as shown at the end of Section I above) they believed that a (say) decrease in the quantity of money would decrease both the velocity of circulation and the level of real output as well as the price level. Thus part of what Friedman presents as a difference between Keynes and the quantity theory is really a difference between these "runs."

Let me also say that presentations of the Keynesian theory of unemployment usually begin with an analysis based on the assumption of absolute wage and price rigidity. However, the basic question here at issue is whether these presentations have gone on to generalize the theory to the case of wage and price flexibility.

---

[10] In Friedman's n. 20, this interpretation of Keynes is slightly modified—but not in a way that really affects the following criticism.

The clear implication of Friedman's interpretation (esp. pp. 15, 18-21) is that Keynesian economics provided no such generalization. But Friedman achieves this interpretation only by overlooking the chapter in the *General Theory* devoted to—and indeed, entitled—"Changes in Money Wages,"[11] by overlooking those portions of interpretations of Keynes that he does cite in which the implications of wage and price flexibility are analyzed within the Keynesian system (for example, Tobin 1947, pp. 585-86;[12] Patinkin 1951, sec. 14; Leijonhufvud 1968, pp. 319 ff., 340 ff.),[13] and, finally, by overlooking entirely the classic interpretation of Keynes by Modigliani, which has provided the basis for so many textbook expositions. Indeed, in this interpretation the case of downward wage and price flexibility that depresses the rate of interest until it ultimately pushes the economy into the "liquidity trap" is even singled out for designation as "the Keynesian case" (Modigliani 1944, sec. 16[A]).[14]

[11] I have long considered this chapter to be the apex of Keynes's analysis (Patinkin 1951, p. 283, n. 38). In support of this interpretation let me cite its opening paragraphs: "It would have been an advantage if the effects of a change in money-wages could have been discussed in an earlier chapter. For the Classical Theory has been accustomed to rest the supposedly self-adjusting character of the economic system on an assumed fluidity of money-wages; and, when there is rigidity, to lay on this rigidity the blame of maladjustment. It was not possible, however, to discuss this matter fully until our own theory had been developed. For the consequences of a change in money-wages are complicated. A reduction in money-wages is quite capable in certain circumstances of affording a stimulus to output, as the classical theory supposes. My difference from this theory is primarily a difference of analysis; so that it could not be set forth clearly until the reader was acquainted with my own methods" (Keynes 1936, p. 257; see also pp. 231-34).

[12] Again, the opening paragraph of this article—entitled "Money Wage Rates and Employment"—indicates the perspective from which the writer approaches the question: "What is the effect of a general change in money wage rates on aggregate employment and output? To this question, crucial both for theory and for policy, the answers of economists are as unsatisfactory as they are divergent. A decade of Keynesian economics has not solved the problem, but it has made clearer the assumptions concerning economic behavior on which the answer depends. In this field, perhaps even more than in other aspects of the *General Theory*, Keynes' contribution lies in clarifying the theoretical issues at stake rather than in providing an ultimate solution" (Tobin 1947, p. 572).

[13] In presenting his interpretation of Keynes, Friedman (n. 7) expresses his indebtedness to Leijonhufvud's book. One might therefore note Leijonhufvud's view that "the most common interpretation is perhaps that, once having adopted the assumption of 'wage-rigidity' and built his model on this assumption, Keynes had little further interest in questions relating to money price flexibility. That this is a superficial explanation is apparent both from our discussion in Chapter II and from the fact that Keynes devoted a large portion of the latter half of the *General Theory* to these problems" (Leijonhufvud 1968, p. 332). One might also note that Leijonhufvud (1968, p. 332, n. 1) supports this view with a reference to my 1951 article, which, as just noted, is also referred to by Friedman.

[14] For reasons elsewhere presented (Patinkin 1965, chap. 14, sec. 3), I do not agree with this identification of Keynesian economics with the "liquidity trap"—an identification which has also been followed by Friedman (pp. 15, 21 ff.). This point is further discussed in the next section.

Friedman (p. 15) identifies Keynesian economics with price rigidity as well as the "liquidity

More specifically, in chapter 19 of the *General Theory*, Keynes analyzes in detail the ways in which a decrease in the wage rate caused by the pressure of unemployment might be expected to increase the level of employment. He argues that the main way is by the reduction in interest caused by the increase in the real quantity of money thus generated—and the consequent increase in investment. After discussing the limitations of this mechanism he concludes:

> There is, therefore, no ground for the belief that a flexible wage policy is capable of maintaining a state of continuous full employment;—any more than for the belief that an open-market monetary policy is capable, unaided, of achieving this result. The economic system cannot be made self-adjusting along these lines. [Keynes 1936, p. 267]

Thus wage rigidities in this chapter are not an *assumption* of the analysis but the *policy conclusion* which Keynes reaches after investigating the results to be expected from wage flexibility.

Let me note that Friedman does state that Keynes qualified his assumption of price rigidity by

> assuming it to apply only to conditions of underemployment. At "full" employment, he shifted to the quantity-theory model and asserted that all adjustment would be in price—he designated this a situation of "true inflation." However, Keynes paid no more than lip service to this possibility, and his disciples have done the same; so it does not misrepresent the body of his analysis largely to neglect the qualification. [P. 19]

Surely, "lip service" is hardly the term to use to describe the detailed analysis of full employment—and the consequent upward wage and price

---

trap." Actually, however, the "liquidity trap" assumes its critical role in Keynesian economics only in the case of price flexibility.

For examples of Keynesian macroeconomic-textbook analyses of wage and price flexibility under conditions of unemployment, see Klein (1947, pp. 87–90), Dillard (1948, chap. 9), Hansen (1949, pp. 122–29), McKenna (1955, chap. 12), Dernburg and McDougall (1960, pp. 144–47), Siegel (1960, pp. 225–31), Ackley (1961, pp. 191–98, 377–93), and Shapiro (1966, pp. 477–87). These discussions refer not only to the indirect effect of a wage decrease on the demand for commodities via the rate of interest but also to the direct (Pigou or real-balance) effect. Needless to say, my own discussions of these problems have included both of these effects of wage and price flexibility—and have interpreted the difference between Keynesian and classical economics within this context (see the next section). I might, however, note that I have also analyzed the case of absolute wage and price rigidity and have—for this case—drawn the contrast between Keynes and the classics in terms of the "reversal of roles" of y and p with respect to the question as to which is constant and which is variable (Patinkin 1965, chap. 13, sec. 4, esp. p. 331).

movement—which Keynes provides in the *General Theory* (1936, pp. 295-306; see also pp. 118-19, 171-74, 239-41, 289-91, 328). Indeed, despite the fact that he wrote during a period of mass unemployment, Keynes warns of the danger that wages will begin to rise with increasing unemployment even before full employment is reached (1936, p. 301). Furthermore, the upward flexibility of the wage rate under conditions of full employment is one that is basic to Modigliani's interpretation of Keynes (1944, pp. 189, 201-2)—and indeed to the standard textbook expositions of Keynesian economics. For obvious reasons, the case of full employment has concerned Keynesian economics much more since World War II than before. But to write today and "neglect as a qualification" the extensive Keynesian literature (particularly during World War II) on the inflationary gap—and the upward price movements it generates—is indeed to misrepresent the nature of this analysis.[15]

I think I can best summarize Keynes's own view of the role of price—and output—variations in his system by citing the paragraph with which he ends chapter 20 ("The Employment Function") of the *General Theory*:

> There is, perhaps, something a little perplexing in the apparent asymmetry between Inflation and Deflation. For whilst a deflation of effective demand below the level required for full employment will diminish employment as well as prices, an inflation of it above this level will merely affect prices. This asymmetry is, however, merely a reflection of the fact that, whilst labour is always in a position to refuse to work on a scale involving a real wage which is less than the marginal disutility of that amount of employment, it is not in a position to insist on being offered work on a scale involving a real wage which is not greater than the marginal disutility of that amount of employment. [Keynes 1936, p. 291]

Returning to the case of unemployment, let me now examine the evidence Friedman adduces in support of his interpretation of the role of price and wage rigidity in the Keynesian system. In this context Friedman writes:

> Keynes embodied this assumption [of wage rigidity] in his formal

[15] On Keynes's own contributions to this literature, see Klein (1947, chap. 6). Friedman (n. 11) claims to find support for his interpretation in Holzman and Bronfenbrenner's survey article (1963) in which (contends Friedman) "theories of inflation stemming from the Keynesian approach stress institutional, not monetary, factors." This contention is hardly consistent with Holzman and Bronfenbrenner's discussion (under the heading of "Demand Inflation") of "Keynesian inflation theory" in terms of the inflationary gap of the "Keynesian cross" diagram (1963, p. 53)—or with their detailed description of the literature which subsequently developed on this question (1963, pp. 55-59).

model by expressing all variables in wage units, so that his formal analysis—aside from a few passing references to a situation of "true" inflation—dealt with "real" magnitudes, not "nominal" magnitudes (Keynes 1936, pp. 119, 301, 303). [P. 18][16]

This passage reflects two basic and related misunderstandings. First, to "express all variables in wage units"—that is, to deflate nominal quantities by the wage rate—is surely not to assume that this unit is constant! This is clear from such passages in the *General Theory* as the following:

> Consumption is obviously much more a function of (in some sense) *real* income than of money income. . . . A man's real income will rise and fall . . . with the amount of his income measured in wage-units. . . . As a first approximation, therefore, we can reasonably assume that if the wage-unit changes, the expenditure on consumption corresponding to a given level of employment will, like prices, change in the same proportion. [Keynes 1936, p. 91; italics in original]

In a similar vein we find:

> Unless we measure liquidity-preference in terms of wage-units rather than that of money (which is convenient in some contexts), similar results [that is, the increased demand for nominal transactions balances] follow if the increased employment ensuing on a fall in the rate of interest leads to an increase in wages, *i.e.,* to an increase in the money value of the wage-unit. [1936, p. 172; see also pp. 248–49]

As a final example, let me cite the following:

> But if the quantity of money is virtually fixed, it is evident that its quantity in terms of wage-units can be indefinitely increased by a sufficient reduction in money-wages. [1936, p. 266]

And to those passages can be added all those cited above in which Keynes discusses the effect of full employment—and the approach thereto—on the wage unit.

Similarly, to express a model in "real magnitudes" does not mean to assume that wages and prices are rigid or exogenously determined. It is, instead, simply to assume that there is no money illusion in the system

[16] The references to the *General Theory* provided here by Friedman are not to passages dealing primarily with the procedure of measuring variables in terms of wage units, but to the allegedly "few passing references to a situation of . . . inflation."

(Patinkin 1954, 1965). Indeed, for this reason I would consider as a priori implausible any model which is *not* expressed in "real magnitudes."[17] Furthermore, this absence-of-money illusion is a necessary condition for the validity of the quantity theory. Thus, both of the quantity-theory models discussed in the preceding section—Friedman's as well as my own—are concerned solely with real variables, including real money balances. But since the nominal quantity of money is given, there is an inverse one-to-one correspondence between the level of these balances and the price level.

The major piece of additional evidence which Friedman brings in support of his interpretation of Keynesian economics is the following:

> A striking illustration [of the treatment of the price level as an institutional datum] is provided in a recent Cowles Foundation Monograph, edited by Donald Hester and James Tobin, on *Financial Markets and Economic Activity* (Hester and Tobin 1967). A key essay in that book presents a comparative static analysis of the general equilibrium adjustment of stocks of assets. Yet the distinction between nominal and real magnitudes is not even discussed. The entire analysis is valid only on the implicit assumption that nominal prices of goods and services are completely rigid, although interest rates and real magnitudes are flexible. [P. 21][18]

[17] Correspondingly, my criticism of Goldfeld (1966) on this issue would be exactly the opposite of Friedman's. Thus, compare my criticism of Arena (1963) in Patinkin (1965, p. 660) with Friedman's (n. 11) criticism of Goldfeld.

[18] In the footnote attached to this passage, Friedman cites—as an example documenting his last sentence—Tobin and Brainard's assumption "that central banks can determine the ratio of currency (or high-powered money) to total wealth including real assets"—and he contends that "if prices are flexible, the central bank can determine only nominal magnitudes, not such a real ratio." In this contention, however, Friedman is not correct. For as I have shown elsewhere, even if prices are flexible, an open-market operation by the central bank will affect the rate of interest—and hence the optimum ratio of money balances to total wealth. The reason the equilibrium rate of interest is affected in such a case—as contrasted with the case in which the quantity of money changes as a result of deficit financing—is that an open-market operation causes a change in the relative quantities of financial assets (measured in real terms) in the equilibrium portfolios of individuals. Now, a change in the price level affects the real value of nominal financial assets in an equiproportionate manner and hence cannot effect such relative changes. Correspondingly, equilibrium can be restored in this case only by variations in the relative rates of return on the various assets so as to make individuals willing to hold them in their changed proportions. The price movement which simultaneously takes place does indeed dampen the extent of the changes in the equilibrium rate(s) of interest, but, for the reasons just explained, it cannot eliminate them entirely. This argument also holds for shifts in liquidity preference as well as for the introduction of financial intermediaries or of new types of financial assets. For further details, see Patinkin (1961, pp. 109–16; 1965, chap. 10, secs. 3–4, chap. 12, secs. 4–6).

Of the five articles which Friedman cites in support of this interpretation of the Keynesian literature (n. 11), three are not relevant to the question at issue, one is relevant but not for the reason adduced by Friedman,[19] and only one is validly cited.

In particular, the three articles by Tobin and Brainard (1967), Brainard (1967), and Gramley and Chase (1965) all explicitly restrict themselves to an analysis of the nature of the stock (or balance-sheet, or asset-portfolio-composition) equilibrium achieved under the assumption that the situation in the market for the flow of current output is taken as given; correspondingly, the assumption of this analysis is not (as Friedman would have us believe) that prices are rigid while real income varies, but that—at the stage of the analysis being presented—both prices *and the flow of current income* are assumed to be held constant.[20] In the illuminating words of Brainard, the concern of these articles can be described as being "analogous to exploring the vertical displacements of the '*LM*' curve which result from monetary actions" (Brainard 1967, p. 99).

On the other hand, a valid criticism can be made of Brainard and Tobin (1968). For though most of this article is devoted to the kind of analysis described in the preceding paragraph, it does contain a section which provides for the endogenous determination of income but not of prices (pp. 112–13). And if it is this section that Friedman has in mind (he provides no specific page references), then he has a point—but only a point. For Brainard and Tobin themselves describe this section as a "primitive extension of the model" (1968, p. 112). A more basic extension—to include the production function and labor market—is not provided; and, as will be shown in the following discussion, it is these which play a vital role in the determination of absolute wages and prices in the Keynesian system.

I definitely agree that Tobin and his colleagues are to be criticized for not having made such an extension in these articles—for one of the primary

[19] I am referring here to Friedman's criticism of Goldfeld (1966); see n. 17 above. What Friedman does not, however, point out—and what is the relevant point—is that Goldfeld's study does not include the price level as an endogenous variable (Goldfeld 1966, p. 136). It should, however, be noted that one of the directions in which Goldfeld indicates that this model might be refined is that "the wage-price nexus might be introduced. This would bring in supply considerations and make the price level endogenous" (1966, p. 197). This point will be further discussed at the end of this section.

[20] See Tobin and Brainard (1967, pp. 59–60), Brainard (1967, pp. 98–100), Gramley and Chase (1965, pp. 221–22). Note also the inclusion of Y as an exogenous variable in Brainard and Tobin (1968, p. 102), in addition to the assumption of a given commodity price level (1968, p. 105). The holding of both Y and p constant at this stage of his analysis is most clear from the methodological discussion in Tobin (1969a, pp. 15–16); see also Tobin's listing of the exogenous variables in the various models he presents here (1969a, pp. 21, 24, 28). As will, however, be shown in the next paragraph, these last two articles are subject to criticism on the point at issue.

tasks of monetary theory is indeed to explain the determination of the wage and price levels.[21] But a far more important question in the present context is whether those Keynesian discussions that do extend the analysis to the labor market assumed (as Friedman contends they did) that the wage and price levels are exogenously determined.

I have already cited the contrary evidence of the analysis of the effects of wage and price flexibility in the theoretical discussions of Keynes and the Keynesians (see above). But, as before, it seems to me that the best way to answer such questions is to examine the empirical writings of the economists involved. In particular, let us see how Keynesian economists treated the wage and price level in their econometric models of the economy as a whole, for the methodology of model building requires the specification of the variables as endogenous or exogenous.

Of particular interest in this context is the work of Lawrence R. Klein, both because of its relative earliness and because of its being explicitly motivated by the desire to provide an empirical expression of the Keynesian system. The first large model (for the United States, 1921-41) constructed by Klein (in the late 1940s) does provide some support for Friedman's contention. For in analyzing the market as a whole, Klein assumes that —because of the lack of competition—"instead of taking price as the adjustment variable here, we take output" (Klein 1950, p. 102; see also pp. 50-57, 85). Nevertheless, the adjustment equation which Klein actually presents is one in which the change in the price level also appears as a variable (1950, p. 102). Furthermore, Klein explicitly treats this price level as an endogenous variable of the system as a whole (1950, p. 105).

In his subsequent work—in the early 1950s—Klein himself criticized the preceding model for giving "inadequate treatment to prices and wages, both absolute and real" and noted that "the postwar inflation showed this deficiency in a striking manner" (Klein and Goldberger 1955, p. 2). Correspondingly, in the model which they proceeded to construct (for the United States, 1929-52) Klein and Goldberger presented a "labor market adjustment equation" which is

[21] However, to maintain a proper perspective on this criticism one should remember that this, after all, is the same Tobin whom Friedman himself (n. 5) cites as being one of the first to point out the key role of the real-balance effect generated by a downward price movement in assuring the existence of a long-run equilibrium position. A characteristic of Friedman's present exposition which may partially explain his losing sight of this aspect of Tobin's work is the fact that Friedman never explicitly refers to the role of the movement of the price level in this equilibrating process; thus see Friedman (pp. 16, 25).

It is also the same Tobin who—in one of his few analyses of a model with a production function and labor market—explains that the "equilibrium absolute price level" is determined at that level "that provides the appropriate amount of real wealth in liquid form" (Tobin 1955, p. 107).

the strategic equation for determining the level of absolute wages and prices in the system. . . .

The main reasoning behind this equation is that of the law of supply and demand. Money wage rates move in response to excess supply or excess demand on the labor market. High unemployment represents high excess supply, and low unemployment below customary frictional levels represents excess demand. [1955, p. 18]

Another relevant factor is the rate of change of prices, for workers take this into account when they bargain for money wages. Thus, the rate of change of the wage rate depends on the volume of unemployment and the rate of change of the price level; and the volume of unemployment, in turn, is essentially determined as the difference between the number of people in the labor force and the input of labor as endogenously determined by the production function. Needless to say, both the wage rate and the price level are endogenous variables of this model (Klein and Goldberger 1955, pp. 17, 34–35, 37, 41, 52).

This theory of wage determination has characterized all of Klein's later work. In the revised version of the Klein-Goldberger model, much the same wage-adjustment equation is associated with the Phillips curve (Klein 1966, p. 239). In the subsequent Wharton model there is a further elaboration on the wage equation, as well as the introduction of a markup equation (which also reflects the demand situation in the market) to explain the movements of the price level (Evans, Klein, and Schink 1967, pp. 33–36). And this is carried over to the Brookings model as well (Duesenberry et al. 1965, pp. 284–85, 311). Thus in all of these models the wage rate and price level continue to be treated as endogenous variables.

That this is true not only of Klein's work can be seen most easily from the tabular survey of macroeconometric models prepared by Nerlove (1966). Of the twenty-five models there described (including the preceding four) the great majority provide for the endogenous determination of the wage and price levels.

I can most easily summarize the findings of this section by noting that they show how misleading is Friedman's contention that

initially, the set of forces determining prices was treated [by Keynesian economics] as not being incorporated in any formal body of economic analysis. More recently, the developments symbolized by the "Phillips curve" reflect attempts to bring the determination of prices back into the body of economic analysis, to establish a link between real magnitudes and the rate at which prices change from their initial historically determined level (Phillips 1958). [P. 32]

First of all, an economic analysis of wage movements was already provided by the *General Theory*. Indeed, the Phillips-curve theory itself is foreshadowed in chapters 19 and 21 of this book. Second, even before the flourishing of the Phillips curve, Keynesian econometric models generally treated the wage rate and price level as endogenous variables of the system. And this has continued to be the case.

One final observation should be made. It has already been indicated in this section that Keynesian economics is concerned with disequilibrium states, with the principal market in disequilibrium being that for labor. Correspondingly, in the Keynesian system—and particularly in the econometric expressions thereof—there is no equilibrium equation for the labor market but rather a dynamic wage-adjustment equation determining the rate of change of the nominal wage rate in response to the state of excess supply in this market. And, as we have seen, it is this equation which plays a vital role in the endogenous determination of nominal wages and prices.

It is, therefore, not surprising that an equilibrium model, without a labor market—and this is the nature of Friedman's model—does not reveal the nature of the endogenous dynamic process by which the time paths of the nominal wage rate and price level have been analyzed in the Keynesian literature.

IV. Concluding Remarks

The standard interpretation of Keynesian economics as developed by Hicks, Modigliani, and Hansen presents as its central message—and basic differentia from classical economics—the possible existence of a position of "unemployment equilibrium." Correspondingly—in order to explain how the level of unemployment remains unchanged in such a position—this interpretation assigns a crucial role to the "liquidity trap." For it is this "trap" that keeps constant the rate of interest, hence the level of aggregate demand, and hence the levels of output and employment in the economy.

Friedman follows this standard textbook interpretation in presenting the "trap"—or, to use (as Friedman does) Keynes's term, the case of "absolute liquidity preference"—as part of "Keynes's basic challenge to the reigning theory" (pp. 15, 21 ff.).[22] All this, it might be noted, is in contrast with

[22] Once again (see n. 12 above) Friedman (n. 7) cites "Leijonhufvud's penetrating analysis" in support of his (Friedman's) view—even though Leijonhufvud's actual position is exactly the opposite! Thus Leijonhufvud writes: "The 'Liquidity Trap' notion is anti-Keynesian not only in that Keynes explicitly rejected the idea that the money-demand function would be perfectly interest-elastic within any range that we would possibly be interested in, but also in its neglect of the downward shift of the entire schedule that, in a continuing state of depression, 'at long last . . . will doubtless come by itself.' Cf. *Treatise, loc. cit.*" (1968, p. 202, n. 26). Similarly, on pp. 160-61 Leijonhufvud rejects interpretations of Keynes that are based on the "liquidity trap."

Keynes's own statement that "whilst this limiting case might become practically important in the future," he knew "of no example of it hitherto" (1936, p. 207).[23]

An alternative interpretation that I have elsewhere developed[24]—and of which I have made use in the preceding section—presents Keynesian economics as the economics of unemployment *dis*equilibrium. More specifically, the fundamental issue raised by Keynesian economics is the stability of the dynamic system: its ability to return automatically to full-employment equilibrium within a reasonable time (say, a year) if it is subjected to the customary shocks and disturbances of a peacetime economy. In this context Keynesian economics contends that as a result of high interest elasticity of the demand for money and low interest elasticity of investment, on the one hand, and distribution and expectation effects, on the other, the automatic adjustment process of the market—even when aided by a monetary policy that pushes the rate of interest down—is unlikely to converge either smoothly or rapidly to the full-employment equilibrium position. And since this interpretation thus frees Keynesian economics from the confines of an equilibrium system, it also frees it from any logical dependence on the existence of a "liquidity trap."

In brief, even if monetary policy could be depended upon to ultimately restore the economy to full employment, there would still remain the crucial question of the length of time it would need. There would still remain the very real possibility that it would necessitate subjecting the economy to an intolerably long period of dynamic adjustment: a period during which wages, prices, and interest would continue to fall, and—what is most important—a period during which varying numbers of workers would continue to suffer from involuntary unemployment. Though I am not aware that he expressed himself in this way, this is the essence of Keynes's position. This is all that need be established in order to justify his fundamental policy conclusion that the "self-adjusting quality of the economic system"—even when reinforced by central-bank policy—is not enough, and that resort must also be had to fiscal policy.

Thus this interpretation takes the debate on the degree of government intervention necessary for a practicable full-employment policy—which is the basic policy debate between Keynes and the classics—out of the realm of those questions that can be decided by a priori considerations of internal

---

[23] This contrast—as well as the passage from Keynes just cited in the text—is further discussed in Patinkin (1965, pp. 349, 352-54, esp. n. 29). This passage is also referred to by Friedman (pp. 25-26).

[24] The following three paragraphs draw freely on the discussions in Patinkin (1951, sec. 14; 1965, chap. 14 and suppl. n. K:3).

consistency and logical validity, and into the realm of those questions that can be decided only by empirical considerations of the actual magnitudes of the relevant economic parameters.

Friedman can undoubtedly point to passages in his article which agree with this last sentence (for example, p. 61). The trouble is that there are many more passages in which he presents quite a different interpretation of the relations between Keynes and the classics. It is these other passages which constitute the major part of his article—and to which, accordingly, my own has been devoted.

I would like to conclude this paper with one observation of an analytical nature on the dynamic equations which Friedman presents in his paper (p. 49). These, unfortunately, are not the structural equations that one might have expected from Friedman's opening statement that the purpose of this paper is to present the theoretical framework implicit in his and Anna Schwartz's book on *A Monetary History of the United States* (1963b).[25] Instead, they are essentially reduced-form equations. The coefficients of these equations are undoubtedly dependent on the elasticities of the structural equations, as well as on their respective speed-of-adjustment parameters. But since Friedman does not specify the nature of this dependence, his dynamic equations do not enable us to investigate what is, after all, one of the basic questions at issue: namely, the way in which—in a given policy context—different assumptions about the various elasticities of demand and dynamic parameters affect the respective time paths of price and output in the system.

[25] Nor, correspondingly, does Friedman's present discussion provide any additional details about the admittedly "tentative" dynamic analysis which he sketched in Friedman and Meiselman (1963, pp. 217–22) and Friedman and Schwartz (1963a, sec. 3). The main point of this analysis is that monetary changes initially generate portfolio-composition (balance-sheet) adjustments, and hence changes in the prices (and hence rates of return) of the assets (including consumer durables) held in the portfolio; these, in turn, generate changes in the demands for commodity flows and hence in their prices and/or output.

In the revised version of his *JPE* papers as reprinted above, Friedman added four paragraphs at the end of section 5 in which he summarizes—without further elaboration—his earlier analysis referred to in the preceding paragraph of this footnote. As in this earlier analysis, Friedman emphasizes that the range of assets over which he carries out his analysis of balance-sheet adjustments is broader than that of Keynesian economics. With this there can be no disagreement. Nor, obviously, would I disagree with the contention that the quantity theorists assumed that a monetary increase increases the demand for commodities even without a prior decrease in the rate of interest on bonds, for this contention can (pragmatically speaking) simply be interpreted as an alternative statement of the real-balance effect (cf. Patinkin [1965, p. 664, n. 44] for an interpretation of Friedman's analysis here in precisely these terms). But what cannot be accepted—for the reasons discussed in Section I above—is any implication that Friedman's analysis here is a proper representation of the traditional quantity theory. On the contrary (as indicated above), this highly sophisticated stock-flow analysis of Friedman's is far closer in its conceptual framework to that of Keynesian monetary theory than to that of the quantity theory.

Comments on the Critics

Milton Friedman

> We are, as I have said, one equation short. Yet it might
> be a provisional assumption of a rigidity of money wages,
> rather than of real wages, which would bring our theory
> nearest to the facts. . . . A theory cannot claim to be a
> *general* theory, unless it is applicable to the case where
> (or, the range within which) money wages are fixed.
> [KEYNES, *General Theory*, p. 276]

Here, in Keynes's own words, is the kernel of my interpretation of the distinctive feature of what I called the "Keynesian challenge to the quantity theory."[1] My discovery of this passage in the *General Theory* in the course of preparing this reply reinforces my confidence that the interpretation is valid. Yet three of the five scholars who have done me the honor of commenting on my article reject that interpretation. I believe that all three are mistaken. I conjecture that Tobin is led into error because he interprets the *General Theory* from a methodological point of view alien to Keynes; Davidson and Patinkin, because they mistake minor themes in the *General Theory* for its central message.

Despite this element of overlap, I reply to each criticism separately, both because the critics support their rejection of my interpretation of Keynes on different grounds, but mainly because this rejection is only a minor theme in some of the comments.

I largely agree with the observations of Brunner and Meltzer, who do not comment in any detail on my interpretation of Keynes. The appearance of disagreement simply reflects their gracious assumption that my objective was much more ambitious than it was. Accordingly, I discuss their comment first.

I am in debt for helpful comments on an earlier draft of this reply to Armen Alchian, Robert Clower, and Robert J. Gordon, and also to Allan Meltzer, Paul Davidson, James Tobin, and Don Patinkin. The usual disclaimer of their responsibility for my mistakes is more than usually relevant.
[1] This passage is imbedded in a discussion of Pigou's *Theory of Unemployment* with which Keynes was contrasting his own theory.

Tobin's comment, like Brunner and Meltzer's, is analytical. Hence, I deal with it next.

In writing this article, I did not intend to engage in doctrinal history and did not express any such intention. I made no attempt to present a comprehensive survey of the development of either the quantity theory or the Keynesian theory. I used references to earlier writers as expository devices to bring out analytical points rather than for their own sake.

Yet both Davidson and Patinkin regard my article as devoted not only to analysis but also to the history of thought—indeed, Patinkin terms this the "major" concern of the paper—and criticize it primarily from this viewpoint. Their contention that I do not present a fully documented account of the contributions of individual scholars, and of the temporal succession of ideas, is entirely correct. That was not my aim, and I should have made it crystal clear that it was not. In my own defense, however, the very absence of such documentation for statements that I intended to be analytical but that Patinkin in particular interprets as concerned with doctrinal history might well have been regarded as evidence of my intentions rather than my performance.

However, both Davidson and Patinkin object not only to what they regard as my forays into the history of thought but also to my analytical interpretation of the doctrines I discuss. In this respect, both seem to me mistaken.

I deal with Davidson first, because his criticism is simpler.

Though I leave Patinkin to the last, that is the reply that concerns me most. This is only one of three articles in which Patinkin has, as I see it, given a misleading impression not only of my work but, more important, of the Chicago tradition that inspired that work (Patinkin 1969a, 1972a). And one of those articles served as the foundation for the even more misleading discussion of that tradition by Harry Johnson in his Ely lecture (Johnson 1971). Accordingly, I am pleased to have this opportunity to document a Chicago tradition that is more distinctive, more important, and more encompassing than readers of Patinkin's and Johnson's articles might suppose.

One reward from writing this reply has been the necessity of rereading earlier work, in particular the *General Theory*. The *General Theory* is a great book, at once more naïve and more profound than the "Keynesian economics" that Leijonhufvud contrasts with the "economics of Keynes."

The heart of the *General Theory* is an extremely simple hypothesis— that a highly unstable marginal efficiency schedule of investment and a liquidity preference function that is highly elastic at low rates of interest and unstable at higher rates of interest are the key to short-run economic movements. That is what gives investment its central role, what makes the consumption function and the multiplier the key concepts, what enables Keynes to develop his theory for 165 pages without having to introduce the quantity of money.

Of course, the hypothesis is oversimplified. But Keynes was no Walrasian seeking, like Patinkin, and to a lesser extent Tobin, a general and abstract system of all-embracing simultaneous equations. He was a Marshallian, an empirical scientist seeking a simple, fruitful hypothesis. And his was a new, bold, and imaginative hypothesis, whose virtue was precisely how much it could say about major problems on the basis of so little. Of course, his assumptions were not in literal correspondence with reality. If they had been, he would have been condemned to pedestrian description; his whole theory would have lost its power. Of course, he could be wrong. There is no point to any scientific theory that cannot be. The greater the range of evidence that, if observed, would contradict a theory, the more precise are its predictions and the better a theory it is *provided it is not, in fact, contradicted.*

I believe that Keynes's theory is the right kind of theory in its simplicity, its concentration on a few key magnitudes, its potential fruitfulness. I have been led to reject it, not on these grounds, but because I believe that it has been contradicted by evidence: its predictions have not been confirmed by experience. This failure suggests that it has not isolated what are "really" the key factors in short-run economic change.

The *General Theory* is profound in the wide range of problems to which Keynes applies his hypothesis, in the interpretations of the operation of modern economies and, particularly, of capital markets that are strewn throughout the book, and in the shrewd and incisive comments on the theories of his predecessors. These clothe the bare bones of his theory with an economic understanding that is the true mark of his greatness.

Rereading the *General Theory* has not only reinforced my confidence in the validity of the interpretation in my article; much more important, it has also reminded me what a great economist Keynes was and how much more I sympathize with his approach and aims than with those of many of his followers.

Brunner-Meltzer

Apparently, I failed to make clear the purpose and scope of my article. It does not, as Brunner and Meltzer assume, present a fully developed theory that is intended to have as implications all of the empirical regularities that those of us working in this area have isolated. My aim was much less ambitious. It was to outline a general approach that could suggest what empirical issues required study, an approach that could then be elaborated in further detail in connection with such empirical studies.[2] I viewed the article as supplementing, not replacing, my other writings, as another piece of a continuing endeavor, not as the final word.

In particular, the so-called common model, which occupies four pages in the article, receives far more attention than it deserves, not only from Brunner and Meltzer but also from the other commentators. This model was specifically designed to bring out the *defects* in both main approaches. For that very reason, it suppressed all complications not relevant for that purpose and was introduced as "a highly simplified aggregate model." My list of unresolved problems ends by stressing that "the central common defect of the two approaches" is that neither "has anything to say about the factors that determine the proportions in which a change in nominal income will, in the short run, be divided between price change and output change" (pp. 29, 44). Yet Brunner and Meltzer have interpreted my presenting the "common model" as meaning that I believe it is desirable and necessary "to divide macroeconomic problems into two sets—unemployment in which prices are fixed *or* inflation in which output is fixed"! Since, like them, I believe the exact opposite, I must have failed dismally to convey what I intended.

In combining the two articles into a National Bureau of Economic Research Occasional Paper, I was led by some initial reactions to the first article to include four additional paragraphs on the difference between our approach and the Keynesian approach. If these paragraphs had been in the original article, they might well have removed some of Brunner and Meltzer's misconceptions.[3]

With this background, I can deal briefly with Brunner and Meltzer's summary of the "four types of criticisms" they offer to my approach.

1. "The restrictions that he imposes on the standard theory to remove any short-term effect of changes in interest rates, fiscal variables, and the stock of securities are not well supported by evidence."

Granted. I never said they were. Indeed, I did not impose them, except in the one section on "The Common Model," and there not on empirical grounds but for the analytical purpose of highlighting what I regard as the key difference between the quantity theory and the income-expenditure theory. Note that for this purpose I also neglected "stochastic distur-

---

[2] Aside from the frequent references to "framework," "abstract level," "highly simplified," etc., note the explicit statement, "still other parts of the theoretical framework are developed more fully in the course of the empirical analysis of some of the issues raised in the other chapters of the book from which this paper is abstracted" (p. 48, n. 31).

[3] See pp. 27–29 above.

bances." I surely did not do that because I regarded their unimportance as "well established by the evidence." I really am puzzled that Brunner and Meltzer could have inflated the role of the common model as much as they did.

2. "The framework does not imply some of the main propositions that have been developed in recent years. . . . For example, there is no mention of the variability of the lag in monetary policy. The gradual adjustment of the price level following the adjustment of real output is either assumed or is not obtained at all."

Unless I am greatly mistaken this is wrong. I may not have mentioned "the variability of the lag in monetary policy," but as figure 3 of my paper illustrates, the framework does imply a lag that depends on the path of the monetary disturbances fed into the system. Hence, even in the system as explicitly written, the framework does imply variability of the lag, and surely it can be taken for granted that stochastic disturbances must be added to all of the equations before they are used to interpret historical data, which would add still another source of variability. There is a sense in which the gradual adjustment of the price level is assumed, but surely this feature is consistent with, if not implied by, equations (45), (46), and (48).

3. "The framework ignores some main developments in economic theory during the past ten years that have important bearing on the issues discussed . . . [such as the introduction of] cost of acquiring information, cost of search, and adjustment."

I plead guilty. I agree that these have been important developments. But I must confess that even on further consideration they seem to me irrelevant to my limited purpose, except to the extent that they indirectly motivate the emphasis that I give to anticipated rates of change. In this connection I might well have referred to the important writings of Stigler, Alchian, and others.

4. "The explanation of fluctuations in prices and output has very little relation to the static theory of prices and output."

This criticism baffles me. For example, Brunner and Meltzer say, "No doubt a set of postulates can be introduced to reconcile the two, but only at the cost of eliminating interest rates and the negatively sloped *IS* curve from the 'common model' or including interest rates in the adjustment equation." And again, "His differential equations describing the adjustment of output contain neither real balances nor relative prices (including interest rates)."

But of course interest rates are in the adjustment equation for nominal income (eq. [48]), as I say explicitly (pp. 52, 53) referring back to the demand for money equation in an earlier section, which includes three different interest rates plus the rate of change of prices. And so also, by the same argument, is wealth, the channel through which the real balance effect operates. Further, the adjustment equation for nominal income enters the adjustment equation for output, so these variables are all in that equation as well.[4]

* * *

All in all, I agree with Brunner and Meltzer that the framework I present is only a beginning. Their own specific model, as outlined in Brunner (1970) and Brunner and Meltzer (1971, 1972) is a special extension and development of that framework. I applaud and welcome their efforts in that direction, without necessarily accepting the details of their model.

Tobin

1. The Main Issue between Monetarists and Neo-Keynesians

Substantively, the most important point in Tobin's comment is his contention that the main issue between "monetarists and the neo-Keynesians" is "the shape of the LM locus"—namely, that what he regards as characteristic monetarist propositions require the LM curve to be vertical, whereas neo-Keynesian propositions rest on the LM curve being positively sloped. I thought that I had disproved this contention in

[4] Similarly, I am baffled by their n. 9 in which they regard these differential equations as implying a modification of the monetary rule I have long supported of a fixed rate of growth of the quantity of money, as implying that "the appropriate rate of growth of money is no longer a constant but a variable dependent on past monetary policy."

It has no such implication except for the transition to a constant rate of monetary growth and that requires no modification of what they call the Simons-Friedman tradition. Henry Simons before me, and I in his footsteps, recognized that how one should move to a constant growth path depends on where you start, that it would have been absurd to append a constant growth path to the 1933 money stock, for example, or to the 1948 money stock, that it was desirable to start the long-run growth path from a position of rough monetary equilibrium, not from a position of significant disequilibrium.

In purely mathematical terms, the initial position determines the transient part of the solution to the differential equations. Constant monetary growth is a prescription for the permanent part.

detail in an article on "Interest Rates and the Demand for Money," published in 1966 (reprinted in Friedman 1969). Since Tobin apparently finds that answer unsatisfactory, I shall comment first on this key point.

In my 1966 article, I concluded, "In my opinion, no 'fundamental issues' in either monetary theory or monetary policy hinge on whether the estimated elasticity [of demand for money with respect to the interest rate] can for most purposes be approximated by zero or is better approximated by —.1 or —.5 or —2.0, provided it is seldom capable of being approximated by —∞" (Friedman 1969, p. 155).

Of the six propositions that Tobin uses to illustrate the opposite contention, it is revealing that one of the three that he alleges to be monetarist is about the effects of real magnitudes on real magnitudes, whereas what I regard as truly "characteristic monetarist" propositions are about the effect of nominal magnitudes on nominal and real magnitudes and are not among any of his six.[5] His third allegedly monetarist proposition asserts that the demand for real balances depends solely on real income. I have never argued that, and I do not know any other monetarist who has. In any event, I demonstrated in my 1966 article that a divorce between monetary and real factors, of the kind embodied in his propositions *a, b,* and *c,* is entirely consistent with a positively sloping *LM* curve.[6] Having done so, I stressed that I did not myself believe that a model which involved such a divorce was "the most useful, or even *a* useful model to interpret reality. On the contrary," I wrote, "...I am myself persuaded that it is far more useful to introduce interactions between the real and monetary sectors" (Friedman 1969, p. 151).

Of Tobin's remaining three propositions, I accept his propositions *d* and *f* as both correct and entirely consistent with a monetarist view (as I shall demonstrate below) but as not in any way a necessary implication of

[5] His proposition *a* comes closest to containing a "characteristic monetarist" proposition, but even that is marred by overstatement. I know of no monetarist who regards velocity as an unchangeable constant apart from stochastic disturbances and hence who would regard a change in *M* as both a necessary and sufficient condition for a change in Tobin's *Yp.* I have elsewhere tried to list "systematically the central propositions of monetarism" (Friedman 1970*b*, pp. 22–26).

[6] In the 1966 article I noted that in the flexible price, full-employment version of the Hicks *IS-LM* model, the "divorce of money from real factors in the sense under discussion requires that there be a way of expressing the equations comprising the theoretical model such that it has a subset of equations sufficient to determine the real magnitudes which do not contain as separate variables either the nominal quantity of money or the price level. In that case, the system of equations simultaneously determining the real and monetary variables can be dichotomized into one set which determines the level of real income and the interest rate and a second set which together with the solution of the first set determines the level of nominal income and the price level, and this is true regardless of whether the demand equation for money in the second set has the interest rate as one of its variables" (Friedman 1969, p. 150).

a positively sloped *LM* curve.[7] His proposition *e* is partly factually correct, partly factually wrong, but in any event is a pure assertion that is not dependent in any way on the *LM* curve, which is drawn in real terms, hence cannot imply anything about price changes.[8]

I fear Tobin is right that his six propositions are "the stuff of macro-economics courses all over the country." Yet they conceal rather than reveal why both monetarists and neo-Keynesians accept the *LM* curve as positively sloped and nonetheless come out with very different conclusions on many issues, particularly the effects of fiscal and monetary policy. Perhaps it will clarify matters if, instead of analyzing Tobin's propositions further, I try to translate a truly characteristic monetarist proposition into Tobin's simple *IS-LM* terms.

Some five years ago, I examined in a number of *Newsweek* columns the likely effect of tax increases that were being recommended as a means of curbing inflation—recommendations that led to the tax surcharge enacted in 1968. Herewith excerpts from two columns, with numbers added in parentheses to facilitate reference.

"I do not share the widespread view that a tax increase which is not matched by higher government spending will necessarily have a strong braking effect on the economy.

(1) "True, higher taxes would leave taxpayers less to spend. But this is only part of the story. If government spending were unchanged, more of it would now be financed by the higher taxes, and the government would have to borrow less. *The individuals, banks, corporations or other lenders from whom the government would have borrowed now have more left to spend or to lend—and this extra amount is precisely equal to the reduction in the amount available to them and others as taxpayers.* If they spend it themselves, this directly offsets any reduction in spending by taxpayers. (2) If they lend it to business enterprises or private individuals—as they can by accepting a lower interest rate for the loans—the resulting increase in business investment, expenditures on residential building, and so on indirectly offsets any reduction in spending by taxpayers.

(3) "To find any *net* effect on private spending, one must look farther beneath the surface. Lower interest rates make it less expensive for people to hold cash. Hence, some of the funds not borrowed by the Federal government may be added to idle cash balances rather than spent or loaned. In addition, it takes time for borrowers and lenders to adjust to

[7] Because the effects he attributes to a positively sloped curve could be completely offset by price and wage flexibility which shifted the curve.

[8] The factually wrong part is the assertion that the quantity of money and velocity tend to move in opposite directions; generally, they move in the same direction.

reduced government borrowing. (4) However, any net decrease in spending from these sources is certain to be temporary and likely to be minor.

(5) "To have a significant impact on the economy, a tax increase must somehow affect monetary policy—the quantity of money and its rate of growth" (*Newsweek*, January 23, 1967, p. 86; italics in original, numbers added).

"Whether deficits produce inflation depends on how they are financed. (6) If, as so often happens, they are financed by creating money, they unquestionably do produce inflationary pressure. (7) If they are financed by borrowing from the public, at whatever interest rates are necessary, they may still exert some minor inflationary pressure. (8) However, their major effect will be to make interest rates higher than they would otherwise be" (*Newsweek*, August 7, 1967, p. 68; numbers added).

To translate:

For points 1, 2, 3, and 4 implicitly, as for point 7 explicitly, it is assumed that the quantity of money or its rate of growth is not affected by the rise in taxes. Hence, what is involved, in Tobin's terms, is a leftward shift in the IS curve (part of his proposition d) which tends to lower the interest rate (point 2). If prices are assumed unaffected, the LM curve is unchanged, but since it slopes positively, the effect is to reduce real income (point 3). If prices were to decline, the LM curve would shift to the right, adding to the downward pressure on the interest rate but offsetting the downward pressure on real income.

So far, Tobin would, I believe, agree completely. The difference begins with item 4. Why "certain to be temporary"? Because the leftward shift in the IS curve is a once-for-all shift, even though the reduced deficit or increased surplus produced by a tax rise with no change in government spending were to continue indefinitely. Put in monetarist terms, the lowered interest rate resulting from the federal government's absorbing a smaller share of annual savings will reduce velocity; the transition to the lower velocity reduces spending for a given money stock (Tobin's proposition f), but once the new velocity is reached there is no further downward pressure.

Why "likely to be minor"? Because the monetarist view is that "saving" and "investment" have to be interpreted much more broadly than neo-Keynesians tend to interpret it, that the categories of spending affected by changes in interest rates are far broader than the business capital formation, housing construction, and inventory accumulation to which the neo-Keynesians tend to restrict "investment." Hence, even a fairly substantial tax increase will produce only a minor shift in the IS curve.[9] Further, while

[9] Note that what is at issue is not primarily the "elasticity" of saving or investment, though

the *LM* curve slopes positively, it is very far from being horizontal, so that the reduction in income associated with a "minor" shift in the *IS* curve will also be minor.

Of course, the terms "temporary" and "minor" are highly imprecise. We get closer to a rigorous statement by comparing the changes resulting from a reduced or increased deficit without any change in monetary growth with those that result when a change in the deficit is matched by a dollar-for-dollar change in monetary growth (points 6, 7, and 8). To interpret these, we must shift gears from the reduction in the deficit assumed in the first excerpt to the increase in the deficit assumed in the second.

Point 7 is the counterpart of the first excerpt: a deficit financed by borrowing, involving, in Tobin's terms, a once-for-all shift to the right in the *IS* curve, a higher interest rate, a higher velocity, and a higher level of spending for a given monetary growth path. Point 6 involves financing the deficit by creating money, which shifts the *LM* curve to the right (so long as prices are assumed constant). But this is not a once-for-all shift. So long as the deficit continues, and continues to be financed by creating money, the nominal money stock continues to grow and the *LM* curve (at initial prices) continues to move to the right. Is there any doubt that this effect must swamp the effect of the once-for-all shift of the *IS* curve? Of course, if prices react, we get into a new set of issues. The rightward movement of the *LM* curve is then offset, but also we need to introduce a distinction between nominal and real interest rates, and the simple *IS-LM* diagram will no longer do.

We may put this point differently. Assume a one-year increase in the deficit, with the budget then returning to its initial position. If this is financed by borrowing from the public with no change in monetary growth, then, in the most rigid Keynesian system, the *IS* curve moves to the right and then back again; real and nominal income rise for one year, then return to their initial values. If the one-year increase in the deficit is financed by creating money, the *LM* curve moves to the right as well, *and stays there* after the *IS* curve returns to its initial position. If prices remain constant, real and nominal income stay at a higher level indefinitely. If, as is more reasonable, prices ultimately rise, real income may return to its initial level, but nominal income will stay at a higher level indefinitely. Surely, to paraphrase a remark of Tobin's in another connection, the monetary effect is "alchemy of a much deeper significance" than the fiscal effect.

---

monetarists would probably set that elasticity higher than neo-Keynesians, but rather the absolute magnitude affected (the position of the relevant investment and saving curves).

But what about the evidences of debt created in the first case? Do they not stay permanently? As Tobin says, "Is a 'rain' of Treasury bills...of no consequence for the price level, while a 'rain' of currency inflates prices proportionately?" The answer is that the evidences of government debt are largely in place of evidences of private debt—people hold Treasury bills instead of bills issued by, for example, U.S. Steel. The total nominal volume of debt grows by less—and I believe much less—than the size of the deficit. Moreover, even this growth is offset by two other factors: the increase expected in future tax liabilities accompanying the growth of the government debt, which Tobin refers to; and the reduction in the physical volume of assets created because of lowered private productive investment. On the other hand, the dollar bills are a net addition to the total nominal volume of assets.

This analysis is, of course, greatly oversimplified. The effects of changes in asset structure are far more complex. They clearly deserve investigation and cannot be simply dismissed. Yet, I believe that even these brief remarks indicate that they are of a different order than the effect of financing deficits by creating money.[10]

So far as this particular analysis is concerned, the difference between Tobin and myself, if there is one, is partly different empirical assumptions; mostly, whether one considers only the impact effect of a change or the cumulative effect. This same difference arises in another connection and is discussed further in section 4 below on the "first-round effect." At any rate, the main issue between us clearly is not and never has been whether the *LM* curve is vertical or has a positive slope.

Emphasis on the "first-round effect" by the Keynesians and neo-Keynesians contributes, I believe, to their tendency to regard prices and wages as an institutional datum and to neglect the effects of price flexibility. But it may be that, at least for the neo-Keynesians, I was mistaken in regarding their treatment of price flexibility as *the* main issue between them and the monetarists. Perhaps the emphasis on first-round effect is *the* main issue and their treatment of price flexibility a minor corollary.

Tobin objects to my interpretation of the main issue because he "had thought that both monetarists and neo-Keynesians agreed that short-run variations of money income . . . were generally divided between changes in output and changes in price. . . . It is equally a caricature of the neo-Keynesian view to say that p is an 'institutional datum' in the short run. Keynes certainly did not make this assumption. . . . Keynes did not even assume a constant wage rate."

[10] In terms of real rather than nominal magnitudes, the difference can be interpreted as reflecting the effect of using different tax structures to finance government expenditures.

These objections seem to me largely beside the point. I said, "Whatever the first group [the neo-Keynesians] may say in their asides and in their qualifications, they treat the price level as an institutional datum in their formal theoretical analysis" (p. 20). I did not intend this statement to mean that neo-Keynesians assert that prices and wages are in fact constant, or even that in their empirical work they do not introduce relations designed to predict the movements of prices and wages. If I gave that impression, Tobin is right to correct it. Treating the price level or the wage level as an institutional datum, or, as Keynes did, as the "numeraire," is not equivalent to asserting that wages or prices are constant. It means, rather, that the theory in question has nothing to say about what determines the wage level; that the forces determining the wage level are forces abstracted from in the theory. This is clearly reflected in the fact that the relations neo-Keynesians introduce into their empirical work to predict prices and wages tend to be largely ad hoc (see also point 11 in Appendix 2 below).

It is important to distinguish between the logical implications of a theory and the statements about observable phenomena that a professed adherent of the theory may make. As Keynes says, "We can keep 'at the back of our heads' the necessary reserves and qualifications and the adjustments which we shall have to make later on" (Keynes 1936, p. 297). Of course, both the neo-Keynesians and Keynes himself recognize that, as a factual matter, changes in income are partly in prices and partly in output; and, of course, both have instructive ideas and insights about the factors that determine the division in particular cases. But Keynes's formal theory, as I demonstrate more fully in my reply to Davidson, has nothing to say about what determines the absolute price or wage level, though it does have some implications for the behavior of prices relative to wages. Tobin's statement to the contrary in his footnote 5 is wrong. The elasticity Tobin refers to is purely definitional, and Keynes's discussion of it consists simply of expressing an arithmetical identity in terms of elasticities (see n. 15 in my reply to Davidson). Similarly, Tobin's assertion later on that "Keynes certainly included in his system a relationship between real output and the price level, derived from a theory of labor demand and supply" is correct about the price level in wage units; it is wrong about the price level in money units.

2. Tobin's Interpretation of My Words

Much of the rest of Tobin's criticism of my article leaves me utterly baffled. We seem to be talking at cross-purposes. I disagree far less with the substance of what he says than with the views that he attributes to me—which repeatedly seem to me in clear and present conflict with what I have written. And, no doubt, he has the same difficulty with my remarks (see also Tobin 1970; Friedman 1970*c*).

Let me try to document my bafflement with some specific examples.

a) Tobin devotes nearly a third of his comment to analyzing the implications of my "third way" for real income, real saving, and real investment. He treats my model as if it had been developed for that purpose.

Yet I stated that this third way "involves bypassing the breakdown of nominal income between real income and prices and using the quantity theory to derive a theory of nominal income rather than a theory of either prices or real income" (p. 34). I discussed briefly the real model Tobin elaborates and concluded that "for both empirical and theoretical reasons, I am inclined to reject this way of marrying the real and the nominal variables and to regard the saving-investment sector as unfinished business, even on the highly abstract general level of this paper" (p. 40).

Is Tobin's reaction not equivalent to criticizing a proposed cure for the measles because it does not also cure the mumps?

b) TOBIN: Friedman "doubts that the real rate should really be regarded as a constant in the short run [for analyzing real investment and saving]. . . . Friedman finds it easy to accept the assumption of his model that the only short-run fluctuations of nominal interest rates relevant to the demand for money are those associated with the inflation premium. This is not consistent with his acknowledgment that real rates relevant for investment and saving decisions vary in the short run."

FRIEDMAN: "It seems entirely satisfactory to take the anticipated real interest rate . . . as fixed for the demand for money. There, the real interest rate is at best a supporting actor. Inflation and deflation are surely center stage. Suppressing the variations in the real interest rate . . . is unlikely to introduce serious error. The situation is altogether different for saving and investment. Omitting the real interest rate in that process is to leave out Hamlet" (p. 40).

c) TOBIN: "This relates the procyclical movement of velocity to the procyclical movement of interest rates—superficially, at least, the orthodox Keynesian interpretation which Friedman has so stubbornly resisted for so long."

FRIEDMAN (in a 1959 article on "The Demand for Money" [reprinted in Friedman 1969] to which Tobin's "so long" presumably refers): "These results [about the cyclical movements of velocity and interest rates] are of the kind that might be expected if the returns on alternative ways of holding assets were the chief factor other than permanent income affecting desired cash balances. . . . The remaining movement in velocity, though . . . it may well be accounted for by movements in interest rates, is much too small to reflect any very sensitive adjustment of cash balances to interest rates" (Friedman 1969, pp. 136, 137).

d) FRIEDMAN: "On an analytical level, it [the quantity theory] is an analysis of the factors determining the quantity of money the community wishes to hold; on an empirical level, it is the generalization that changes in desired real balances (in the demand for money) tend to proceed slowly and gradually or to be the result of events set in train by prior changes in supply, whereas, in contrast, substantial changes in the supply of nominal balances can and frequently do occur independently of any changes in demand" (p. 3).

Tobin gives six alternative meanings of "the long-run quantity theory." One of them, his number 4, can be regarded as corresponding to the "analytical" level in my statement. None of them corresponds to the "empirical" level (his item 3 on first reading can be read as if it does, but his further explanation makes it clear that he does not interpret it that way).

3. *What Explains the Difficulty of Communication?*

One explanation for the failure of communication that long appealed to me is the one I gave in my article, namely, that our qualification of our statements "by referring to their effect on *nominal* income . . . appeared meaningless to economists who implicitly identified nominal with real magnitudes. Hence they have misunderstood our conclusions" (p. 27). But that explanation must clearly be rejected since it can hardly apply to Tobin's present comment.

The alternative that now appeals to me is that the difficulty is a different approach to the use of economic theory—the difference between what I termed a Marshallian approach and a Walrasian approach in an article I wrote many years ago (Friedman 1949, reprinted in Friedman 1953). From a Marshallian approach, theory is, in Marshall's words, "an engine for the discovery of concrete truth." In this view, "Economic theory . . . has two intermingled roles: to provide 'systematic and organized methods of reasoning' about economic problems; to provide a body of substantive hypotheses, based on factual evidence, about the 'manner of action of causes.' In both roles the test of the theory is its value in explaining facts, in predicting the consequences of changes in the economic environment. Abstractness, generality, mathematical elegance—these are all secondary, themselves to be judged by the test of application" (Friedman 1953, pp. 90–91). On this view, there is no such thing as "the" theory, there are theories for different problems or purposes; there is nothing inconsistent or wrong about using a theory that treats the real interest rate as constant in analyzing fluctuations in nominal income but using a theory that treats the real interest rate as variable in analyzing fluctuations in real income; the one theory may be more useful for the one purpose, the other theory for the other. We lose generality by this procedure but gain simplicity and precision.

From a Walrasian approach, "abstractness, generality, and mathematical elegance have in some measure become ends in themselves, criteria by which to judge economic theory. Facts are to be described, not explained. Theory is to be tested by the accuracy of its 'assumptions' as photographic descriptions of reality, not by the correctness of the predictions that can be derived from it" (Friedman 1953, p. 91). If the real interest rate enters one part of the model it must be used in all, hence it is logically inconsistent and presumably invalid to regard it as constant for one purpose but as variable for another.

The economic principle of equating marginal costs in all directions in order to achieve minimum cost for given output applies to the use of theory just as much as to other productive activities. Generality reduces cost in one direction, specificity in another. Just where the right margin comes is a matter of judgment about which scholars may differ. Presumably, we all tend to develop our own methodological style or bias. The items in section 2 labeled *a* and *b*, are consistent with the hypothesis that Tobin's style goes farther in Walras's direction than mine does and that this difference in methodological style is an important reason why we seem to talk at cross-purposes.

4. *First-Round Effects*

Further indirect evidence in support of this hypothesis is provided by Tobin's discussion of whether "the genesis of new money makes a difference" in the effect of the new money on the economy, whether "an increase in the quantity of money has the same effect whether it is issued to purchase goods or to purchase bonds." The basic issue is ancient— whether the "first-round effect" of a change in the quantity of money largely determines the ultimate effect. As John Stuart Mill put a view very much like Tobin's in 1844, "The issues of a *Government* paper, even when not permanent, will raise prices; because Governments usually issue their paper in purchases for consumption. If issued to pay off a portion of the national debt, we believe they would have no effect" (Mill 1844, p. 589).

Tobin's concentration on the first-round effect also parallels the emphasis by von Mises in his theory of the cycle. For example, Lionel Robbins, in his Misean analysis of the Great Depression, says, "In normal times, expansion and contraction of the money supply comes, not *via* the printing press and government decree, but *via* an expansion of credit through the banks. . . . This involves a mode of diffusion of new money radically different from the case we have just examined—a mode of diffusion which may have important effects" (Robbins 1934, pp. 35–36).

Of course, Tobin is right that the way the quantity of money is increased will affect the outcome in some measure or other. If one group of individuals receives the money on the first round they will likely use it for different purposes than another group of individuals. If the newly printed money is spent on the first round for goods and services it adds directly at that point to the demand for such goods and services, whereas if it is spent on purchasing debt it has no such immediate effect on the demand for goods and services. Effects on the demand for goods and services come later as the initial recipients of the "new" money themselves dispose of it. Clearly, also, as the "new" money spreads through the economy, any first-round effects will tend to be dissipated. The "new" money will be merged with the old and will be distributed in much the same way.

One way to characterize the Keynesian approach is that it gives almost exclusive importance to the first-round effect. This leads it to attach importance primarily to flows of spending rather than to stocks of assets. Similarly, one way to characterize the quantity-theory approach is to say that it gives almost no importance to first-round effects.

The empirical question is how important the first-round effects are compared to the ultimate effects. Theory cannot answer that question. The answer depends on how different are the reactions of the recipients of cash via different routes to larger cash balances, on how rapidly the larger money stock is distributed through the economy, how long it stays at each point in the economy, on how much the demand for money depends on the structure of government liabilities, and so on. Casual empiricism yields no decisive answer. Tobin can say, "The monetization of commercial loans . . . seems to me to be alchemy of much deeper significance than semi-monetization of Treasury bills" (Tobin 1965*a*, p. 467). But I could answer, "True, but remember that the transactions velocity of money may well be over twenty-five to thirty times a year, to judge from the turnover of bank deposits, so the first round covers at most a two-week period, whereas the money continues circulating indefinitely." Maybe the first-round effect is so strong that it dominates later effects; but maybe it is highly transitory. We shall have to examine empirical evidence systematically to find out.

The issue looks different to Tobin. "The crucial issue," he writes, "is whether government interest-bearing time debt is of *any* significance" (my italics). If that is the crucial issue, then of course he is right. Government interest-bearing time debt is of some significance. But although he phrases the issue that way, on reflection Tobin will undoubtedly agree that the crucial issue is not whether government interest-bearing time debt is of any significance but whether it is of enough significance to introduce significant error into a relation between money and income—or, put differently, whether knowledge of the sources of the change in money permits an economically and statistically significant improvement in predictions of the future course of income.

Despite his repeated assertions that the effect is significant in this sense, Tobin has not, so far as I know, presented any systematic empirical evidence in support of that assertion. It has long seemed to me that the apparently similar response of income to changes in the quantity of money over a long span of time in different countries and under different monetary systems established something of a presumption that the first-round effect was not highly significant. More recently, several empirical studies designed explicitly to test the importance of the first-round effect have supported this presumption.[11]

Perhaps other studies will reverse this tentative conclusion. In any event, the importance of the first-round effect will be provided by empirical evidence, not by argumentation or theory.

Davidson

Paul Davidson reproaches me for having neglected "several important chapters in Keynes's *General Theory*"—namely, chapters 12, 17, 20, and 21. Having reread those chapters, and Davidson's comments, I am unrepentant.

The four chapters Davidson refers to contain many correct, interesting, and valuable ideas, although also some wrong ones, and many shrewd observations on empirical matters, particularly the operation of financial

---

[11] Cagan investigated the first-round effect on interest rates. He was able to identify the existence of such an effect, but it was of minor quantitative importance. Auerbach found no evidence of a first-round effect on nominal income of the division of the change in the quantity of money between high-powered money and bank credit, or the division of high-powered money between financing current government expenses and debt redemption. Bordo, in a thesis underway dealing with the pre–World War I period for the United States, finds at best very limited traces of the first-round effect (see Auerbach 1969; Cagan 1972; Bordo, in preparation). I am indebted to Anna Schwartz for calling to my attention the 1844 quotation from John Stuart Mill with which I began this section.

markets. But all four chapters are strictly peripheral to the main contribution of the *General Theory*. They contain a sequence of organized but uncoordinated comments on their several subjects, and none makes any contribution to the formal theory of the book. Far from being in any way inconsistent with my interpretation of Keynes's views, they reinforce that interpretation, particularly with respect to the key role that Keynes assigned to the liquidity trap.

Let me document this judgment by considering Davidson's own six-item summary of his critique "from the Keynesian view"—the first three referring to "basic factors which Friedman omits," the fourth to a "misspecification," the fifth and sixth to "two of Friedman's assertions about Keynes's model [that] are incompatible with the *General Theory*."

The three basic factors I am said to omit are:

1. "The essence of uncertainty."

This is simply wrong. Uncertainty may not be explicitly mentioned, but it is certainly taken for granted throughout the analysis. Indeed, the assumption that there exists a demand for a finite amount of real-cash balances itself implies the existence of uncertainty.[12] In exactly the same sense I could be said to omit "the existence of men who calculate," since I nowhere state explicitly that the analysis is for a society of such men (and women). Surely, a technical article for technical economists can take some things for granted.

Davidson justifies his assertion that "in Friedman's framework, . . . *all expectations* are realized and therefore there is no uncertainty" by referring to my statement that "at a long-run equilibrium position, all anticipations are realized." But this is a definition of long-run equilibrium, not an assumption about the real world. In any event, my paper is largely devoted to the problem of short-run adjustment. I introduced the concept of "long-run equilibrium" solely as a preliminary step in sketching a theory of the short-run "adjustment process." This is a straw man if I ever saw one (see also point 2 below).

Keynes emphasizes "uncertainty" in his chapter 12 primarily to stress the importance of expectations about the future for the marginal efficiency of capital. This is the point also of his remark in chapter 21, to which Davidson refers, that "the importance of money essentially flows from its being a link between the present and the future" (Keynes 1936, p. 293). I regard as the major new items in my paper the "third approach" of a "monetary theory of nominal income" and the section on the "adjust-

---

[12] Compare my statement, "It is worth noting that both reasons [for holding money] depend critically . . . on the existence of individual uncertainty" (Friedman 1969, p. 3).

ment process." The rest is mostly a retelling of a well-known story. Both new items give a key role to expectations about the future movements of prices, output, money, and income, and to the consequences of deviations between actual magnitudes and anticipated magnitudes. Thus they extend the role of anticipations from the market for investments and loans, with which Keynes dealt, to a broader range of markets.

In a respect that Davidson regards as distinctively Keynesian, therefore, my paper is more Keynesian than the *General Theory*!

Yet, as noted in my reply to Brunner and Meltzer, these extensions owe much more to recent work that has been done on information and search, and to my own work on the consumption function, than they do to Keynes.

2. "The existence of particular market institutions, organizations, and constraints...which exist only because uncertainty is present."

The gravamen of Davidson's complaint under this heading is an alleged incompatibility of "the Walrasian auctioneer and flexible money-wages and prices" with uncertainty and a stable monetary system. "Thus," he concludes, "these institutions cannot be used to close logically the Keynesian system."

A methodological answer to this complaint is given by Keynes: "After we have reached a provisional conclusion by isolating the complicating factors one by one, we then have to go back on ourselves and allow, as well as we can, for the probable interactions of the factors amongst themselves. This is the nature of economic thinking" (Keynes 1936, p. 297). The long-run equilibrium in which, as I put it, "all anticipations are realized" and that is determined by "the earlier quantity theory plus the Walrasian equations of general equilibrium" is not a state that is assumed ever to be attained in practice. It is a logical construct that defines the norm or trend from which the actual world is always deviating but to which it is tending to return or about which it tends to fluctuate. The hypothesis that the logical construct does specify the norm or trend in this sense is entirely compatible with the existence of uncertainty, just as the hypothesis that $s = \frac{1}{2}gt^2$ specifies the law of falling bodies is entirely compatible with the existence of air. This does not of course mean that the hypothesis is correct. That is a question of fact to be determined by the consistency of the hypothesis with experience. But the hypothesis cannot validly be rejected on the purely a priori grounds on which Davidson rejects it.[13]

[13] Of course, as Davidson notes, there may be and are "false trades" and "disappoint-ments" "in the real world," just as there may be and is air pressure. But the relevant issue is not whether there are false trades and disappointments but whether such false trades and disappointments are "sufficiently" important to change "significantly" the trend about which the observed magnitudes fluctuate, or instead tend to be of the nature of random

The substantive fallacy that underlies Davidson's belief in the incompatibility of flexible wages and prices with "uncertainty and a stable monetary system" is the confusion between flexibility and instability that has done so much to impede understanding of the desirability of flexible exchange rates. A price may be flexible, in the sense that it can and does change promptly in response to changes in demand and supply and that there are no institutional obstacles to its changing, yet be relatively stable, because demand and supply are relatively stable over time (e.g., this was the case with the exchange rate of the Canadian dollar in the 1950s). Violent instability of prices in terms of a specific money would greatly reduce the usefulness of that money; however, flexibility of prices in terms of that money has no such effect.

Keynes does not make Davidson's mistake. Whereas Davidson says flatly, "A 'perfect' labor market with flexible prices would be incompatible with a system where there are contracts, and money is used as a store of value," Keynes says that "the fact that contracts are fixed, and wages are usually somewhat stable, in terms of money unquestionably plays a large part in attracting to money so high a liquidity premium," and he goes on to refer to "the relative stability...in the future money-cost of output." He then argues that flexible wages and prices would in practice be highly unstable because, to simplify and summarize, the marginal efficiency schedule is highly unstable and the liquidity preference schedule is highly elastic so that it will take wide fluctuations in money-wages and prices "to establish a relation between the rate of interest and the marginal efficiency of capital that would maintain investment at the critical level" (Keynes 1936, pp. 236, 237, 370). Keynes does not treat instability in wages and prices as a logical implication of flexibility and uncertainty per se; he presents it as an empirical hypothesis that may be, as I believe it is, false. Its plausibility even to Keynes rested on the omission of adjustment mechanisms from his theoretical system that were added later (notably, the Keynes and Pigou real wealth effects, and the role of permanent income in the consumption function).

Keynes's recognition of the logical consistency of flexibility, uncertainty, and the use of money is demonstrated by his continued belief in the desirability of flexible exchange rates (Keynes 1936, p. 270).

3. The third basic factor I am said to omit is "the existence of money which, in an uncertain world, has a dual function—namely, a medium of exchange and a store of value."

---

disturbances that largely average out over time. The answer need not, of course, be the same for all problems or under all circumstances. Unfortunately, armchair reasoning cannot settle such issues.

Clearly I did not omit this—indeed, one of Patinkin's main criticisms of my article is that I treated the asset role of money as consistent with the quantity theory, whereas, in his view, it is Keynesian.

Davidson's real criticism is that I did not recognize that "money has two essential properties, namely (*a*) a zero (or negligible) elasticity of production and (*b*) a zero (or negligible) elasticity of substitution" and that "the existence of a money possessing these properties underlies Keynes's basic propositions that (*a*) as a purely theoretical matter if there is uncertainty there need not exist, in a monetary, production economy, a long-run equilibrium position characterized by full employment of labor; (*b*) stickiness of the money-wage rate is necessary if money is to play its peculiar role in such an economy; and (*c*) if wages and prices are flexible, 'the quantity of money is, indeed, nugatory in the long period.'"[14]

Let us take a deep breath and see if we can sort out this jumble of ideas.

In the first place, Keynes himself never says that the two properties Davidson refers to are essential properties of an asset money. He says that they "commonly characterize money as we know it" and that they are essential to attribute "a peculiar significance to the money-rate of interest," the peculiar significance in turn being required to justify the

[14] In a footnote, Davidson says, "Friedman 'summarily' dismisses propositions *a* and *b* as already having been proved false while ignoring proposition *c* altogether."

I am puzzled by this remark in view of the references I gave to the extensive and excellent literature dealing with propositions *a* and *b* (pp. 15, 16, 25). I did not introduce Davidson's proposition *c* in my article, so of course I ignored it. But in any event, it is not an independent proposition. It is simply a statement of the converse of proposition *a*.

In discussing the effect of money-wage reductions, Keynes said that they would increase employment directly "only if the community's marginal propensity to consume is equal to unity" (Keynes 1936, p. 261). In effect, the proof of the falsity of proposition *a* that I referred to can be regarded as a demonstration that if necessary (that is, if Keynes's mechanisms via liquidity preference, the rate of interest, and investment are not sufficient) this condition can always be satisfied. If "equilibrium" is regarded as described by a fixed price level and a fixed nominal quantity of money, then the Pigou effect means that there will always exist a price level low enough so that wealth is high enough so that the marginal propensity to consume is unity.

I have long regarded an alternative way to assure the same result as a more elegant answer on a purely theoretical level, though of not much greater practical significance than the real balance effect. The alternative involves widening our perspective to accept as equilibrium positions states of the world in which prices are falling or rising at a fixed rate. In that case, for a fixed quantity of money, falling prices make income as viewed by the consumer (say Y_1) higher than income defined by the value of productive resources (say Y_2), because Y_1 includes not only Y_2 but also the capital gain from the increasing real value of cash balances. Consumers can then add to their wealth a fraction of Y_1 equal to the capital gain on cash balances, yet spend on consumption the whole of Y_2. Hence there will always exist a rate of price fall which will enable Y_1 to exceed Y_2 at full employment by the difference between the amount that consumers, when fully employed, want to add to their wealth and the amount that the business community wants to add to physical capital when there is full employment.

possibility that there will not exist a long-run equilibrium position characterized by full employment—a very different proposition from Davidson's (Keynes 1936, pp. 229-30).

In the second place, neither alleged property of money is essential for an asset money and neither has in fact characterized actual moneys. With respect to a zero elasticity of production, over most of the world's history, money has consisted of a commodity that was capable of being produced by the exertion of labor, often at roughly constant costs (the cowrie shells so widely used as money in Asia and Africa and the wampum of the American Indians are the most obvious primitive examples, metallic moneys the most obvious modern examples). Keynes himself recognized this with respect to a gold standard but dismissed the possibility except for "a country of which gold-mining is the major industry" (Keynes 1936, p. 230). But surely this is wrong. In a gold-standard world, a country that does not have literal gold mines has the economic equivalent in industries capable of producing goods for export, and these are likely to account for a larger fraction of employment than literal gold mines.

With respect to a zero elasticity of substitution, Keynes became enmeshed in a confusion between two kinds of prices—the purchase price of an asset (its capital value) and the price of the service flow yielded by the asset (its rental value)—that has more recently been a key element in the dispute over the contentions of Pesek and Saving about inside money and outside money (see Pesek and Saving 1967, p. 118; Johnson 1969, p. 37; Friedman and Schwartz 1970, pp. 114-16).

This confusion is brought out by Keynes's comparison of money with other "pure rent factors, the production of which is completely inelastic," and so in this respect share the first property he attributes to money. He differentiates the two by the alleged zero elasticity of substitution of money, saying that "as the exchange value of money rises there is no motive or tendency, as in the case of rent factors, to substitute some other factor for it" (Keynes 1936, p. 231). But this is equally true for rent factors if what changes is their capital value as a result of a change in the interest rate used to discount future rents. If the annual rent charged for the services of a piece of land remains the same relative to the annual rent charged for the services of other productive services, there will be no tendency to substitute other factor *services* for land *services*, even though the price of an acre of land goes up sharply. On the other hand, if the annual rental value of a piece of land rises relative to the rental value of other productive sources, there will be an incentive to substitute other services for land services, even though the price of an acre of land does not change. Similarly, if the annual cost of holding money increases, because for example of a more rapid rate of inflation, there will be a tendency to substitute the service of other factors for money, even at the same price level. Money and "pure rent factors" are on all fours.

With respect to the elasticity of substitution in response to a change in rental value rather than in response to a change in capital value, it is Keynes who assumes a high elasticity (infinite when liquidity preference is absolute) and the quantity theorists who are (incorrectly) charged with assuming a zero elasticity of substitution.

In the third place, Keynes recognizes, as Davidson does not, that these two properties are not sufficient for his proposition about long-run equilibrium. The two properties are stated initially in terms of the nominal quantity of money, so Keynes goes on to ask whether the conclusion that these two properties prevent falling prices from adding to employment is "upset by the fact that" falling wages and prices will add to the real stock of money. He admits the theoretical possibility but argues that the possibility is not likely to be realized for several reasons, of which "the most fundamental consideration" is the high elasticity of the liquidity preference function—the liquidity trap (Keynes 1936, pp. 231–33).

In my interpretation of Keynes, I put great emphasis on highly elastic liquidity preference, calling this his "special twist" and "a key element" in his proposition about long-run equilibrium. Davidson does not refer to "absolute liquidity preference," yet two of the three statements of Keynes to which he gives page references when he first introduces this proposition about long-run equilibrium assign a key role to absolute liquidity preference. One quotation is particularly pertinent: If wages are flexible, "there will...be only two possible long-period positions—full employment and the level of employment corresponding to the rate of interest at which liquidity preference becomes absolute (in the event of this being less than full employment)" (Keynes 1936, p. 191). The impression given by this quotation is confirmed by all the other statements I have been able to find in the *General Theory* bearing on the issue, and assembled in my Appendix 1 below.

I am not sure I have understood Davidson's own position (as distinct from his interpretation of Keynes), but if I have it seems to stand theory on its head. He appears to *start* from the proposition that there does not exist a long-run equilibrium position characterized by full employment, and then try to *deduce* the empirical characteristics of money (and other elements of the economy) from that proposition. But perhaps I have misunderstood him.

4. Davidson says that I misspecify "the demand function for money and the supply processes for altering the money supply" because my omission

of "*planned* expenditures as a specific independent variable can lead to wrong theoretical constructs and policy implications" and because I do not treat "the supply of money and debt and production offer contracts" as "intimately and inevitably related."

I, like every other scientist, readily grant, even know, that any simplification of whatever character "can lead to wrong theoretical constructs and policy implications." But Davidson makes no case for attaching particular significance to the simplification in the demand function that he singles out.

On the supply function, Davidson confuses money with credit. There is no necessary connection between a change in the quantity of money and in the volume of outstanding debts—as is crystal clear when the change in the quantity of money reflects either gold discoveries or the printing of fiat money by government to pay for current expenses.

5 and 6. The two assertions of mine that Davidson regards as incompatible with the *General Theory* are "5. Keynes assumed that before full employment all adjustments to changes in demand take place via quantity changes," and "6. The price analysis underlying Keynes's model is 'arbitrary' and has 'no underpinning in economic theory' " (the words in single quotes are from my article).

Re 5, Keynes of course recognized that increases in income were in practice divided between price and quantity changes and stated explicitly that the "wage-unit," that is, money wages, "may tend to rise before full employment." But, as he said, while these phenomena have "a good deal of historical importance, . . . they do not readily lend themselves to theoretical generalizations" (Keynes 1936, p. 302). He drew a sharp distinction between such changes in money wages and "a condition which might be appropriately designated as one of true inflation" which occurs "when a further increase in the quantity of effective demand produces no further increase in output" (Keynes 1936, p. 303). He did not incorporate any changes in the wage unit in his formal theoretical structure but simply added, as a verbal qualification, recognition of this possibility and some discussion of how it might occur. This discussion is all reasonable and sensible, but I believe that I have done no violence to Keynes's theory by neglecting these qualifications in discussing his central structure. Of course, the use of a wage unit to express all quantities does not require that money wages be regarded as in fact constant or rigid. It simply means that changes in money wages are exogenous to the theoretical system and are to be explained by other factors.

Re Davidson's point 6, Keynes's discussion of the price level *relative* to the wage level does have a theoretical underpinning in the law of diminishing returns, and this does play a critical role in his theory, leading him to regard a reduction in real wages as a necessary condition for a rise in employment. This aspect of his theory has stimulated a great deal of empirical work on the behavior of real wages during the business cycle, which has failed to confirm his hypothesis. There is no clear negative relation between real wages and the level of employment over the course of the cycle of the kind that Keynes postulates. The kind of framework that I use, which introduces a distinction between real wages as measured ex post and real wages as viewed ex ante by employer and employee, can explain this result without contradicting the basic notion of diminishing returns. During an expansion, when the actual rate of price rise exceeds the anticipated, it is possible for real wages as viewed by employers to fall (because they deflate wages by the price of the product they produce) and thus induce them to increase employment, and for real wages as viewed by employees to rise (because they deflate wages by cost of living) and thus induce them to increase the amount of labor offered. This result can be regarded as implied by information and search theory. The actual result ex post can be either a rise or a fall in measured real wages.

But the behavior of prices relative to wages is a very different question from the behavior of the absolute price or wage level, and it is one that I abstracted from entirely in my article. The relevant issue is whether Keynes had a theory of the absolute price level that was not "arbitrary." Davidson says, "Keynes skillfully constructed the elasticities of output, wages, and prices from traditional price theory concepts. Empirical estimates of these elasticities would go a long way toward answering some of the questions on the adjustment process which Friedman raises in the concluding section of his paper. Unfortunately, such elasticity concepts are not specified at all in Friedman's framework."

This is nonsense pure and simple. The elasticities are simply definitions; the formula connecting them that Davidson cites is a truism derived from the identities that the price in money is equal to the price in wage units times the money-wage rate and that the price in wage units is equal to total demand in wage units divided by output. The formula is a bit complex only because two of the three elasticities it contains are defined with respect to the change in aggregate demand in money and one with respect to the changes in aggregate demand in wage units.[15] These elasticities and this truism are "specified" as much—whatever that may mean—in my framework as they are in Keynes's. They are pure arithmetic and are

---

[15] Keynes defines: p_w = price of goods in wage units, O = output, W = wage rate in money:

completely empty both theoretically and empirically. To regard them as a "theoretical underpinning" for Keynes's assumptions about the price level is on a par with regarding $(a + b)^2 = a^2 + 2ab + b^2$ as theoretical underpinning for the law of falling bodies.

I thus remain persuaded that Keynes's assumption about the absolute price or wage level is "arbitrary" and has no "theoretical underpinning," however useful, or mischievous, that assumption may be.[16]

$$D_w = p_w O = \text{aggregate demand in wage units,} \tag{1}$$
$$p = p_w W = \text{price of goods in money,} \tag{2}$$
$$D = D_w W = \text{aggregate demand in money,} \tag{3}$$
$$e_p = d \log p / d \log D = \text{elasticity of price with respect to } D,$$
$$e_o = d \log O / d \log D_w = \text{elasticity of output with respect to } D_w,$$
$$e_w = d \log W / d \log D = \text{elasticity of wages with respect to } D.$$

From (1) and (2),

$$p = \frac{D_w W}{O}. \tag{4}$$

Taking logs, we have

$$\log p = \log D_w - \log O + \log W. \tag{5}$$

Differentiate with respect to $\log D$ and replace relevant symbols with elasticities:

$$e_p = \frac{d \log D_w}{d \log D}(1 - e_o) + e_w. \tag{6}$$

But, from (3),

$$\log D_w = \log D - \log W, \text{ or} \tag{7}$$

$$\frac{d \log D_w}{d \log D} = 1 - e_w. \tag{8}$$

Substituting in (6), we have

$$e_p = (1 - e_w)(1 - e_o) + e_w, \tag{9}$$

or

$$e_p = 1 - e_o(1 - e_w), \tag{10}$$

which is Keynes's formula (Keynes 1936, p. 285).

[16] In the epilogue which Davidson added after reading the first draft of my reply, he asks a series of "when did you beat your wife" questions. For the record, let me answer them succinctly.

a) My general framework does not assume an exogenous money supply in any relevant sense (see sec. 3). One simplified model, used for a special purpose, takes money supply to be exogenous. I have done work on the factors determining the money supply and have encouraged much work by others on this subject.

b) I have answered this question in my response to Davidson's point 2 and in n. 13.

c) Keynes, as I have explained, has no theory of the absolute level of prices.

d) Talk is not a substitute for evidence. I know no empirical study of the demand for money that has ever identified variables corresponding to "the finance motive," let alone found them to have a significant influence. An attempt to do so would certainly be an appropriate piece of research. In view of Davidson's strong a priori feelings on this issue, I hope that he will be led to investigate the question systematically.

Patinkin

Patinkin's (1969*a*) article on "The Chicago Tradition, the Quantity Theory, and Friedman" served as an important source for Harry Johnson's 1970 Richard T. Ely lecture (Johnson 1971). Patinkin—both in his 1969 article and in the present comments—and Johnson criticize me for linking my work to a "Chicago tradition" rather than recognizing that, as they see it, my work is Keynesian. In the course of their criticism, they give a highly misleading impression of the Chicago tradition. Grant for the sake of the argument—as I do not in fact grant—that my 1956 "Restatement" (see "The Quantity Theory of Money—a Restatement," in Friedman 1956; reprinted in Friedman 1969, pp. 51-67), which is the main object of criticism in Patinkin's 1969 article, had nothing whatsoever of the flavor of the Chicago tradition. That would indict my perception, or integrity, or scholarship, but it would in no way contradict the existence of an important Chicago tradition in the field of money that had a great influence on subsequent work in monetary economics and on my own work in particular. Similarly, it might justify Johnson's charge that I engaged in "scholarly chicanery," but it would not justify his charge that the "University of Chicago oral tradition" was my "invention."

Whether I conveyed the flavor of that tradition or not, there was such a tradition; it was significantly different from the quantity theory tradition that prevailed at other institutions of learning, notably the London School of Economics; that Chicago tradition had a great deal to do with the differential impact of Keynes's *General Theory* on economists at Chicago and elsewhere; and it was responsible for the maintenance of interest in the quantity theory at Chicago. My restatement *is* a restatement of the quantity theory and is not Keynesian in any meaningful sense of that term.

One reason Patinkin gives such a misleading view of both the Chicago school tradition and of my theoretical framework is his propensity to take the "quantity theory" to mean one thing and one thing only, namely, the long-run proposition that money is neutral, even though he fully recognizes, indeed insists, that the quantity theorists (myself included) were concerned mostly with short-run fluctuations. My explicit statement of what I mean by the quantity theory (quoted in my reply to Tobin, p. 145) is not referred to by Patinkin; he interprets almost all my references to the quantity theory as if I meant by it what he means by it. For example, he criticizes me for "not presenting the long-run quantity theory in the most general way that one can, once one has decided to reformulate it" and proceeds in the very next paragraph to document this criticism by referring to a model which I said—and he even quotes this statement—"refers to a short period"![17]

A second, and closely related, reason why Patinkin gives a misleading view of both the Chicago school tradition and of my framework is his emphasis on the role of the interest rate in the demand function for money as "one of the central issues of monetary economics." He regards the inclusion of the interest rate in the demand function for money as distinctively Keynesian and its neglect as a key omission in pre-Keynesian monetary theory. The contrast between that alleged omission and my inclusion of the interest rate in the demand function for money is a major ground on which he criticizes my "persistent refusal to recognize" that my "analytical framework is Keynesian." As I show below, the inclusion of the interest rate in the demand for money is not distinctively Keynesian. But, far more important for the present purpose, the inclusion of the interest rate is a minor feature of my framework, and its exclusion would have been a minor feature of pre-Keynesian monetary theory. As I also show below, the inclusion or exclusion of the interest rate in the demand function for money is not the respect in which my work is in the Chicago tradition. That tradition influenced my work primarily with respect to the interpretation of short-run movements, the reasons for the Great Depression, and the role of monetary and fiscal policies.

In arguing that inclusion of the interest rate in the demand for money is "Keynesian," Patinkin implicitly takes everything in the *General Theory* as *ipso facto* "Keynesian," as we use that term. Keynes was a quantity theorist long before he was a Keynesian, and he continued to be one after he became a Keynesian. Many parts of the *General Theory* are a continuation of his earlier interests and beliefs. The fact that Patinkin can find parallels between some of my discussion of the demand for money and Keynes's discussion in the *General Theory* does not establish that my discussion is therefore Keynesian. I shall argue, rather, that those parts of the *General Theory* are a direct outgrowth of Keynes's earlier quantity-theory views.

A more fundamental reason for Patinkin's emphasis on long-run "neutrality," the interest rate, and the real balance effect, and for his slighting the short-run context of most of my framework is that Patinkin, even more than Tobin, is Walrasian, concerned with abstract complete-

---

[17] For another striking example, see his discussion of the comment he quotes from my article (p. 51), in which he regards as an advantage of his own model that it demonstrates "the validity of the quantity theory," meaning by that simply the long-run neutrality of money, a result that is wholly irrelevant to my quotation in which I used "quantity-theory approach" in my sense, not his.

ness, rather than Marshallian, concerned with the construction of special tools for special problems.

In a recent article, "On the Short-Run Non-Neutrality of Money in the Quantity Theory," Patinkin (1972a) cites evidence that he regards as decisively contradicting my interpretation that Fisher and quantity theorists "simply took over Marshall's assumption" that "prices adjust more rapidly than quantities." Yet I regard the evidence he cites as strikingly confirming my interpretation. One sample of his evidence will do:

"The sequence of effects visualized by Fisher" after an increase in the quantity of money is "as follows:

"1. Prices rise.

"2. Velocities of circulation (V and V') increase; the rate of interest rises, but not sufficiently.

"3. Profits increase, loans expand, and the Q's [i.e., the real volume of trade] increase.

"4. Deposit currency (M') expands relatively to money (M).

"5. Prices continue to rise; that is, phenomenon No. 1 is repeated. Then No. 2 is repeated, and so on."

I described Marshall's assumption as being "that prices adjust more rapidly than quantities, indeed, so rapidly that the price adjustment can be regarded as instantaneous. An increase in demand (a shift to the right of the long-run demand curve) will produce a new market equilibrium involving a higher price but the same quantity. The higher price will, in the short run, encourage existing producers to produce more with their existing plants, thus raising quantity and bringing prices back down toward their original level, and, in the long run attract new producers and encourage existing producers to expand their plants, still further raising quantities and lowering prices. Throughout the process, it takes time for output to adjust but no time for prices to do so" (p. 17). Is not Fisher's sequence precisely the counterpart for the aggregate to this analysis for a particular product?

Further proof is that just prior to listing the five steps that Patinkin quotes, Fisher states that "an increase in currency cannot, even temporarily, very greatly increase trade. . . . [A]lmost the entire effect of an increase of deposits must be seen in a change of prices" (Fisher 1911, pp. 62–63).

Consider how a Keynesian would describe the effects of an increase in the quantity of money. It would go:

1. Interest rates fall.
2. Investment increases.

3. Output and real income increase.
4. Consumption increases.

It is not clear when he would come to the statement "prices rise," but it would surely be late in his list. Moreover, his step number 1 implies that velocity falls, but he would be most unlikely ever to refer to that phenomenon.

Is this not precisely the contrast that I drew between the quantity theorists and the Keynesians when I said that Keynes "deviated from Marshall . . . in reversing the roles assigned to price and quantity" (p. 18)?[18]

I must plead guilty to one careless expression that Patinkin quotes and that does lend itself to the interpretation that I was accusing the quantity theorists of assuming strict neutrality in the short run. This was my statement: "There is nothing in the logic of the quantity theory that specifies the dynamic path of adjustment, nothing that requires the whole adjustment to take place through P rather than through k or y." In light of my quotation above about Marshall's assumption (which is separated from the prior sentence by only one paragraph), I intended this sentence to refer to the instantaneous market equilibrium and to the assertion that "throughout the process, it takes time for output to adjust but no time for prices to do so"; it is not intended to mean that there are no effects on output during the process. But my wording is ambiguous and I should have been more careful.

Patinkin goes on also to quote my statement: "It was widely recognized that the adjustment during what Fisher, for example, called 'transition periods' would in practice be partly in k and in y as well as in P. Yet this recognition was not incorporated in formal theoretical analysis." He italicizes the last sentence for emphasis and asserts, "The facts of the case, however, are quite different," giving as evidence that "Fisher wrote incomparably more on his monetary proposals for mitigating the cyclical problems of the 'transition period' than on the long-run proportionality of prices to money. This concentration on short-run analysis was even more true for the policy-oriented Chicago quantity-theory school of the 1930s and 1940s."

The issue here is one that we have already encountered in my replies to Tobin and Davidson (and that is discussed also in points 7 and 11 of Appendix 2 below). There can be a great difference between what is implied by or contained in a formal theory, what proponents of the theory

[18] The references in Patinkin's article to statements by Chicago economists, Pigou, Keynes, Robertson, and Lavington, all equally strike me as clearly confirming my interpretation.

may believe it implies or contains, and what they write about. Of course, Fisher, the Chicago monetary economists, and the host of other economists who studied business cycles wrote a great deal about short-run movements and constructed many ingenious theories about business cycles that have much to teach us. In particular, Fisher's distinction between nominal and real interest rates, which dates back to some of his earliest writing, remains a seminal and penetrating insight. Yet, so far as I know, none of this voluminous writing and none of these theories provide a formal theoretical extension of the quantity theory to explain the division of changes in nominal income between changes in prices and in output or of changes in the quantity of money between changes in velocity, in prices, and in output, just as none of Keynes's extensive discussion of changes in money-wage rates prior to the point of full employment provides a formal theoretical analysis of such changes.

Rather than continuing to examine Patinkin's remarks in detail, I believe it will contribute more to clarify the issues raised by Patinkin if I address myself directly to the two key questions: (1) What was the distinctive quality of the Chicago tradition as it affected my own writings? (2) What are the quantity theory antecedents of Keynes's and my writings on the demand for money? I shall therefore relegate further detailed comments on those of Patinkin's statements that do not bear directly on these two issues to Appendix 2.

1. *The Chicago Tradition*

I was myself first strongly impressed with the importance of the Chicago tradition during a debate on Keynes between Abba P. Lerner and myself before a student-faculty seminar at the University of Chicago sometime in the late 1940s (or perhaps early 1950s). Lerner and I were graduate students during the early 1930s, pre-*General Theory*; we have a somewhat similar Talmudic cast of mind and a similar willingness to follow our analysis to its logical conclusion. These have led us to agree on a large number of issues—from flexible exchange rates to the volunteer army. Yet we were affected very differently by the Keynesian revolution—Lerner becoming an enthusiastic convert and one of the most effective expositors and interpreters of Keynes, I remaining largely unaffected and if anything somewhat hostile.

During the course of the debate, the explanation became crystal clear. Lerner was trained at the London School of Economics, where the dominant view was that the depression was an inevitable result of the prior boom, that it was deepened by the attempts to prevent prices and wages from falling and firms from going bankrupt, that the monetary authorities had brought on the depression by inflationary policies before the crash and had prolonged it by "easy money" policies thereafter; that the only sound policy was to let the depression run its course, bring down money costs, and eliminate weak and unsound firms.

By contrast with this dismal picture, the news seeping out of Cambridge (England) about Keynes's interpretation of the depression and of the right policy to cure it must have come like a flash of light on a dark night. It offered a far less hopeless diagnosis of the disease. More important, it offered a more immediate, less painful, and more effective cure in the form of budget deficits. It is easy to see how a young, vigorous, and generous mind would have been attracted to it.

It was the London School (really Austrian) view that I referred to in my "Restatement" when I spoke of "the atrophied and rigid caricature [of the quantity theory] that is so frequently described by the proponents of the new income-expenditure approach—and with some justice, to judge by much of the literature on policy that was spawned by the quantity theorists" (Friedman 1969, p. 51).

The intellectual climate at Chicago had been wholly different. My teachers regarded the depression as largely the product of misguided governmental policy—or at least as greatly intensified by such policies. They blamed the monetary and fiscal authorities for permitting banks to fail and the quantity of deposits to decline. Far from preaching the need to let deflation and bankruptcy run their course, they issued repeated pronunciamentos calling for governmental action to stem the deflation— as J. Rennie Davis put it, "Frank H. Knight, Henry Simons, Jacob Viner, and their Chicago colleagues argued throughout the early 1930's for the use of large and continuous deficit budgets to combat the mass unemployment and deflation of the times" (Davis 1968, p. 476).

They recommended also "that the Federal Reserve banks systematically pursue open-market operations with the double aim of facilitating necessary government financing and increasing the liquidity of the banking sructure" (Wright 1932, p. 162). There was nothing in these views to repel a student; or to make Keynes attractive. On the contrary, so far as policy was concerned, Keynes had nothing to offer those of us who had sat at the feet of Simons, Mints, Knight, and Viner.

It was this view of the quantity theory that I referred to in my "Restatement" as "a more subtle and relevant version, one in which the quantity theory was connected and integrated with general price theory and became a flexible and sensitive tool for interpreting movements in aggregate economic activity and for developing relevant policy prescriptions" (Friedman 1969, p. 52).

I do not claim that this more hopeful and "relevant" view was restricted to Chicago. The manifesto from which I have quoted the recommendation for open-market operations was issued at the Harris Foundation lectures held at the University of Chicago in January 1932 and was signed by twelve University of Chicago economists. But there were twelve other signers (including Irving Fisher of Yale, Alvin Hansen of Minnesota, and John H. Williams of Harvard) from nine other institutions.[19] I have done no exhaustive research on the policy views at the time of economists at other institutions. But we do know that the London School view, really the Austrian view of Ludwig von Mises, had many adherents—including Gottfried Haberler, who was at the time a visiting lecturer in economics at Harvard and who gave a talk on "Money and the Business Cycle" at the same Harris Foundation lectures.

To assure you (and myself) that this is not simply hindsight, let me quote from pre-Keynesian publications about the depression, reflecting the London-Austrian view and the Chicago view.

Lionel Robbins's *The Great Depression* (1934) is an extraordinarily lucid and penetrating analysis of the depression from the Austrian point of view.[20] Published in 1934, large stretches of it make instructive reading today, especially the analysis of the consequences of restrictive foreign and domestic policies. But when it comes to the role of money and to causes and cures of the depression, here is what he has to say:

"If we take deflation to mean a deliberate curtailment of the supply of money, there seems to be no evidence of its existence on a large scale either before or since the slump commenced. . . . Since the slump, Central Banks and Governments have vied with each other in promoting policies calculated to bring about easy money conditions" (p. 17).

"It is clear that the authorities of the Federal Reserve Bank and the Bank of France did nothing to prevent their increased reserves [as a result of gold inflows during the depression] from becoming effective. It is not really sensible, therefore, to attribute what happened after 1929 to their policy" (p. 23).

"A fluctuation of the kind described in the last chapter [the alleged inflation of the twenties] is bound to be followed by a period of extensive depression" (p. 55). But it "does not explain why [the slump] has been so severe." Robbins goes on to argue that "no single explanation of this phenomenon will be sufficient" (p. 56), gives a long catalog of special

[19] However, several of these were Chicagoans at one remove, for example, Charles D. Hardy and Harold G. Moulton of Brookings Institution.

[20] Compare the footnote in the *General Theory*, "It is the distinction of Prof. Robbins that he, almost alone, continues to maintain a consistent scheme of thought, his practical recommendations belonging to the same system as his theory" (Keynes 1936, p. 20).

factors intensifying the depression, and turns to "certain tendencies of policy . . . which have greatly enhanced these difficulties" (p. 65). After stressing restrictions on international trade, he turns to wage policy. "If profitability is to be restored, costs must be cut and the capital resources rehabilitated" (p. 69).

"In earlier depressions this has been the rule. . . . But at the outset of this depression other measures were adopted" (p. 69) to keep up wage rates.

"Now this policy was the reverse of what was needed. . . . The maintenance of wage rates and dividends was at the expense of capital. . . . Consumption is maintained at the expense of capital. . ." (p. 71).

"In the present depression . . . we eschew the sharp purge. We prefer the lingering disease. . . .

"The moment the boom broke in 1929, the Central Banks of the world, acting obviously in concert, set to work to create a condition of easy money, quite out of relation to the general conditions of the money market. . . . The process of liquidation was arrested" (p. 73).

"It is agreed that to prevent the depression the only effective method is to prevent the boom" (p. 171). There is needed "a greater flexibility of wage rates" (p. 186). "Our main contention [is] the necessity for the elimination of all kinds of inflexibility" (p. 189).

Compare this with what Jacob Viner said in early 1932 in his Harris Foundation lecture:

"The Federal Reserve Board has revealed to the outsider no greater capacity [than other Central Banks] to formulate a consistent policy, unless a program of drift, punctuated at intervals by homeopathic doses of belated inflation and deflation and rationalized by declarations of impotence, can be accepted as the proper constituents of central bank policy. While the New York Federal Reserve Bank has made more effort than any other central banking institution to develop a program and a technique of credit control with a view to stabilization, it has at critical moments found itself at cross-purposes with, and inhibited from action by, a Federal Reserve Board with an attitude toward its functions resembling with almost miraculous closeness that of the Bank of England during its worst period" (Wright 1932, p. 28).

Even more pertinent is a talk Viner delivered in Minneapolis on February 20, 1933, on "Balanced Deflation, Inflation, or More Depression" (Viner 1933). While agreeing with Robbins on the harm done by wage and price rigidity, and in particular by the Hoover Administration pressure against wage reductions, he also spoke vigorously against letting the cure take its course:

"We have already had three years of patient waiting, probably three years too much. It is arguable that even dangerous remedies now threaten less risk of disaster than does continuance of inaction" (p. 10).

"Had it not been for this campaign of fear . . . it would have been sound policy on the part of the federal government deliberately to permit a deficit to accumulate during depression years, to be liquidated during prosperity years. . . . The outstanding though unintentional achievement of the Hoover Administration in counteracting the depression has in fact been its deficits of the last two years, and it was only its own alleged fears as to the ill effects of these deficits, and the panic which the big business world professed to foresee if these deficits should recur, which have made this method of depression finance seriously risky" (pp. 18-19).

"I will use the term inflation to mean an increase in the total amount of spendable funds, whether consisting of coin, paper money, or bank deposits subject to check.

"The basic argument for inflation is that it would operate to raise product-prices more than cost-prices, would in this way restore a profit margin for business, and thus would bring about an increased volume of production and of employment. Against inflation many things are urged. . . .

"I can see little force in most of these objections. . . " (p. 20).

"It is often said that the federal government and the Federal Reserve system have practiced inflation during this depression and that no beneficial effects resulted from it. What in fact happened was that they made mild motions in the direction of inflation, which did not succeed in achieving it, did not succeed even in accomplishing 'reflation'; but which probably did slow up somewhat the rate of price decline . . . [p. 21]. At no time . . . since the beginning of the depression has there been for so long as four months a net increase in the total volume of bank credit outstanding. On the contrary, the government and Federal Reserve bank operations have not nearly sufficed to countervail the contraction of credit on the part of the member and non-member banks. There has been no net inflation of bank credit since the end of 1929. There has been instead a fairly continuous and unprecedentedly great contraction of credit during this entire period" (p. 22).

"Assuming for the moment that a deliberate policy of inflation should be adopted, the simplest and least objectionable procedure would be for the federal government to increase its expenditures or to decrease its taxes, and to finance the resultant excess of expenditures over tax revenues either by the issue of legal tender greenbacks or by borrowing from the banks" (p. 24).

However, Viner adds, such a policy might be vitiated by "general fear of an early departure from the gold standard and therefore a flight from the dollar." In light of this, "if going off the gold standard were as simple a matter for us as for England and Canada, I would not only advocate it, but if the mere cessation of gold payments did not suffice to lower substantially the internal purchasing power of the dollar I would recommend its accompaniment by increased government expenditures financed by the printing press or by loans" (p. 25).

However, "the actual process of going off the gold standard, while it is under way, is extremely painful, costly, panic-breeding. . . . In this country, it would undoubtedly require weeks, if not months, of public and congressional debate, during which utter confusion would be likely to prevail. . . .

"If we are to have inflation, therefore, we must have it within the gold standard" (p. 27).

Two weeks after Viner spoke these words, the United States was off the gold standard! Another graphic illustration of why economists should not let their amateur judgments of political feasibility overrule their professional judgments of economic desirability.[21]

But this is a digression. My main point is different. What, in the field of interpretation and policy, did Keynes have to offer those of us who learned their economics at a Chicago that was filled with these views? Can anyone who knows my work read Viner's comments and not see the direct links between them and Anna Schwartz's and my *Monetary History* (1963b), or between them and the empirical *Studies in the Quantity Theory of Money* (1956)? Indeed, as I have read Viner's talk for the purposes of this paper, I have myself been amazed to discover how precisely it foreshadows the main thesis of our *Monetary History* for the depression period, and have been embarrassed that we made no reference to it in our account. Can you find any similar link between Robbins's comments and our work?

I shall not defend my "Restatement" as giving the "flavor of the oral tradition" at Chicago in the sense that the details of my formal structure have precise counterparts in the teachings of Simons and Mints. After all, I am not unwilling to accept some credit for the theoretical analysis in that article. Patinkin has made a real contribution to the history of thought by examining and presenting the detailed theoretical teachings of Simons and Mints, and I have little quarrel with his presentation. But I certainly do defend my "Restatement" as giving the "flavor of the oral tradition" at

---

[21] The other famous example, of course, is Keynes's advocacy of a tariff in 1931 as a second-best solution to Britain's departure from the gold standard, which he ruled out as not feasible politically, only to see it happen very shortly.

Chicago in what seems so me the much more important sense in which, as I said, the oral tradition "nurtured the remaining essays in" *Studies in the Quantity Theory of Money,* and my own subsequent work. And, in any event, it is clearly not a tradition that, as Johnson charges, I "invented" for some noble or nefarious purpose.

2. *Keynes and the Quantity Theory*

Is everything in the *General Theory* Keynesian? Obviously yes, in the trivial sense that the words were set down on paper by John Maynard Keynes. Obviously no, in the more important sense that the term Keynesian has come to refer to a theory of short-term economic change—or a way of analyzing such change—presented in the *General Theory* and distinctively different from the theory that preceded it. To take a noncontroversial example: in his chapter 20 on "The Employment Function" and elsewhere, Keynes uses the law of diminishing returns to conclude that an increase of employment requires a decline in real-wage rates. Clearly that does not make the "law of diminishing returns" Keynesian or justify describing the "analytical framework" of someone who embodies the law of diminishing returns in his theoretical structure as Keynesian.

In just the same sense, I maintain that Keynes's discussion of the demand curve for money in the *General Theory* is for the most part a continuation of earlier quantity theory approaches, improved and refined but not basically modified. As evidence, I shall cite Keynes's own writings in the *Tract on Monetary Reform* (1923)—long before he became a Keynesian in the present sense.

a) Absolute Liquidity Preference

There is one respect—and I believe only one—in which the discussion of the demand curve for money in the *General Theory* is distinctively Keynesian and that is the importance attached to "absolute liquidity preference" or a high-interest elasticity of the demand for money. This element is distinctively Keynesian in the double sense that it is, so far as I know, introduced for the first time in the *General Theory* and also, as I stated in the "Theoretical Framework," that it can "be regarded as a direct consequence of his assumption about the relative speed of adjustment of price and quantity" (p. 20).

Patinkin objects to my treating "the case of 'absolute liquidity preference'—as part of 'Keynes's basic challenge to the reigning theory.' " He cites as counterevidence Keynes's own statement (which I also quoted) that "whilst this limiting case might become practically important in the future" he knew "of no example of it hitherto." However, the right hand apparently knows not what the left does. In the very next paragraph, Patinkin says, "Keynesian economics contends that as a result of high-interest elasticity of the demand for money. . . ." Pray tell how that statement differs from mine that Keynes "treated velocity as if in practice its behavior frequently approximated that which would prevail in this limiting case" (p. 26)?

More important, Patinkin does not quote the sentence immediately following Keynes's disclaimer, to wit, "Indeed, owing to the unwillingness of most monetary authorities to deal boldly in debts of long term, there has not been much opportunity for a test" (Keynes 1936, p. 207).[22] Neither does Patinkin note that, so far as I can discover, this is the only disclaimer in the *General Theory;* while there are repeated statements in the opposite direction, such as, to pick only one, "The most stable, and the least easily shifted element in our contemporary economy has been hitherto, and may prove to be in the future, the minimum rate of interest acceptable to the generality of wealth-owners" (Keynes 1936, p. 309).

One consequence of my rereading large parts of the *General Theory* in the course of writing this reply has been to reinforce my view that absolute liquidity preference plays a key role. Time and again when Keynes must face up to precisely what it is that prevents a full-employment equilib-rium, his final line of defense is absolute liquidity preference. To document this point, I have assembled the relevant quotations in Appen-dix 1. The first quotation is from page 172 because Keynes does not introduce liquidity preference or the quantity of money, with only trivial exceptions, until page 166. I do not see how anyone can read through these quotations and come to any other conclusion than that his "special twist" was highly elastic liquidity preference and that this "was a key element in Keynes's proposition" about the possibility that there might not be a

---

[22] As Allan Meltzer points out, this comment was in line with views that had long been held by Keynes.

"Keynes of the *Treatise* and even more Keynes of the *Essays in Persuasion* was scornful of the analysis and policies of bankers, central as well as private. In the *Treatise*, Keynes talked repeatedly and at length about the inadequacies of monetary policy during the interwar period and the limitations imposed by bankers. . . .

"Keynes's views on the subject of monetary policy, central banks, and the liquidity trap were much the same when he wrote the *General Theory*. The main point Keynes makes about the possibility of a liquidity trap and the breakdown of monetary policy is sandwiched between two statements that are critical of central bankers for not acting boldly and for not dealing in long-run debts" (Meltzer 1970, pp. 46–47).

full-employment equilibrium even with flexible prices. Patinkin sees the fly on the barn door but not the door!

b) Stocks versus Flows and Interest-Rate Effects

Patinkin argues that the liquidity-preference analysis of the *General Theory* differs from the earlier quantity-theory approach in two key respects: first, that it "is concerned with the optimal relationship between the stock of money and the stocks of other assets, whereas the quantity theory . . . was primarily concerned with the direct relationship between the stock of money and the flow of spending on goods and services."

Second, the two theories treated differently "the influence of the rate of interest on the demand for money. For, though quantity theorists did frequently recognize this influence, they did not fully integrate it into their thinking."

With respect to the first point, Patinkin does not correctly describe the analysis in the *General Theory*. The liquidity function includes both M_1, which is treated as strictly a function of "the flow of spending on goods and services," as well as M_2, which is treated as related to the stock of other assets.

In his *Tract on Monetary Reform* (1923), Keynes discusses the amount of cash people wish to hold, saying that it "depends partly on the wealth of the community, partly on its habits. Its habits are fixed by its estimation of the extra convenience of having more cash in hand as compared with the advantages to be got from spending the cash or investing it. . . . The matter cannot be summed up better than in the words of Dr. Marshall." There follows a lengthy quotation from Alfred Marshall's *Money, Credit, and Commerce,* including: "Let us suppose that the inhabitants of a country . . . find it just worth their while to keep by them on the average ready purchasing power to the extent of a tenth part of their annual income, together with a fiftieth part of their property" (Keynes 1923, pp. 78–79).

This is precisely the liquidity preference function of the *General Theory* (p. 199):

$$M = M_1 + M_2 = L_1(Y) + L_2(r),$$

except that Marshall expressed the M_2 part as a fraction of wealth, whereas Keynes expresses it as a function of the interest rate. So Patinkin's first point reduces to his second.

With respect to the second, Patinkin states that the "rate of change of the price level as one of the alternative rates of return which affect the

demand for money . . . was not systematically integrated into our thinking until the work of Friedman and his associates, particularly Cagan
(1956)." Patinkin is clearly wrong, at least if "our" includes the Keynes of
Monetary Reform. Keynes has an excellent and explicit discussion of
inflation as a tax and of the effect of the tax on the quantity of real
balances demanded. "The public," he writes, "discover that it is the
holders of notes who suffer taxation . . . and they begin to change their
habits and to economize in their holding of notes" (Keynes 1923, p. 51).

Keynes also uses Germany as "an illustration of the extraordinary
degree in which the money rate of interest can rise in its endeavor to keep
up with the real rate, when prices have continued to rise for so long and
with such volume that, rightly or wrongly, everyone believes that they will
continue to rise further" (Keynes 1923, p. 26). The remark already quoted
about "the advantages to be got from . . . investing" cash is further
evidence that he recognized the role of the interest rate. True, he discussed
the role of the rate of inflation explicitly, and of the interest rate only
implicitly, but that was because his book was so largely devoted to an
analysis of post-World War I inflations and their implications for
exchange rates. True, also, he did not write down an explicit demand
function with the rate of interest as an argument, but neither did he write
one down with the anticipated rate of inflation as an argument.

Patinkin is correct when he says "quantity theorists paid little, if any,
attention to the effects on the rate of interest . . . of shifts in the tastes of
individuals as to the form in which they wish to hold their assets." This
indeed was a Keynesian development that reflected what I regard as
Keynes's critical assumption that prices were an institutional datum. The
quantity theorists (including Keynes in *Monetary Reform*) found it
natural to regard changes in the quantity of money as affecting prices in
the first instance, and to regard the interest rate as determined by saving
and investment or lending and borrowing. Monetary changes affected the
interest rate by producing inflation (or deflation), which shifted the saving
and investment functions by leading lenders to demand higher (or lower)
nominal rates and borrowers to be willing to pay higher (or lower) nominal
rates. Because the Keynesians take the price level as an institutional
datum, they regard a change in the interest rate as the means whereby
people are induced to hold a larger or smaller quantity of money. Hence
the Keynesians were led to place greater importance than the quantity
theorists on the role of changes in the interest rate in the economy's
adjustment to monetary change.

But this valid point is a final, and decisive, piece of evidence against
Patinkin's claim that my "analytical framework is Keynesian." For in this

respect the treatment in my "Restatement" and in my "Theoretical Framework" (except where I am discussing the Keynesian theory) is the quantity-theory treatment. I too pay no attention to "the effects on the rate of interest" of shifts in the demand function for money. I too tend to minimize changes in market interest rates as the primary channel through which changes in the quantity of money affect spending, output, and prices. To go further, in the "Restatement" I do not even consider the effect of changes in the quantity of money on interest rates. In the "Theoretical Framework" I do, but only (in the passage I added to the NBER version that is referred to in my reply to Brunner and Meltzer) to show how the quantity-theory and income-expenditure approaches "can be readily reconciled on a formal level" (p. 28).

I conjecture that Patinkins's insistence on labeling my analytical framework Keynesian ultimately reflects his concentration on "neutrality." For if he interprets my framework as in the "quantity-theory" tradition, he cannot continue to regard "the quantity theory" as synonymous with the long-run neutrality of money, since my framework is clearly and obviously not about that—just as I believe the writings of earlier quantity theorists, from Ricardo and Thornton to Keynes, were not about that either. So cut down the forest to let the "neutrality tree" stand proud and tall.

Appendix 1

Quotations from the *General Theory* Related to Absolute Liquidity Preference

1. "Circumstances can develop in which even a large increase in the quantity of money may exert a comparatively small influence on the rate of interest" (p. 172).

2. "In the extreme case where money-wages are assumed to fall without limit in face of involuntary unemployment through a futile competition for employment between the unemployed labourers, there will, it is true, be only two possible long-period positions—full employment and the level of employment corresponding to the rate of interest at which liquidity-preference becomes absolute (in the event of this being less than full employment)" (p. 191).

3. "This, indeed, is perhaps the chief obstacle to a fall in the rate of interest to a very low level" (p. 202).

4. "The long term rate may be more recalcitrant when once it has fallen to a level which . . . is considered 'unsafe' by representative opinion. . . . [A] domestic rate of interest dragged up to a parity with the *highest* rate . . . prevailing in any country belonging to the international system may be much higher than is consistent with domestic full employment. . . .

"M_2 may tend to increase almost without limit in response to a reduction of r below a certain figure. . . .

"*Any* level of interest which is accepted with sufficient conviction as *likely* to be durable will be durable. . . .

"[I]t may fluctuate for decades about a level which is chronically too high for full employment. . . .

"The difficulties in the way of maintaining effective demand at a level high enough to provide full employment, which ensue from the association of a conventional and fairly stable long-term rate of interest with a fickle and highly unstable marginal efficiency of capital, should be, by now, obvious to the reader" (pp. 203-4).

5. "There is the possibility, for the reasons discussed above, that, after the rate of interest has fallen to a certain level, liquidity-preference may become virtually absolute. . . . In this event the monetary authority would have lost effective control over the rate of interest. But whilst this limiting case might become practically important in future, I know of no example of it hitherto. Indeed, owing to the unwillingness of most monetary authorities to deal boldly in debts of long term, there has not been much opportunity for a test" (p. 207).

6. "What would this involve for a society which finds itself so well equipped with capital that its marginal efficiency is zero and would be negative with any additional investment; yet possessing a monetary system, such that money will 'keep' and involves negligible costs of storage and safe custody, with the result that in practice interest cannot be negative; and, in conditions of full employment, disposed to save?

". . . the position of equilibrium, under conditions of *laissez faire*, will be one in which employment is low enough and the standard of life sufficiently miserable to bring savings to zero" (pp. 217-18).

7. "We have assumed so far an institutional factor which prevents the rate of interest from being negative. . . . In fact, however, institutional and psychological factors are present which set a limit much above zero to the practicable decline in

the rate of interest . . . , which in present circumstances may perhaps be as high as 2 or 2½ percent on long term" (pp. 218–19). (At the time Keynes wrote, consol yields in the United Kingdom were around 3 percent.)

8. "It seems, then, that the *rate of interest on money* plays a peculiar part in setting a limit to the level of employment" (p. 222).

9. "We come to what is the most fundamental consideration in this context, namely, the characteristics of money which satisfy liquidity-preference. For, in certain circumstances such as will often occur, these will cause the rate of interest to be insensitive, particularly below a certain figure, even to a substantial increase in the quantity of money in proportion to other forms of wealth" (p. 233).

10. "The significance of the money-rate of interest arises, therefore, out of the combination of the characteristics that, through the working of the liquidity-motive, this rate of interest may be somewhat unresponsive to a change in the proportion which the quantity of money bears to other forms of wealth measured in money. . ." (p. 234).

11. "If . . . money wages were to fall without limit whenever there was a tendency for less than full employment . . . there would be no resting place below full employment until either the rate of interest was incapable of falling further or wages were zero" (pp. 303–4).

12. "The most stable, and the least easily shifted, element in our contemporary economy has been hitherto, and may prove to be in future, the minimum rate of interest acceptable to the generality of wealth owners" (p. 309).

13. "The destruction of the inducement to invest by an excessive liquidity-preference was the outstanding evil, the prime impediment to the growth of wealth, in the ancient and medieval worlds" (p. 351).

Appendix 2

Comments on Some of Patinkin's Other Detailed Criticisms

Except where otherwise indicated, all quotations are from Patinkin's comment.

1. "Milton Friedman's article . . . has two concerns. The first and—from the viewpoint of the space devoted to it—major one is the chapter in the history of monetary doctrine which deals with . . . the quantity theory and Keynesian monetary theory."

That was not my intention in the article under discussion, and I made no attempt to survey the relevant literature exhaustively. I was, and am, interested primarily in the analytical differences between the two approaches, and used references to literature to illuminate them. That is, I was concerned with "doctrinal aspects of monetary theory" but not with "the history of monetary doctrine"—though Patinkin treats these terms as synonymous.

2. Patinkin sees confession of error in my failure in the 1968 and 1970 essays to "mention either the Chicago school or its individual members."

No such thing. The 1956 essay was the introduction to a series of studies done as Ph.D. theses at Chicago. The Chicago background was relevant. It was not relevant to the later articles.

3. "No evidence is given in support of this assertion about the nature of the income version of the transactions approach"—that it stresses that money is held and can be regarded as a way station between the Fisher and the Cambridge version.

In line with point 1, I did not intend this to be a statement about the history of doctrine. Clearly, as an analytical matter, it can be regarded as a way station.

4. "Friedman . . . has claimed too little . . . in the context of his identification of the quantity theory with the short-run assumption that real income is constant."

As already explained, I identified the quantity theory rather with the assumption that prices react more rapidly than output. The assumption Patinkin attributes to me, I introduced only in the "simple model" designed to highlight the problem of the missing equation.

5. "In view of the crucial role that Friedman assigns to the real-balance effect in assuring the long-run equilibrium of the system, I would prefer introducing this effect explicitly into the commodity-demand functions."

But for the most part I was concerned with the short run, not the long run, and I never have believed that the real balance effect is of much empirical significance for the short run.

6. (Continuation of quotation in point 5.) "This would also seem to provide an expression of Friedman's view that 'the key insight of the quantity-theory approach is that such a discrepancy [that is, between the nominal quantity of money demanded and supplied] will be manifested primarily in attempted spending.' "

It would provide an erroneous expression, in my opinion. I believe the real balance effect plays a negligible role in this process. The substitution effect between money and other assets is, I believe, the key factor. This is a particularly clear example of Patinkin's propensity to identify the quantity theory with long-run neutrality.

7. "Friedman achieves this interpretation [that Keynes assumed rigid wages

and prices and did not generalize the theory to the case of wage and price flexibility] only by overlooking the chapter [chap. 19] in the *General Theory* . . . entitled 'Changes in Money Wages' " which "I [Patinkin] have long considered . . . to be the apex of Keynes's analysis" and in which Patinkin believes an economic analysis of wage movements was already provided.

Chapter 19 of the *General Theory* correctly points out that the argument that wage cuts will increase employment cannot be generalized directly from a single industry to the economy as a whole without taking into account effects on demand. It then lists various possible effects of wage cuts on the propensity to consume, the marginal efficiency of capital, and the rate of interest, stresses that the only significant positive effect (in Keynes's system) is by increasing the real quantity of money and thereby lowering the rate of interest, and points out that this is subject to the same limitations as monetary policy—that is, the liquidity trap. It ends with some reflections on the appropriate policy, which Keynes concludes to be rigid wages.

There are intelligent, thoughtful comments in the chapter, but to call it "the apex of Keynes's analysis" is an insult to Keynes. The chapter adds nothing important to the rest of the Keynesian apparatus; it rather illustrates how that apparatus can be applied to a particular problem and gives a basis for regarding rigid wages as not only an observable phenomenon but also a desirable policy. (See also my reply to Davidson.)

8. "Thus wage rigidities in this chapter [chap. 19 of the *General Theory*] are not an *assumption* of the analysis but the *policy conclusion* which Keynes reaches after investigating the results to be expected from wage flexibility."

Agreed. That is precisely what I said: "When there was no full-employment equilibrium, there was also no equilibrium nominal price level; something had to be brought in from outside to fix the price level; it might as well be institutional wage rigidity. Put differently, flexible nominal wages under such circumstances had no economic function to perform; hence they might as well be made rigid" (pp. 18–19).

9. "To 'express all variables in wage units' . . . is surely not to assume that this unit is constant."

Of course not. But it does mean that the system of equations or relations expressed in wage units provides no information on the money value of the wage unit. That has to be brought in from outside, which is precisely my point. (See also section 1 of my reply to Tobin.)

10. "Furthermore, this absence-of-money illusion is a necessary condition for the validity of the quantity theory."

Only in Patinkin's sense of that term, not my sense.

11. "Even before the flourishing of the Phillips curve, Keynesian econometric models generally treated the wage rate and price level as endogenous variables of the system," which, in Patinkin's view, contradicts my interpretation of Keynes as assuming wage rigidity.

The crucial question is not whether such equations are included in the models but whether they are ad hoc or derivable from Keynes's theoretical system. The price equations generally simply link prices to costs, mainly wages. This equation can be regarded as derivable from Keynes's system. But the wage equations are either purely ad hoc or, insofar as they are derivable from any theoretical system, it is the pre-Keynes classical system rather than Keynes's. For example, Patinkin refers approvingly to Klein's comment that "the main reasoning behind this equation is that of the law of supply and demand. Money wage rates move in response to excess demand on the labor market." The "law of supply and demand" is hardly Keynesian! More important, Klein misapplies it. The "classical law," *as taken over by Keynes*, would connect *real-wage rates*, not *money-wage rates*, with excess supply or demand. Klein's inclusion of the rate of change of prices in the equation, which Patinkin cites, is a move toward the correct classical inclusion of real wages, but if it went wholly in that direction it would leave money wages and money prices either undetermined or a simple inheritance from past history—which is precisely what I say Keynes's system assumes.

12. "Friedman cites 'Leijonhufvud's penetrating analysis' in support of his (Friedman's) view [that the liquidity trap plays a crucial role in Keynes's system]—even though Leijonhufvud's actual position is exactly the opposite."

This is careless textual interpretation. What I actually said in the footnote to which Patinkin refers was, "I am indebted to a brilliant book by Leijonhufvud (1968) for a full appreciation of the importance of this proposition [that, 'as an empirical matter, prices can be regarded as rigid—an institutional datum—for *short-run economic fluctuations'*] in Keynes's system. This subsection and the one that follows, on the liquidity preference function, owe much to Leijonhufvud's penetrating analysis."

That is literally true and in no way whatsoever implies either that I agree with every conclusion Leijonhufvud reaches or that he agrees with my conclusions. In fact, I believe that Leijonhufvud's "penetrating analysis" justifies a different conclusion about the role of absolute liquidity preference in Keynes's system than the one Leijonhufvud reaches (that it plays no important role), and I am strongly confirmed in that conclusion by my rereading of Keynes (see quotations in Appendix 1).

References

Ackley, Gardner. *Macroeconomic Theory.* New York: Macmillan, 1961.

Allais, M. "A Restatement of the Quantity Theory of Money." *A.E.R.* (December 1966), pp. 1123-57.

Andersen, Leonall, and Carlson, Keith. "A Monetarist Model For Economic Stabilization." *Review* (Federal Reserve Bank of Saint Louis) 52, no. 4 (April 1970): 7-25.

Andersen, Leonall C., and Jordan, Jerry L. "Monetary and Fiscal Actions: A Test of Their Relative Importance in Economic Stabilization." *Review* (Federal Reserve Bank of Saint Louis) (November 1968), pp. 11-23.

Angell, James. "Money, Prices, and Production: Some Fundamental Concepts." *Q.J.E.* (November 1933), pp. 39-76.

Arena, John J. "The Wealth Effect and Consumption: A Statistical Inquiry." *Yale Econ. Essays*, no. 2 (1963), pp. 251-303.

Auerbach, Robert. "The Income Effects of the Government Deficit." Ph.D. dissertation, Univ. Chicago, 1969.

Bailey, Martin J. *National Income and the Price Level.* New York: McGraw-Hill, 1962.

Baumol, W. J. "The Transactions Demand for Cash: An Inventory Theoretic Approach." *Q.J.E.* (November 1952), pp. 545-56.

Bordo, Michael. "The Effects of the Sources of Change in the Money Supply on the Level of Economic Activity." Ph.D. dissertation, Univ. Chicago, in preparation.

Brainard, William. "Financial Institutions and a Theory of Monetary Control." In *Financial Markets and Economic Activity.* Cowles Foundation Monograph 21. New York: Wiley, 1967.

Brainard, William, and Tobin, James. "Pitfalls in Financial Model Building." *A.E.R.* (May 1968), pp. 99-122.

Brown, A. J. "Interest, Prices, and the Demand Schedule for Idle Money." *Oxford Econ. Papers* 2 (May 1939): 46-69. Reprinted in *Oxford Studies in the Price Mechanism,* edited by T. Wilson and P. W. S. Andrews. London: Oxford Univ. Press, 1951.

Brunner, Karl. "The Role of Money and Monetary Policy." *Review* (Federal Reserve Bank of Saint Louis) 50, no. 7 (July 1968): 8-24.

———. "The 'Monetarist Revolution' in Monetary Theory." *Weltwirtschaftliches Archiv* 105, no. 1 (1970): 1-30.

Brunner, Karl, and Meltzer, Allan H. "Predicting Velocity." *J. Finance* (May 1963), pp. 319-34.

———. "Liquidity Traps for Money, Bank Credit, and Interest Rates." *J.P.E.* 76, no. 1 (January/February 1968): 1-37.

———. "A Monetarist Framework for Aggregate Analysis." *Kanstanzer Symposium on Monetary Theory and Monetary Policy,* vol. 1, 1971.

———. "Money, Debt, and Economic Activity." *J.P.E.* 80 (September/October 1972): 951-77.

Cagan, Phillip. "The Monetary Dynamics of Hyperinflation." In *Studies in the Quantity Theory of Money,* edited by Milton Friedman. Chicago: Univ. Chicago Press, 1956.

————. *Determinants and Effects of Changes in the Stock of Money, 1875–1960.* New York: Columbia Univ. Press (for Nat. Bur. Econ. Res.), 1965.

————. *The Channels of Monetary Effects on Interest Rates.* New York: Nat. Bur. Econ. Res., 1972, in press.

Chandler, Lester V. *An Introduction to Monetary Theory.* New York: Harper, 1940.

————. *The Economics of Money and Banking.* 2d ed. New York: Harper, 1953.

Chow, Gregory C. "On the Long-Run and Short-Run Demand for Money." *J.P.E.* 74 (April 1966): 111–31.

Clower, R. W. "The Keynesian Counter-Revolution: A Theoretical Appraisal." In *The Theory of Interest Rates*, edited by F. H. Hahn and F. Brechling. London: Macmillan, 1965.

————. "Reconsideration of the Microfoundations of Monetary Theory." In *Monetary Theory*, edited by R. W. Clower. Middlesex: Penguin, 1969. Original in *Western Econ. J.* 6 (December 1967): 1–8.

Culbertson, J. M. "United States Monetary History: Its Implications for Monetary Theory." *Nat. Banking Rev.* (March 1964), pp. 372–75.

Davidson, P. "Keynes's Finance Motive." *Oxford Econ. Papers* 17 (March 1965): 47–65.

————. "A Keynesian View of Patinkin's Theory of Employment." *Econ. J.* 77 (September 1967): 559–78.

————. "Money, Portfolio Balance, Capital Accumulation, and Economic Growth." *Econometrica* 36 (April 1968): 291–321.

————. "A Keynesian View of the Relationship between Accumulation, Money, and the Money-Wage Rate." *Econ. J.* 79 (June 1969): 300–323.

————. *Money and the Real World.* New York: Wiley, 1972.

Davis, J. Rennie. "Chicago Economists, Deficit Budgets, and the Early 1930's." *A.E.R.* 58 (June 1968): 476–82.

DeLeeuw, Frank, and Kalchbrenner, John. "Comment." *Review* (Federal Reserve Bank of Saint Louis), vol. 51, no. 4 (April 1969).

Dernburg, Thomas, and McDougall, Duncan. *Macro-Economics.* New York: McGraw-Hill, 1960.

Dillard, Dudley. *The Economics of John Maynard Keynes.* New York: Prentice-Hall, 1948.

Duesenberry, James; Fromm, Gary; Klein, Lawrence R.; and Kuh, Edwin. *The Brookings Quarterly Econometric Model of the United States.* Chicago: Rand McNally, 1965.

Eckstein, Otto, and Feldstein, Martin. "The Fundamental Determinants of Interest Rates." *Rev. Econ. and Statis.* (November 1970), pp. 365–75.

Evans, Michael; Klein, Lawrence; and Schink, George. *The Wharton Econometric Forecasting Model.* Wharton School of Finance and Commerce Studies in Quantitative Economics, no. 2. Philadelphia: Univ. Pennsylvania Press, 1967.

Fisher, Irving. *Appreciation and Interest.* New York: Macmillan, 1896. Reprint. New York: Kelley, 1961.

————. *The Rate of Interest.* New York: Macmillan, 1907.

————. *The Purchasing Power of Money.* New York: Macmillan, 1911. Rev. ed. 1920. 2d rev. ed. 1922. Reprint. New York: Kelley, 1963.

————. "Money, Prices, Credit, and Banking." *A.E.R.* (June 1919), pp. 407-9.

Friedman, Milton. "The Marshallian Demand Curve." *J.P.E.* 57 (December 1949): 463-95. Reprinted in Friedman (1953).

————. *Essays in Positive Economics.* Chicago: Univ. Chicago Press, 1953.

————. "The Quantity Theory of Money—a Restatement." In *Studies in the Quantity Theory of Money,* edited by M. Friedman. Chicago: Univ. Chicago Press, 1956. Reprinted in Friedman (1969).

————. *A Theory of the Consumption Function.* Princeton, N.J.: Princeton Univ. Press (for Nat. Bur. Econ. Res.), 1957.

————. "The Supply of Money and Changes in Prices and Output." In *The Relationship of Prices to Economic Stability and Growth.* U.S. Congress, Joint Economic Committee, Compendium, 1958. Reprinted in Friedman (1969).

————. "The Demand for Money: Some Theoretical and Empirical Results." *J.P.E.* 67 (August 1959): 327-51. Reprinted as Occasional Paper 68 (New York: Nat. Bur. Econ. Res., 1959). Reprinted Friedman (1969).

————. "The Lag in Effect of Monetary Policy." *J.P.E.* 69 (October 1961): 447-66. Reprinted in Friedman (1969).

————. *Price Theory.* Chicago: Aldine, 1962.

————. "Interest Rates and the Demand for Money." *J. Law and Econ.* 9 (October 1966): 71-85. Reprinted in Friedman (1969).

————. "The Monetary Theory and Policy of Henry Simons." *J. Law and Econ.* (October 1967), pp. 1-13. Reprinted in Friedman (1969).

————. "Money: Quantity Theory." In *International Encyclopedia of the Social Sciences.* New York: Macmillan and Free Press, 1968. (*a*)

————. "The Role of Monetary Policy." *A.E.R.* (March 1968), pp. 1-17. (*b*) Reprinted in Friedman (1969).

————. *The Optimum Quantity of Money and Other Essays.* Chicago: Aldine, 1969.

————. "A Theoretical Framework for Monetary Analysis." *J.P.E.* 78 (March/April 1970): 193-238. (*a*)

————. *The Counter-Revolution in Monetary Theory.* Occasional Paper 33, Institute of Economic Affairs for the Wincott Foundation. London: Tonbridge, 1970. (*b*)

————. "Comment on Tobin." *Q.J.E.* 84 (May 1970): 318-27. (*c*)

————. "A Monetary Theory of Nominal Income." *J.P.E.* 79 (March/April 1971): 323-37.

Friedman, Milton, and Meiselman, David. "The Relative Stability of Monetary Velocity and the Investment Multiplier in the United States, 1897-1958." In *Stabilization Policies.* Englewood Cliffs, N.J.: Prentice-Hall, 1963.

Friedman, Milton, and Schwartz, Anna. "Money and Business Cycles." *Rev. Econ. and Statis.*, suppl. (February 1963), pp. 32-64. (*a*) Reprinted in Friedman (1969).

————. *A Monetary History of the United States, 1867-1960.* Princeton, N.J.: Princeton Univ. Press (for Nat. Bur. Econ. Res.), 1963. (*b*)

————. *Monetary Statistics of the United States.* New York: Columbia Univ. Press (for Nat. Bur. Econ. Res.), 1970.

Goldfeld, Stephen M. *Commercial Bank Behavior and Economic Activity.* Amsterdam: North-Holland, 1966.

Goodhart, C. A. E. "The Importance of Money." *Bank of England Q. Bull.* (June 1970), pp. 159-98.

Gramley, Lyle, and Chase, S. B., Jr. "Time Deposits in Monetary Analysis." *Federal Reserve Bull.* 51 (October 1965): 1380-1406. Reprinted in *Targets and Indicators of Monetary Policy*, edited by Karl Brunner. San Francisco: Chandler, 1969.

Gupta, Suraj. "Expected Rate of Change of Prices and Rates of Interest." Ph.D. dissertation, Univ. Chicago, 1964.

Haberler, Gottfried. *Prosperity and Depression.* 3d ed. Geneva: League of Nations, 1941.

Hahn, F. H. "Some Adjustment Problems." *Econometrica* 38 (January 1970): 1-17.

———. "Equilibrium with Transactions Costs." *Econometrica* 39 (May 1971): 417-40.

Hansen, Alvin. *Monetary Theory and Fiscal Policy.* New York: McGraw-Hill, 1949.

Heller, H. R. "The Demand for Money: The Evidence from the Short-Run Data." *Q.J.E.* (May 1964), pp. 291-303.

Hendershott, Patric H. *The Neutralized Money Stock.* Homewood, Ill.: Irwin, 1968.

Hester, Donald, and Tobin, James, eds. *Financial Markets and Economic Activity.* Cowles Foundation Monograph 21. New York: Wiley, 1967.

Hicks, John R. "A Suggestion for Simplifying the Theory of Money." *Economica*, n.s. 2 (February 1935): 1-19.

———. "Mr. Keynes and the Classics: A Suggested Interpretation." *Econometrica* 5 (April 1937): 147-59. Reprinted in *Readings in the Theory of Income Distribution*, edited by W. Fellner and B. F. Haley. Homewood, Ill.: Irwin, 1951.

Holzman, Franklyn D., and Bronfenbrenner, Martin. "Survey of Inflation Theory." *A.E.R.* (September 1963), pp. 593-661.

Jaffé, W. "Walras' Theory of *Tâtonnement:* A Critique of Recent Interpretations." *J.P.E.* 75 (February 1967): 1-19.

Johnson, Harry G. "The *General Theory* after Twenty-five Years." *A.E.R.* (May 1961), pp. 1-17.

———. "The Neo-classical One-Sector Growth Model: A Geometrical Exposition and Extension to a Monetary Economy." In *Essays in Monetary Economics.* London: Allen & Unwin, 1967. (*a*)

———. "Neutrality of Money in Growth Models: A Reply." *Economica* (February 1967), pp. 73-74. (*b*)

———. "Inside Money, Outside Money, Income, Wealth, and Welfare in Monetary Theory." *J. Money, Credit, and Banking* 1 (February 1969): 30-45.

———. "The Keynesian Revolution and the Monetarist Counter-Revolution." *A.E.R.* 61 (May 1971): 1-14.

Kaldor, N. "Speculation and Economic Stability." In *Essays on Economic Stability and Growth*, by N. Kaldor. London: Duckworth, 1960. Original in *Rev. Econ. Studies* 6 (1939): 1-27.

Keran, Michael. "Monetary and Fiscal Influences on Economic Activity—the Historical Evidence." *Review* (Federal Reserve Bank of Saint Louis) 51, no. 11 (November 1969): 5-23.

Keynes, John Maynard. *Tract on Monetary Reform.* London: Macmillan, 1923.

———. *A Treatise on Money.* London: Macmillan, 1930.

———. "On the Theory of a Monetary Economy." *Festschrift für A. Spiethoff.*

Munich: Duncker & Humblot, 1933. Reprinted in *Nebraska J. Econ. and Bus.* 2 (Autumn 1963): 7–9.

―――. *The General Theory of Employment, Interest, and Money.* London: Macmillan, 1936.

―――. "The Ex-ante Theory of the Rate of Interest." *Econ. J.* 49 (December 1937): 663–69. (*a*)

―――. "The General Theory." *Q.J.E.* 51 (February 1937): 209–23. (*b*) Reprinted in *The New Economics*, edited by S. E. Harris. New York: Knopf, 1947.

Klein, L. R. *The Keynesian Revolution.* New York: Macmillan, 1947. 2d ed. New York: Macmillan, 1966.

―――. *Economic Fluctuations in the United States, 1921–41.* Cowles Commission Monograph, no. 11. New York: Wiley, 1950.

Klein, L. R., and Goldberger, A. A. *An Econometric Model of the United States.* Amsterdam: North-Holland, 1955.

Konig, H. "Demand Function, Short-Run and Long-Run Function, and the Distributed Lag." *Zeitschrift Gesamte Staatswissenschaft* (February 1968), pp. 124 ff.

Koyck, L. M. *Distributed Lags and Investment Analysis.* Amsterdam: North-Holland, 1954.

Laidler, David. *The Demand for Money: Theories and Evidence.* Scranton, Pa.: Internat. Textbook, 1970.

Laurent, Robert. "Currency Transfers by Denominations." Ph.D. dissertation, Univ. Chicago, 1969.

Leijonhufvud, Axel. *On Keynesian Economics and the Economics of Keynes.* London: Oxford Univ. Press, 1968.

Levhari, D., and Patinkin, D. "The Role of Money in a Simple Growth Model." *A.E.R.* (September 1969), pp. 713–53.

McKenna, Joseph P. *Aggregate Economic Analysis.* New York: Holt, Rinehart & Winston, 1955.

Martin, P. W. *The Flaw in the Price System.* London: King, 1924.

Marty, Alvin. "The Optimal Rate of Growth of Money." *J.P.E.* 76, pt. 2 (July/August 1968): 860–73.

Meltzer, Allan H. "The Demand for Money: The Evidence from the Time Series." *J.P.E.* 71 (June 1963): 219–46.

―――. "Monetary Theory and Monetary History." *Schweizerische Zeitschrift Volkswirtschaft und Statis.* 4 (Spring 1965): 409–22.

―――. "Public Policies as Causes of Fluctuations." *J. Money, Credit, and Banking* 2 (February 1970): 45–55.

Metzler, Lloyd. "Wealth, Saving, and the Rate of Interest." *J.P.E.* 59 (April 1951): 93–116.

Mill, John Stuart. Reviews of books by Thomas Tooke and R. Torrens. *Westminster Rev.* 41 (June 1844): 579–93.

Mitchell, W. C. *Business Cycles.* New York: Nat. Bur. Econ. Res., 1927.

Modigliani, Franco. "Liquidity Preference and the Theory of Interest and Money." *Econometrica* 12 (January 1944): 45–88. Reprinted in *Readings in Monetary Theory*, edited by F. A. Lutz and L. W. Mints. Homewood, Ill.: Irwin, 1951.

Moore, B. J. *An Introduction to the Theory of Finance.* New York: Free Press, 1968.

Mundell, Robert A. "A Fallacy in the Interpretation of Macro-economic Equilibrium." *J.P.E.* 73 (February 1965): 61–66.

Muth, J. F. "Optimal Properties of Exponentially Weighted Forecasts." *J. American Statis. Assoc.* (June 1960), pp. 299–306.

Nerlove, Marc. *Distributed Lags and Demand Analysis.* Agriculture Handbook no. 141. Washington: Dept. Agriculture, 1958.

———. "A Tabular Survey of Macro-econometric Models." *Internat. Econ. Rev.* (May 1966), pp. 127-75.

Ohlin, B. "Some Notes on the Stockholm Theory of Savings and Investment, pt. II." *Econ. J.* 47 (June 1937): 221–40.

Okun, Arthur M. "Comment." *Rev. Econ. and Statis.,* suppl. (February 1963), pp. 72–77.

Patinkin, Don. "The Indeterminacy of Absolute Prices in Classical Economic Theory." *Econometrica* (January 1949), pp. 1–27.

———. "Price Flexiblity and Full Employment." In *Readings in Monetary Theory,* edited by F. A. Lutz and L. W. Mints. Homewood, Ill.: Irwin, 1951. Revised version of an article that originally appeared in *A.E.R.* (September 1948), pp. 543–64.

———. "Keynesian Economics and the Quantity Theory." In *Post-Keynesian Economics,* edited by Kenneth Kurihara. New Brunswick, N.J.: Rutgers Univ. Press, 1954.

———. "Financial Intermediaries and the Logical Structure of Monetary Theory." *A.E.R.* (March 1961), pp. 95–116.

———. *Money, Interest, and Prices.* 2d ed. New York: Harper & Row, 1965.

———. "The Chicago Tradition, the Quantity Theory, and Friedman." *J. Money, Credit, and Banking* 1 (February 1969): 46–70. (*a*)

———. "Money and Wealth: A Review Article." *J. Econ. Literature* (December 1969), pp. 1140–60. (*b*)

———. "On the Short-Run Non-Neutrality of Money in the Quantity Theory." *Banca Nazionale Lavoro Q. Rev.* (March 1972), pp. 3–22. (*a*)

———. "Keynesian Monetary Theory and the Cambridge School." In *Issues in Monetary Economics,* edited by Harry G. Johnson and A. R. Nobay. Proceedings of the Money Study Group Conference, Bournemouth, February 1972. Oxford: Oxford Univ. Press, 1972. (*b*) This paper also appears, without appendix, in *Banca Nazionale Lavoro Q. Rev.* (June 1972).

Pesek, Boris P., and Saving, Thomas R. *Money, Wealth, and Economic Theory.* New York: Macmillan, 1967.

Phelps, Edmund S., et al. *The New Micro-Economics Foundations of Employment and Inflation Theory.* New York: Norton, 1970.

Phillips, A. W. "The Relation between Unemployment and the Rate of Change of Money Wage Rates in the United Kingdom, 1861-1957." *Economica* (November 1958), pp. 283–99.

Pigou, A. C. "The Value of Money." *Q.J.E.* (November 1917), pp. 38–65. Reprinted in *Readings in Monetary Theory,* edited by F. A. Lutz and L. W. Mintz. Homewood, Ill.: Irwin, 1951.

———. "Economic Progress in a Stable Environment." *Economica,* n.s. (August 1947), pp. 180–88.

Reeve, Joseph E. *Monetary Reform Movements.* Washington: American Council on Public Affairs, 1943.

Robbins, Lionel. *The Great Depression.* London: Macmillan, 1934.

Robertson, D. H. *Money.* 4th ed. London: Pitman, 1948.

Samuelson, Paul A. *Foundations of Economic Analysis.* Cambridge, Mass.: Harvard Univ. Press, 1947.

―――. "The Role of Money in National Economic Policy." In *Controlling Monetary Aggregates.* Boston: Federal Reserve Bank of Boston, 1969.

Shapiro, Edward. *Macroeconomic Analysis.* New York: Harcourt Brace, 1966.

Sidrauski, M. "Rational Choice and Patterns of Growth in a Monetary Economy." *A.E.R.* (May 1967), pp. 534-44. (*a*)

―――. "Inflation and Economic Growth." *J.P.E.* 75 (December 1967): 796-810. (*b*)

Siegel, Barry. *Aggregate Economics and Public Policy.* Homewood, Ill.: Irwin, 1960.

Smith, Warren L. "On Some Current Issues in Monetary Economics: An Interpretation." *J. Econ. Literature* 8, no. 3 (September 1970): 767-82.

Snyder, Carl. "On the Statistical Relation of Trade, Credit, and Prices." *Rev. Inst. Internat. Statis.* (October 1934), pp. 278-91.

Solow, R. M. "A Contribution to the Theory of Economic Growth." *Q.J.E.* (February 1956), pp. 65-94.

―――. "On a Family of Lag Distributions." *Econometrica* (April 1960), pp. 393-406.

Stein, J. L. "Money and Capacity Growth." *J.P.E.* 74 (October 1966): 451-65.

Tobin, James. "Money Wage Rates and Employment." In *The New Economics,* edited by Seymour Harris. New York: Knopf, 1947.

―――. "A Dynamic Aggregative Model." *J.P.E.* 63 (April 1955): 103-15.

―――. "The Interest Elasticity of Transactions Demand for Cash." *Rev. Econ. and Statis.* (August 1956), pp. 241-47.

―――. "Liquidity Preference as Behavior toward Risk." *Rev. Econ. Studies* 25 (February 1958): 65-86.

―――. "The Monetary Interpretation of History." *A.E.R.* (June 1965), pp. 464-85. (*a*)

―――. "Money and Economic Growth." *Econometrica* (October 1965), pp. 671-84. (*b*)

―――. "A General Equilibrium Approach to Monetary Theory." *J. Money, Credit, and Banking* 1, no. 1 (February 1969): 15-29. (*a*)

―――. "The Role of Money in National Economic Policy." In *Controlling Money.* Boston: Federal Reserve Bank of Boston, 1969. (*b*)

―――. "Money and Income: Post Hoc Ergo Propter Hoc?" *Q.J.E.* 84 (May 1970): 301-17, and "Rejoinder," pp. 328-29.

Tobin, James, and Brainard, William C. "Financial Intermediaries and the Effectiveness of Monetary Controls." In *Financial Markets and Economic Activity.* Cowles Foundation Monograph 21. New York: Wiley, 1967. Reprinted from *A.E.R.* (May 1963): 383-400.

―――. "Pitfalls in Financial Model Building." *A.E.R.* (May 1968), pp. 99-122.

Uzawa, H. "On a Neo-classical Model of Economic Growth." *Econ. Studies Q.* (September 1966), pp. 1-14.

Viner, Jacob. *Balanced Deflation, Inflation, or More Depression.* Minneapolis: Univ. Minnesota Press, April 1933.

Von Neumann, John. "A Model of Economic Equilibrium." *Rev. Econ. Studies* 33, no. 1 (1945-46): 1-9.

Walters, A. A. "A Survey of Empirical Evidence." In *Money in Britain, 1959-1969*, edited by David R. Croome and Harry G. Johnson. London: Oxford Univ. Press, 1970.

Warburton, Clark. "The Volume of Money and the Price Level between the World Wars." *J.P.E.* 53 (June 1945): 150-63. Reprinted in *Depression, Inflation, and Monetary Policy: Selected Papers, 1945-1953.* Baltimore: Johns Hopkins, n.d.

Weintraub, S., and Habibagahi, A. "Keynes and the Quantity Theory Elasticities." *Nebraska J. Econ. and Bus.* 10 (Spring 1971): 13-25.

Working, H. "New Concepts concerning Future Markets and Prices." *A.E.R.* 52 (June 1962): 431-60.

Wright, Quincy, ed. *Gold and Monetary Stabilization.* Harris Foundations Lectures, 1932. Chicago: Univ. Chicago Press, 1932.

Zwick, Burton. "The Adjustment of the Economy to Monetary Changes." *J.P.E.* 79, no. 1 (January/February 1971): 77-96.

Contributors

Milton Friedman is Paul Snowdon Russell Distinguished Service Professor at the University of Chicago.

Karl Brunner is professor of economics at the Graduate School of Management, University of Rochester, and the editor of the *Journal of Money, Credit, and Banking.*

Allan Meltzer is Maurice Falk Professor of Economics and Social Science at the Graduate School of Industrial Administration, Carnegie-Mellon University.

James Tobin is Sterling Professor of Economics at Yale University.

Paul Davidson is professor of economics at Rutgers University.

Don Patinkin is professor of economics at the Hebrew University of Jerusalem.

186

Index